## Advance praise for *Awhi Mai Awhi*

CW00540173

"*Awhi Mai Awhi Atu* is a precious gi
Filled with honesty and vitality, this
holy ground for women, men and c
hopeful relationship with each other a
my life has been shaped by 'earth-writing. This collection of womens
writing is the best type of 'earth-writing'; written from, and written for,
incarnational embodiment. Here women reflect deeply and powerfully
on their own embodied relationship with the earth and with the Creator
and Redeemer of all. Each reflection ends by grounding this wisdom in a
gift of incarnational invitation for the reader – practical steps we can all
take to live more humbly and hopefully in loving relationship with God's
earth. This collection is a beautiful celebration of the loving compassion
perceived and expressed by the women of these islands as well as a clear
call to join with the work of God's Spirit in safeguarding the integrity of
God's creation and to sustain and renew the life of the earth."

*Bishop Eleanor Sanderson*
*(Pihopa Awhina, Diocese of Wellington)*

"This is an astonishing book. The living water of the Spirit ripples
through its pages in the lives so generously shared, the stories gifted,
the poems and prayers offered, the invitations extended to walk with
others on pathways to fuller, more just and fruitful participation in the
life of the earth and its creator, life-giver and restorer. This kete taonga
could not have been assembled anywhere else than Aotearoa, nor by
anyone else than those, tangata whenua and tangata tititi, who have
known and are learning to know God and the ways of God in this land.
In its diversity and creativity this collection is a stunning witness to that
persistent bubbling and way-making of the water of life. I am grateful for
this rich gift and pray that it may be widely and warmly received."

*George Wieland, Director of Carey Centre for*
*Mission Research and Formation*

"In our time of planetary and human crisis, the words and witness of
this book speak of hope, nurturing us to new life in the midst of chaos –
even in the darkest of times. They stir us to renewed vigour in caring for
earth, caring for people. The diversity of voices expresses the interwoven
fabric of our multicultural society founded on Te Tiriti. I am delighted
and moved that these words have grown out of the wellspring of life – te
puna o te ora – within this land of Aotearoa New Zealand. May they
inspire all who read them."

*Julianne Hickey, Director of Caritas Aotearoa New Zealand, 2012-2022*

"I am impressed with the variety of women whose voices we hear in Silvia Purdie's book, their depth of faith, and the innovative ways they care for creation as an expression of their love for the Creator. The poetry and hands-on suggestions make the book both evocative and practical. These wonderful women encourage and challenge me."

—*Rev. Dr. Lynne Baab, author of a host of books including Joy Together: Spiritual Practices for Your Congregation*

"We need not just theology but stories. This book is full of vibrant stories of women of God, caring for creation in many different ways. They come from varied backgrounds in age, culture, and life experience, but I find myself challenged and inspired by them. I hope you will too!"

*Rev. Dave Bookless, Director of Theology, A Rocha International and Lausanne Global Catalyst for Creation Care. Author of Planetwise: Dare to Care for God's World*

# Awhi Mai Awhi Atu

## *Women in Creation Care*

### Silvia Purdie, editor

**Foreword by Ruth Valerio**

Philip
Garside
Publishing Ltd.

Email Silvia at: silvia.purdie@gmail.com

Paperback International edition 2022:
ISBN 9781991027122

Also available

New Zealand paperback: ISBN 9781991027115
Paperback print-on-demand USA: ISBN 9798831833799
PDF: ISBN 9781991027139
ePub: ISBN 9781991027146
Kindle/Mobi: ISBN 9781991027153

Philip Garside Publishing Ltd
PO Box 17160
Wellington 6147
New Zealand
books@pgpl.co.nz — www.pgpl.co.nz

Cover illustration:
Photograph of Cross from the Chapel of Tarore, Ngatiawa River Monastery, Waikanae by Shaun Lawson.
Background: Photograph of native bush on Te Ahumairangi section of the Northern Walkway, Wellington by Alexander Garside.

# Contents

# Foreword: Ruth Valerio

Dr. Ruth Valerio is a passionate voice for faith-based environmental action around the world. She is the author of several books which are gutsy and easy-to-read, practical and theologically rich. Ruth founded Eco Church as Churches and Theology Director for A Rocha UK. She is now Tearfund's Global Advocacy and Influencing Director.

Yesterday I went for a walk with my eldest daughter, home from university where she is studying zoology. We took binoculars and went to a nature reserve: a wetland site on an estuary that leads to the sea. For some inexplicable reason, of all the many walks I've done over the years in my beautiful area of England, this was one place neither of us had been before and we set off with excitement. We are both trying to learn more about birds and were a bit nervous as to whether we would see much and, if we did, would we be able to identify them?! We needn't have worried.

It was a stunning walk that will stay in both our minds for a long time. We were out for hours – far longer than expected – and identified 33 different bird species. Much of that was through asking people with bigger binoculars than ours what they were looking at, and learning on the spot. One of the highlights was large flocks of lapwings, twisting, turning, swooping and swirling across the sky in beautiful shape-shifting formations, their calls ringing out over the estuary. We arrived home cold, hungry but happy, and poured over our bird book to confirm the birds we had seen.

It was a beautiful time: two women, mother and daughter, connecting with each other and with the world around us.

We have been made for connection, for relationship. I am who I am because of my relationship with God and my many relationships with people who have shaped me over the years. Sometimes that shaping has come out of pain. Sometimes those human relationships have warped the God-shaping in me. Nonetheless, they have formed me and made me who I am, and who I will continue to become.

And my relationship with the wider creation is also integral to who I am. Right back in Genesis 1 God creates an earth creature, an earthy one. *Ho adam* ('the adam') is a play on words, with the Hebrew for 'ground' being *adamah*. We are literally made from the earth, humans from the humus. Genesis 2:7 highlights this again: the first human are formed out of the dust of the ground. So we are earth creatures with an intrinsic relationship with the wider natural world.[1]

We are not isolated beings, floating free, independent from everything and everyone around us. Our connectedness places a responsibility on us to nurture our relationships and work for their good health. In the same way that some of my relationships have caused me pain, so I recognise that I can cause others pain and I can damage the relationships that exist within the natural world. So we all have choices to make: will I act for love, justice and compassion? Will I seek to live lightly on this earth?

My role as a director at Tearfund – an organisation that partners with churches in the world's poorest countries to tackle poverty and injustice and respond to disasters – shows me how those connections reach around the world. Those connections can be negative. As the climate crisis ravages through the communities we serve, I see the terrible destruction caused by our addiction to fossil fuels and our inability to live in a way that takes care of the earth and its bounties. I face the stark reality that a person in the UK will take only 6 days to emit the same amount of $CO_2$ that a person in Malawi emits in a year.

But those connections can be positive too. We can make a difference. We can reach out and use our blessings to help others. We can learn from each other and benefit from the wisdom of the generations in cultures very different to our own. I have experienced those connections in reading *Awhi Mai Awhi Atu*. What a humbling privilege for me, living on the other side of the world, to be asked to write the Foreword to this book! It is full of so many inspiring and wonderful women, all drawing on their life experiences to be people who care for the land and the seas and all the creatures – human and wider – that share those spaces.

The radical Latin American educationalist Paulo Freire used a phrase from the Spanish poet Antonio Machado when he stated, "We make the road by walking." Such is the case for each woman you will meet in the following chapters. Such is the case for you too. No woman's experience can be replicated, but as you read, my prayer is that you will be inspired to use your own experiences and connections to walk your road of care for this wonderful but so wounded world that God has made. And know that as you do so, you are in good company.

# Introduction

I te timatanga te Kupu,[2]
i te Atua te Kupu, ko te Atua anō te Kupu.

In the beginning was the Word,
and the Word was God and the Word was with God.

Nāna nga mea katoa i hanga; i a ia te ora.

Through him all things were made; in him was life.

I roto i te pōuri te marama e whiti ana.
In the darkness, the light shines.

In the darkness of destruction and pollution,
the Word speaks Beauty.

In the distancing of Me and Mine,
the Word speaks Community.

In the despair and injustice of climate crisis,
the Word calls God's people to faith, hope and courage.

This is our time to shine, for Christ is our light,
Light of the world, the indestructible light of Life!

## Narrative Eco Missiology

Welcome to *Awhi Mai Awhi Atu: Women in Creation Care*. This collaborative project documents a dynamic emerging mission movement in Aotearoa New Zealand, through the voices of 30 women leading in diverse forms of faith-based environmental action.

Each story is grounded in whakapapa, family origins, and honours the shaping of culture. Each story reflects on childhood experiences and relationships with the natural world and with God. And each story describes initiative and innovation in response to a driving conviction that God cares about the state of the world, both environmental and human, and that God needs Christian people to be part of the solutions. A concluding chapter attempts to articulate the theology that underpins our mission, in conversation together.

This is, then, narrative eco missiology. Missiology because it explores the theology and practice of a mission movement. Eco, short for ecological, used interchangeably with 'creation care'; attending to our relationship with

# Glossary of Te Reo

Te Reo Māori is an official language of New Zealand and is increasingly in common usage. Where Te Reo is used in this book, a translation is either given within the text (or in a bracket) or explained in a footnote. Some frequently used kupu (words) are listed here for easy reference. Untranslated words are likely place names. The macron lengthens the vowel and places emphasis. If the reader is unfamiliar with Te Reo Māori, there is an abundance of tutorials and other resources online.

| | |
|---|---|
| Ao | world, realm. Te Ao Māori means the Māori world/community. |
| Aotearoa | the Māori name for New Zealand |
| Atua | God. This term is used here to refer to the Trinity of Christian faith, the God of the Bible. |
| Awa | river |
| Awhi | embrace |
| Ihu | Jesus |
| Iwi | tribe |
| Kai | food |
| Karakia | prayer |
| Karaiti | Christ |
| Kōrero | talk |
| Mahi | work |
| Manaakitanga | hospitality |
| Mana | prestige, inner power |
| Māori | the indigenous people and culture of Aotearoa |
| Mauri | life force |
| Moana | ocean |
| Mokopuna | grandchildren |
| Pākehā | New Zealanders of European descent[10] |
| Taiao | the natural environment |
| Tāngata | people |
| Te Reo | the Māori language |
| Tiaki | assist |
| Tikanga | culture, ways of doing things |

| | |
|---|---|
| Tūrangawaewae | ancestral home, literally the place where feet stand |
| Wāhine | women |
| Waiata | song |
| Whānau | family – also means 'birth' |
| Whanaungatanga | relationality |
| Whenua | land – also means 'placenta' |

# Dedication

We dedicate this book to ngā tūpuna wahine, our mothers, grandmothers and role models. The world would be a better place now if we had followed your advice! Thank you for believing in us.

Patricia Harris (Amy), Mere Wahine Tai (Ana Lisa), Tumirah (Ani), Margaret Bates (Angela), Nola Bartlett (Anna), Sylvia Carter (Ava), Zhang Xiu Xian (Cathy), Mary Goad (Courtnay), Hazel Slight (Diana), Silaati Aigafou Tealofi, Eleni Talua Mauga and Savali Lauti (Eliala), Claire Russell (Elise), Fualaau Tauāsili Tui-Misikopa (from Vailoa Palauli) and Faaogea Mafuatu-Loli (Vaipu'a, Samoa – Faaolataga), Tina Cairns (nee Hunt – Honey), Hong Mean Sim (Ira), Carmen Yeoh Poh Eng (Iris), Rose Victoria Hume (nee Bradshaw, te taha o tōku Papa, Ko Ngāitahu tōna iwi) and Margaret Kyle O'Brien nee Taplin (i te taha o tōku Mama, Scottish – Jenny), Hōhepine Te Wake (Jacynthia), Joyce McDonald (Jill), Elizabeth Maria Behiels-Bavré (Kristel), Rasoanatoandro ("the beautiful one of the middle of the day" – Lala), Sheila Dunbar (Marg), Elizabeth Hamlin (Marie), Sister Louise O'Kane and Karani Ngapiu (Mina), Elsie Symes Wood and Irene Faul (Nicola), Pauline Parsonson (Olivia), Hingano Hehea Anatohuia Makahili Finau (O'Love), Jessie MacInnes (Robyn), Mary Wilson (Rosemary), Vivienne Ellis (Silvia), Jean Beaumont (Skye).

We gratefully acknowledge the Anglican Women Studies Centre for their assistance and support for this publication.[11]

## Stories

*Poem by Ana Lisa de Jong, Living Tree Poetry[12]*

My story is woven in your story.
Because our paths crossed,
connected, carried on in step,
diverged,
I have become a bigger story.

If we are each of us streams,
then the place we flow into each other
is our rushing river, our brimming over,
our rich heritage.
We have become a grateful history.

And the place we flow out of each other
to put down sweet roots,
our offshoot from the branch, our fertile bush –
our tūrangawaewae –
is where we stand separate but together.

I am glad to be in this river with you.
Your blessing is my drink,
my sustenance your pleasure, twin streams
in differing directions.

We become a waterway of many branched tributaries.
Our stories intertwining, dividing,
becoming bigger.

# Empowered to Serve: Amy Ross

Amy is the Eco Church Co-ordinator for the Wellington Region.[13] She lives in Porirua, with two lively boys, where her husband Daniel is vicar of the Pāuatahanui Anglican Parish.

The five values of A Rocha (and therefore Eco Church NZ) are woven deeply into my personal value system: Christian, conservation, community, cross-cultural, co-operation.[14]

I grew up in a Pākehā family, was born in Auckland and spent a few years there and in Mangawhai before spending my formative years in two key multi-cultural environments: firstly rural and then low decile urban. My university years were also full of interesting and diverse cultural experiences, as have been my 12 years of marriage and ministry with Dan since.

*What kind of childhood did you have?*

When I was aged 6 to nearly 11 my family lived on Aotea (Great Barrier Island). There I went to Okiwi School, a small, predominantly Māori school with a strong emphasis on educating from a Māori worldview. Aotea has a small population and a rural 'feel' and the Christian community we lived in was semi self-sufficient. I imbibed the beauty of Te Ao Māori and Te Reo through school,[15] and was immersed in a creation-centred and charismatic Christian faith through life at Orama Christian Community.[16] The sustainable living, the rhythm of prayer and worship in residential community, and welcoming of people in need, all shaped me to become someone who finds it easy to question a mainstream, urban, nuclear family way of life.

It was also a time of challenge in my family's life. My father nearly died in a building accident soon after we arrived on the Island, and while he recuperated and learned to live with long-term pain, my mother was busy raising myself, my brother and my little sister in the community. Among other responsibilities, Mum was in charge of the community laundry, and my memories revolve around hanging out endless loads of washing after they had been through the hand-wringer!

Our milk was fresh from the cows, thick and creamy, and our drinking water fresh from the sky, harvested from rain on our roof. Tap water was brown from the creek after rain, not for drinking because it gave you giardia (diarrheoa). Fish was fresh, caught regularly by community members. Electricity was a scarce resource produced by the noisy old generator. We made household items last as long as possible, shared and repaired resources, because trips to the mainland were the only way to get new stuff.

As children we had chores but we also had endless hours to roam the rocky shoreline of our bay, the hills that enclosed it like warm, forested arms, and to clamber up the creek to swim under the waterfall. We were free to play mostly unsupervised until the gong rang out for dinner and we'd race back for dinner with 50 others in a big hall filled with noise and laughter. My friends were like siblings as we fought and played. We climbed on roofs, built epic huts, jumped naughtily in the piles of freshly sheared wool in the woolshed reeking of lanolin, sat on pohutakawa[17] boughs reaching lazily out over the incoming tide. We fed the pigs our food scraps and marvelled at the kittens living in the sty.

We didn't go to Scouts, dance or sports lessons, because it was a long drive over gravel roads to get anywhere, but we did not feel the lack of hobbies, because community members were always teaching new skills. Group games, drama, celebrations, visitors, music, worship – someone somewhere was always playing a guitar. And did I mention swimming?! – jumping off the wharf, off the rocky shores, upriver. My memories include little time spent inside our family's private dwelling compared to being outside.

A big change came when we moved back to the mainland. After a rough transition we settled in Point England in the eastern suburbs of Aotearoa's biggest city (Auckland). Renting, then buying, was cheap there because it was a low-decile area. It was extremely multi-cultural – we were one of very few Pākehā families. We lived in three different houses during our family's eight years there.

Being from a white well-educated family with a low income, in an area that is predominantly home to Polynesian, Māori, and other ethnic minorities, had an interesting impact on me. I became extremely conscious of the inequalities that pervade New Zealand society, and yearned to do something to address them. I walked alone the 40 minutes from Point England to Glendowie (a High School in a more affluent suburb) – I was out of zone and no-one else from my school lived near me. This required a thick skin. I would be cat-called as I walked past noisy sociable packs of multicultural teens, and I tried to carry myself proudly while I hefted the musical instrument that I inevitably had to wield for band: a trumpet or french horn. I loved to learn, enjoyed school and the teachers, and worked hard to succeed. I became deputy head prefect and took scholarship exams which earned me money towards university fees.

## How did you develop faith?

I had a Christian friend in Point England who invited me to join her youth group at the Anglican church in Meadowbank when I was 13. For me this was a new kind of church, more broad-minded. My friend's Dad led youth group. He provided me – and my now-husband whom I met there – with the opportunity to explore faith through an intelligent questioning approach without forcing or assuming easy answers. I have found this to be essential to making sense of the relationship between climate change, science and faith. At an age when many young Christians are not allowed to question faith in a way that allows space for ambiguity, I was fortunate to be in a supportive environment that encouraged theological openness and grappling.

I went on to study Geography and Political Studies at university, where I learned about biodiversity loss, damage to natural ecosystems and climate change. I wondered how this connected to my Christian faith. These questions led me to A Rocha. An international network, A Rocha was founded in Portugal in the 1980s at a Field Study centre in the Algarve; A Rocha means 'the Rock' in Portuguese. It is a network of 23 national organisations inspired by God's love, who lead community based projects that connect people to places and help restore and transform them. I was attracted to A Rocha for its core commitments: cross-cultural, Christian, community-based, conservation-focussed, and co-operative.

Newly married, my husband and I moved to the UK to study at All Nations Christian College, a cross-cultural missions training college. I met Dave Bookless, the founder of A Rocha UK, and invited him to speak at our college. He told me about his work in a team that restored a very degraded site in an economically-deprived, multi-cultural inner-city London suburb, to become a thriving hub for nature: Minet Country Park. He inspired me to form a student-led Earthkeepers group at All Nations, who worked to transform aspects of college life to reflect an environmental ethic. The cafeteria food went local and seasonal, with more meat-free meals, a large vegetable garden was planted, a recycled art exhibition raised funds for solar panels, beehives were hosted on college grounds, a biomass boiler was investigated as an sustainable heating source, and outdoor creation care themed worship took place – and more.

We spent a year living in Bradford where I worked with Christians Against Poverty. Being part of the ethical action team in head office gave me the chance to lead a conversion of the office waste system from several hundred combined-waste desk bins to a separated-waste recycling system. Next, my husband went on to train as an Anglican priest, and we lived in Cambridge, UK, where I studied part time and worked for both Cambridge Carbon Footprint and Cambridge Centre for Christianity Worldwide.[18]

I did a Masters in Environmental Management, supervised by the Conservation Advisor for A Rocha International. I was able to visit A Rocha Ghana and research the governance of degraded forest restoration projects in Ghana, Kenya and Uganda. Understanding the impact of climate change in those countries had a huge impact on me, as I saw subsistence farmers losing their livelihoods and migrating onto once-protected state forests. More frequent natural disasters such as floods and droughts were devastating. The relationship between climate change, poverty, people and nature is deep. In Ghana, where faith is integrated culturally into the way of life, Christian environmentalists are leading the way and are widely recognised in the international conservation movement for their work. I found this very inspiring.

Dan and I connected with A Rocha in France, and we stood-in for the house managers at the Les Tourades field study centre one summer. There the expression of Christian conservation included bird-ringing, habitat restoration, leisurely lunches with a deep appreciation of locally-grown produce, artisan farming and viticulture. A healthy environment leads to both healthy bodies and healthy relationships with the land.

Attending both the East African (2015) and European (2017) Lausanne Conferences on Creation Care were incredible highlights for me.[19] I saw how Christians from many diverse cultures, natural environments and socio-economic settings were responding to multiple environmental crises, guided and motivated by their faith. Another important experience was leading a small multi-faith project in Leeds for Cambridge Carbon Footprint. I brought together a group from Jewish, Sikh, Hindu, Muslim, Buddhist, Baha'i, Pagan and Christian communities to plan intergenerational events for the local community. These deepened locals' awareness of how faith interacts with our climate change response; for example how faith can enable the self-sacrifice required to live sustainably.

In the academic world of climate change research, most of the discourse I encountered was devoid of faith-based and religious perspectives. Climate change awareness sprung originally from the physical sciences, and climate research has grown into economics, governance, political studies, sociology and more. However, scholars in the UK at that time seemed more likely to discuss how Aristotle's virtue ethics might help in climate change response than they were to look at faith-based responses. This phenomenon of separating the spiritual and scientific has been deeply challenged in Aotearoa by our bicultural journey. There is an interconnectedness between spirituality and the natural environment that is increasingly acknowledged in public policy through recognition of Māori values, which makes space for deeper conversations about Christian eco-theology.

Eco Church encourages congregation-based expression of environmental action, integrating eco-friendly choices throughout worship and teaching, buildings, facilities and land management, community and global partnerships and sustainable lifestyles.[20] It is led by volunteers within church congregations. I first spearheaded this initiative at St Paul's Church in Cambridge, assisting the congregation to adopt sustainable practices to gain a nationally-recognised award. Starting with a small committed group and eventually enjoying the support of the wider congregation, we made a range of changes over time. Most of these have been lasting, and we had fun doing it! Implementing activities at a congregation scale felt far more inspiring and impactful than just trying to save the planet at a household scale (which often felt inadequate) or simply lobbying government (which felt frustrating and distant). I was also invited to preach, teach and lead workshops in different Christian settings on a faith-based response to climate change and biodiversity loss. We moved to Leeds when my husband took up a parish ministry.

*What challenges have you encountered?*

For many years I had considered myself a Christian environmental activist. However, a crisis of faith, marriage and identity took me on a journey into the limitations inherent in human nature, and our total dependence on God for redemption – environmental or otherwise. Interwoven with all my activities was the arrival of my two sons, one born in Cambridge and one in Leeds. Becoming a parent of two, at the same time as my husband became a church leader with all the associated responsibilities, wreaked havoc with my understanding of my own vocation. Having preached about, written about and responded practically to the urgency of climate change and biodiversity loss for many years, I was blindsided by my own inability to continue to prioritise acting environmentally 'when push came to shove'.

My husband was working more than full-time, we had a low income and were living in an area of socio-economic deprivation where I had few close relationships. I had a baby and a toddler to learn to care for, and also felt heavily the responsibility to offer support to my family still based on the other side of the world. People around us were often more concerned with surviving tough lives day-to-day than with caring for the environment. My health was suffering from the air pollution in Leeds and lack of sleep, I had no resilience to local kindergarten germs, and I seemed to be constantly ill as I struggled to adjust to an unfamiliar climate. I was not used to asking for help, and couldn't voice my struggles to those around me. I was desperately homesick but there was no way out on the horizon. All in all, I felt unable to show leadership in the environmental sphere, or even to maintain a shining example with my household practices. I felt I was failing at my life's work, as I put my energies into simply surviving, hour by hour, day by day.

In an effort to adapt to the situation, we enrolled our children in a local daycare part-time and I managed to carry out a Masters of Social Research, on public perception of green hydrogen energy. I had been working as a research assistant and thankfully secured a grant. My parents-in-law, living 3 hours away, helped where they could and I stayed up all hours to write. Then I began a PhD at the University of Leeds, cycling across the city to get there from our suburb. But I was not finding joy, meaning or hope in trying to solve the world's problems intellectually.

Eventually, my approach to service was forced to change. I went from having a hero complex and trying to save the world by my own strength, to learning that I must operate in humility, with failure as a friend. I learned to have real compassion for myself and others.

I had to drastically reduce my PhD research due to Covid-19 and childcare lockdowns, which allowed for a better balance of life and sustainable household practices. We made the decision to move back to New Zealand, and Dan was appointed as vicar of the Anglican Parish of Pāuatahanui. I am now able to dedicate much more time to raising our two sons. I work part-time for A Rocha as a community coordinator for the Eco Church NZ movement, and there is plenty of room for this movement to grow. I love my work.

I can see how the various threads of my life experience so far have been woven carefully together by God to allow me to make a contribution in this time, in this place. I continue to explore climate justice, including aspects of procedural justice, representation and deliberative democracy, citizen's juries and infrastructure planning. I believe that there are insufficient secular moral resources to supply the grand ambitions being cited by these movements. I firmly believe that the world's religions, and Christians especially, have an important role to play as the crisis becomes more urgent, more widely and deeply understood. Hope can be hard to find outside faith.

*How has your understanding of God changed?*

I have learned that we can trust the unfailing provision of God, and don't have to operate by sheer busyness and willpower alone. God has provided more for our family than I could have dreamed or imagined. We now live in a beautiful location overlooking Porirua Harbour, and I enjoy sharing in Dan's ministry of service to our church and wider community, as well as making the best contribution that I can, with my failings, to Eco Church NZ.

When God gave me the courage to let go of my pride, I learned that it is God who empowers us to serve in the area of creation care. I was shown that intellectual prowess is insufficient to answer the challenges of the world. The life of Christian discipleship is vital, because it is only by rooting ourselves in God's love and provision that we can keep going and make the tough daily choices. We need all the tools of the spiritual disciplines that have been passed down through the centuries to keep us going in this fight to care for our hurting planet.

Now I delight in supporting church life, as I believe that it offers the spiritual community, relationships and theological learning that will support us as people of faith serving the planet. Now I prioritise my private relationship with God even before public ministry, using the tools of prayer, worship, fellowship and especially **rest** (the Sabbath principle) to inspire and fuel our journey of environmental service. Previously, I must admit, I had grown to view these things as distractions from the work of conservation, advocacy, waste reduction and sustainable living. But all are integrated, all are vital. Take heart, fellow worker in the Kingdom, you will fail but you still have a contribution to make!

## Word-Speaker God

*Prayer by Amy Ross*

Creator God,
Life-giver
Word-speaker
Healer
Friend.

In our midst, we read You in the natural world,
and in our friends' lives –
those who love and serve their communities in hope.
You deny despair and eco-anxiety the right to paralyse.
You enable action that restores and protects.
Lord forbid that guilt in our complicity should be the end word.

You offer us your Word –
You say 'Go,
Love My world, its people, our flora and fauna'.
Encourage us as we journey this path.
May our hearts find freedom in You.
Thank you for the gift of one another as companions.
Thank you for the gift of Your Spirit around us.

Gift-giver
Restorer
Nurturer of spirit and hope
Be our guide.
Amen.

### Action Point 1: Become an Eco Church

A growing network of thriving ecologically active churches around Aotearoa who are growing in faithful mission.

- Get the support of church leadership
- Click the 'Connect' button at Eco Church NZ: www.ecochurch.org.nz
- Work through the Eco Church Self Assessment
- Set goals and make an action plan
- Share stories and be part of the network

### Action Point 2: Help young families live sustainably

Families growing in confidence in sustainable living with babies and young children.

- Run workshops on eco parenting
- Gift re-usable nappy starter packs when a new baby is born, or start a nappy library
- Cut out single-use non-compostable items such as wet wipes at church
- 'Sustainable Parenting' blog, Oma Rapeti:
  www.omarapeti.net.nz/blog/post/49464/Sustainable-Parenting
- 'Eco Living' OHbaby magazine:
  www.ohbaby.co.nz/lifestyle/eco-living
- 'Nurturing Eco Kiwis' Kidspot:
  www.kidspot.co.nz/parenting/nurturing-eco-kiwis
- Join 'Zero Waste in NZ!' on Facebook

### Action Point 3: Serve creation together as a congregation

Get your hands dirty! People working together across generations doing an environmental service activity.

- Use congregational worship time to do a practical project, e.g. planting, weeding, stream clean-up
- Include fellowship, fun and food
- Amy: "This is brilliant for time-poor families, to do church and creation care at the same time!"

### Action Point 4: Celebrate eco mission initiatives

The whole church getting in behind environmental action.

- We are great at celebrating birthdays and anniversaries; let's also celebrate our creation care actions: e.g. sharing time in worship for people to say their own steps to sustainability.
- Interview a person or family each month about an initiative they have taken
- Use existing communications, e.g. newsletters, including a regular column about sustainability
- Commit to doing this regularly
- Share stories with the Eco Church NZ community, and join on Facebook.

# Creation Spark: Ana Lisa de Jong

Ana Lisa's poems are inspiring thousands of people every day through Facebook and her Living Tree Poetry website, as well as her printed collections.[21] She lives in Auckland with her husband and daughter and son. She is an administrator for the NZ Defence Force Chaplaincy team, supporting Army, Air Force and Navy chaplains, based in Whenuapai, Auckland.

*What do you know about your ancestry?*

Recently my siblings and I have discovered more about our grandmother who has Māori ancestry. She moved away from her marae and home in the Hokianga as a child, and married into Pākehā (white) families – her first husband (my father's father) died young, and she married again. Her Māori heritage was not widely known or discussed, at least with us grandchildren, although we had an inkling. I started tracing my family tree a few years ago. Through Defence Chaplaincy I got to know Bishop Te Kitohi Pikaahu, Bishop of Te Tai Tokarau, and he put me in touch with our Ngāpuhi relations. In 2019 my sister, mother and I were invited by Bishop Kito to travel to Kamo and meet our Māori whānau for the first time at a Te Tai Tokerau Wananga. That was a precious experience. Later we travelled to the Hokianga and spent time with our new cousins, one acting as a local guide for us, taking us to the marae where we believe my grandmother spent time as a child. Being in the Hokianga, and understanding our links there, felt like a real homecoming, a very emotional experience. I could see my son's face in a great great uncle's photo.

*How does discovering your Māori ancestry change how you feel about this place?*

It explains some things about my sense of connection to nature and the land. We all have a connection to the land, because we are part of creation. But there are some places that just feel like home, like when I went to the Hokianga for the first time. It is wonderful to have a long-standing connection with this land, as well as our settler story. I feel that history.

The other side of my father's family are Welsh, which explains why I resonate so strongly with Celtic spirituality. Like Māori they see creation as a way of connecting with God, through nature around us. I don't know everything about my ancestry. We are not to know everything, or why we are made as we are, but we trust that one day all will be revealed.

*Did you grow up with faith?*

I have always been a very sensate person – I use my senses to experience God and the world around me. I grew up drawing and writing, noticing nature, noticing flowers or the sea, and letting it move me and speak to me. I had a vague understanding of God. My parents didn't go to church but they had grown up in the church and they sent me to Sunday School – partly because it was the thing to do at the time, but my mother is also a very spiritual person and wanted us to have a basic Christian understanding. When I was 13 I went to a pentecostal church service with my friend while I was staying with her in Russell, in the little town hall, still there on the waterfront in Opua. At the service there was a visiting speaker – she was amazing! She prayed for me, prophesied over me, and I was filled with the Holy Spirit. So during my teens I went to a New Life Church, in Orewa. I was given the gift of tongues when filled with the Holy Spirit, and that is still part of my contemplative prayer, an amazing gift.

I met my husband at 16, and fell away from church going, although I kept my sense of connection to God. I talked with my children about the Bible and prayed with them, but when they got to school age I wanted them to know more. So I found a local church, Baptist, and brought my children up there. Our attendance was a bit intermittent. Artistic people don't tend to be very disciplined, not good at doing what we're told! And I am an introvert, so crowds are not my favourite thing. But my children gained an understanding of faith, and it did feed and sustain me. Mothering can be hard, and it is important to be uplifted in worship.

There was a change in pastor in recent years, and I found it increasingly hard to sit and listen, as the teaching did not resonate with me. I started to question more, to think about what I believe. I got to a point where it didn't feel authentic to continue attending and I stopped. For a while I felt guilty about not going to church, but there was also a sense of freedom. Now I am looking for a more contemplative place to go for worship. St Luke's Mt Albert has a monthly contemplative evening service which I am looking forward to, once we are out of Covid lockdown.

Through the lockdown I have been exploring online sources of spiritual food. There are great websites, like Godspace Light which is very much based on honouring creation.[22] I especially love their Taizé services. I discovered Northumbria Community – I pray their Daily Office when I need that calming practice.[23] The NZ journal *Refresh* by Spiritual Growth Ministries is a wonderful resource.[24] And I enjoy the 'Lectio 365' app on my phone, which provides reflections and morning and evening prayer.[25]

### What does faith mean to you now?

I trust in so much more than I understand. To me, this is faith, a willingness to embrace the mystery. Part of our journey as we get older is coming to terms with our lack of surety, and embracing life with a faith based more on trust than absolutes.

Learning more about Māori spirituality, I can see how my trust in the natural environment, and my innate belief in the God spark in everything, was passed down to me from my Māori as much as from my Celtic forebears. In the Māori worldview the world is a vast connected family: humans are children of the earth (Papatūānuku the earth mother) and the sky (Ranginui the sky father), and cousins to all living things. Thus our kinship with nature provides a foundation and a sense of belonging. This marries well with my religious beliefs. As the creator and lover of us all, God loves and inhabits the natural world as much as he does his people.

Just as a true understanding of science gives us a new revelation of our Creator God, an appreciation and affinity with the natural world gives us a deeper connection with God. This informs a respect and proper reverence for the earth, based on our kinship with it, rather than our dominion over it. God's Spirit is teaching us our responsibility for, and connection with, the environment. Sometimes I write about 'heaven being here'. It's not that heaven isn't out there too – God is everywhere – but eternity is as much evident in everything we see around us as it is placed in human hearts. There is a great thread of continuity weaved through all of nature. It is our whakapapa (ancestry), and the whakapapa of every living thing. Our tūpuna (ancestors) are part of that thread and therefore part of us. This is faith that both grounds us to the earth and links us to the heavens, and to the Creator who resides in all. 'Tuia te rangi e tū iho nei. Tuia te papa e takato nei' ('Join sky above to earth below, so people depend on one another').[26]

*What is God doing with the church, do you think?*

God is shaking everything up! God wants to do something new with the church, I strongly feel that. Either we're on board or we're not. This involves eco spirituality, the importance of environment, and us looking at ourselves as guardians or caretakers rather than having dominion over it. God is opening our eyes in all sorts of areas. That could be in a church building, but it is increasingly about how we take God outside the church.

I have joined the Eco Church NZ network, because I know that God is drawing me in that direction. I am interested in the Forest Church concept which is emerging.[27] It is exciting to hear about what churches are doing, both here and around the world. Just like the Ecoschools where kids do schoolwork outside and learn in the environment, churches are now doing that for worship. It can be just as valid to go for a tramp on Sunday and worship in the outdoors together, like an open building. That suits contemplative people like me.

*Why is contemplative prayer important to you?*

It is the practice of viewing all of life through a sacred lens, uncovering the messages hidden in creation. Mechthild of Magdeburg wrote, "The day of my spiritual awakening was the day I saw – and knew I saw – all things in God, and God in all things." I like the line in Laudato Si': "The entire material universe speaks of God's love, God's boundless affection for us. Soil, water, mountains: everything is, as it were, a caress of God."[28]

*Are there ways that anyone can cultivate contemplative prayer?*

Take time for activities that slow down our heartbeats and wake up our spirits. Our soul needs time to catch up with all the rushing we've been doing, all that has been happening. In contemplation you reflect back on everything and you allow yourself to process that. When we slow down and pay attention, we start to hear the Word. God's Word is forever speaking. My spirit takes part in that eternal ongoing conversation carrying on everywhere around us. It is the creation spark in the heart of everything: "In the beginning was the Word, and the Word was with God, and the Word was God." (John 1:1).

In some traditions meditation is about not thinking, trying to put yourself in a place of non-attachment and mental focus. I don't do that. I do it my way or not at all! If we work hard to pray in a specific way we miss what God is saying. I allow my thoughts to go anywhere and everywhere. From that, for me comes the prompt to write – others may be prompted to paint or draw or sing. Being still and quiet helps us move into a listening place. But don't be strict. Do it in a way that works for you. Eventually we realise that we can hear this continual Word anywhere: cooking, doing the washing, playing with the children.

The Word is always speaking back to God, sometimes in lament, oftentimes in praise and worship, so how do we hear it? We slow down to listen. We transfer that hearing to what we create, in word and art and in our daily living. Creativity is a way of tapping in to the eternal Word.

*So there is a strong link for you between prayer and creativity?*

The Word is God's creative energy which is always speaking, and that energy is still creating every day. We are co-creators with that whenever we express ourselves creatively. That can be anywhere: in our relationships, our dialogue with people, the things we enjoy doing, gardening, dance, exercise, making things, from doing carpentry to making a poem or a piece of art. Wherever we are being creative and something is coming about from what we are doing, then we are expressing God's creativity.

*How can people become more creative?*

The poet's job is to be receptive. You wait for it to come, whatever it is, and you go with it. Poets often say they don't know what a poem is going to be about. It becomes something you didn't expect – and you don't always like it. It is an unfolding, an unravelling. You go with it. That is the magic of it.

We feel at one with our true nature when we give ourselves permission to be creative. There is a deep sense of being in tune with the world around us. Once we have found our 'voice' we cannot mute it. There is a healing power. In the undamming of that river we join the flow of creation. We feel a pleasure deep inside that resonates with the underlying joy of the universe. God takes pleasure in us.

*What can help someone get over the "I can't" message?*

You have to get judgement and self judgement out of the way. Any art is freedom of expression. We have to stop ourselves thinking: "Is this good? Is it what other people expect?" First, don't do it for anyone else. Second, don't look at it to judge it. The benefit is more in the process than the product. Focus on the freedom that creativity is giving you. It only matters that we are creating for our own sake and for the Creator who instilled in us our desire and ability. Ironically, when we are no longer creating art to impress

The New Zealand Defence Force is central to the New Zealand government's response to climate change, particularly around the Pacific, and that will grow as we face more climate disasters. Defence does what the government asks them to do – where there's a need we will go and help. There will be more and more of a need, sadly. We have deepening relationships with our Pacific neighbours.[31]

*Climate change, and the anxiety it brings, is such a big thing for our world today. What is the role of creativity and contemplation?*

When we face big questions, like climate change, creativity is a way to tap in to what God is saying on the subject. When we tap into God – through writing or art or music or contemplative prayer – we hear his encouragement. God is always giving us space, always encouraging us that what we are doing is worth it! I feel God is prompting people to do things in different and new ways to respond to the challenges we are facing.

We trust that God will keep on teaching us and showing us how to make a difference. God has made us each unique, to make a unique contribution. Some are practical people and organisers. I'm a contemplative, but I am also an activist through my poetry. I speak out about what I feel is most important. We need to believe in each other and what we all bring to the table.

There is a huge sense of hopelessness out there. It is especially hard for young people. It takes time to learn to trust God in every circumstance.

*Do you get exhausted?*

Contemplation and creativity comes from a place of self care. Don't make art or prayer into a chore. For me it is life giving – if I'm feeling tired I write a quick poem and feel refreshed. Learn to listen to yourself. Make yourself a priority. Find those things that refuel you.

Creativity is restorative. It is a response to the awe we feel about what see around us and what we hear from God. Paul calls us to focus on what is good and beautiful, and that releases energy.[32] People tell me I am wise, but I am incredibly ordinary. Anyone can be creative. No one is ordinary. We are all unique and amazing!

## No Explanation

*Poem by Ana Lisa de Jong, Living Tree Poetry*

We believe.
We believe in the sun rising
and falling,
in the birds and the trees,
the ocean's hum registering far within.
The way a seashell put to the ear
draws from us a dozen memories,
of childhood, of floating on the currents,
of waves against a beach.

So personal, individual,
we travel on a raft of longings
and remembrances.

Therefore we believe.

We honour the faiths
of our forebears,
the rituals of our parents,
their graces and their prayers,
and we remember
our grandparent's gestures,
their hopes placed in us,
hands upon our foreheads.

That we believe, and hardly know
how our totality is made of hums,
and snatches of song and prayer,
of snapshots in the memory,
the graces of our surrounds.

Therefore we believe,
and might not be able to give
credit to the source,
or define with clear descriptors
enough to satisfy the judges, the evangelists,

who would have us learn
a different story off their tongues,
and declare it
as our own soul's speech.
Yes, we each believe.

We believe in the sun rising
and falling, in the birds and trees,
all the common denominators that make us human,
in need of meaning.

And what means life to one
may not register with another.
But who are we to question,
or refute
the way the Spirit moves
in the eternal dance –
the song we each uniquely hear,
the private steps we follow.

## Action Point 5: Nurture creativity
Release gifts of creativity in ourselves and others to inspire creation care.
- Workshops and creative space. Invite an recycled arts team such as Rangiwahia Environmental Arts Centre Trust (React): www.rangienviroartscentre.org
- Include creative options in creation care events and worship services, especially on special Sundays such as St Francis day
- Celebrate poetry, writing, photography, art, drama etc. through displays, websites & social media, etc.
- Join Track Zero 'Arts inspiring climate action': www.trackzero.nz
- Explore online resources such as the Centre of Contemporary Art[33]

## Action Point 6: Slow down, rest and pray
Sustain resilience and wellbeing with rhythms of rest and contemplative prayer.
- Hold a Quiet Day, or Art Retreat.
- See a Spiritual Director, or invite one to preach.
- Spiritual Growth Ministries, for prayer resources and retreats: www.sgm.org.nz
- Centre for Contemplation: www.cac.org

# At the Forefront: Angela Pennington

Kia ora, I am a 31 year old Pākehā wahine living in Ōtautahi, Christchurch, New Zealand. My family are from here, but I grew up on a five acre block in the small southern town of Waimate, where my dad was the local GP. Today I work as an Architectural graduate, and by the time this is published will have a newborn and a three year old daughter with my husband Chris. Both Chris and I were raised in Christian families and have been attending Grace Vineyard since 2008 whenever we lived in Christchurch.[34]

*How did you get started with creation care?*

Creation Care at Grace Vineyard started in July 2017. I'd been on a bit of a journey learning about waste. I came to the realisation that if it hasn't been burned or recycled, all the plastic ever made still exists somewhere in the ocean or landfill. That was life-changing for me. At that time it was not mainstream thinking, which made things tricky, but look where we are now!

The waste at our church events was a really big thing for me. I remember a combined celebration service for all our campuses, at a large park with a massive marquee. Seeing so many rubbish bins overflowing with coffee cups upset me. It was just a mess. I felt that this was not what Jesus would want, not how we should be managing it. Waste was not on our radar as a church at the time, but our leadership supported me to take an initiative.

I started with Plastic Free July in 2017. Then we arranged an enviro film screening at church, with help from a couple of people from our life group. I didn't expect many people to come. We held it in the main auditorium and set out a few rows at the front, but as more and more people arrived we had to open up more and more seats. Over 100 people attended! I was blown away. I was especially excited that people came who don't normally attend church. Our community was seeing that the church cared about issues that were important to them too!

For the first year or so it was just me leading things, with a few other interested people we had gathered. But I wanted to create a core team. It helped that one of our pastors was involved from the start and had a strong environmental interest. We hosted an evening for anyone in our congregation who thought that caring for creation was part of following Jesus. From this we formed a Creation Care team for Grace Vineyard.

We decided to divide responsibilities amongst our core team based on people's interests. For example, if someone wanted to run a Biketober event, they would lead the project, rather than me doing it all. We had one team member from a World Vision background, another who worked in carbon certification, and another who was a soil scientist passionate about planting programmes.

We host regular evenings to gather the whole team together for a fun evening. We have great sustainably sourced food, and opportunities to connect with others. We've run a couple of film nights. We had popcorn and hot chocolate at the last one, with discussion before and after the film – that was fun. The best thing about these evenings was that people discovered, "Hey, there are all these other people in church who care about the same things as me!" They suddenly realised they were not alone, and it was OK to think of this as a Christian issue.

*How has your church culture shifted?*

The wider culture has changed quite significantly. That has been helped by wider changes, such as the ban on plastic bags which awakened a number of Kiwis to plastic being a problem. Whole societal change on environmental issues has helped us make changes within church. It's easier for our leaders to create change if they know that people are more likely to be open to it.

We started becoming aware of the rubbish we produce as a church – how much and what type. The environment had not previously been considered or the longer-term impact of products we were buying. This wasn't necessarily intentional – church staff were busy, and people weren't aware of the importance. So we tried to change the products we were using as they came on our radar. Things like changing from plastic plates for shared lunches to compostable wheat straw plates. They were cheaper, came from a waste product, could be composted after use, and were easier than having to wash every plastic plate before recycling.

Grace Vineyard is a large church, which means it takes time to change things, but we have seen significant change. We're a big ship to turn, but once we start turning we can have large-scale impact. One example is changing the type of paper we use. We use a lot of paper, and now all that paper has recycled content, and in turn gets recycled. We also reduced how often we print the church newsletter that is handed out at the door on Sundays – it's now a monthly newsletter instead of weekly. Small repeated actions can create a big change.

A woman in the church accounts team was passionate about reducing waste and part of our Creation Care team, which was very helpful. I would say things like, "We need to buy some compost bins" and it was helpful having an advocate in the finance department. She knew who to talk to, and the correct processes such as how to get a purchase order. Several years on, we now have a staff member who has environmental sustainability as part of his job description, which is a massive step. I'm so grateful to our leadership for doing this.

## What helps you make the connections for people?

It is important to start with our church's values. We do a lot of local mission, which has a positive impact on the communities around us, but we started to realise that the **natural** environment was negatively impacted by us being there. People could see that as God's vessels our impact on a place should be holistically positive.

We also connected through our commitment to global mission. Our church sends money to missionaries overseas to help people who are suffering. We talked about how we could soon be sending money to people who are climate change refugees. Wouldn't it be better to take action now which could help prevent climate change, rather than sending money later when we've messed it up?

Probably every Christian would agree that we are called to care for the poor; it'd be pretty hard to argue that's not what Jesus calls us to do. So even if Christians adamantly believe that we're not called to care for the environment for its own sake, realising how climate change impacts poor communities can be a really good motivator for those just starting on this journey. It is a place of agreement to start conversations.

Creation care is also an evangelism tool. There are a lot of people who are passionate about environmental issues, and environmental anxiety is a real thing. People are looking for answers and hope in this whole crisis. What if the church could be an example and a hope to guide that? If we don't address this, it could also have the opposite effect and become a roadblock for the environmentally aware person attending a church service for the first time.

Taking action on creation care issues can also have a positive impact on the mental health of people in our congregation. Instead of being paralysed by fear of the effects of climate change, we can influence the outcome when we make these changes. Conversely, when you live in a way that doesn't align with your values, we often see negative mental health impacts. Realising that our values around the environment align with God's desire to bring restoration and thriving to the earth – this brings peace.

I always try to bring a message of hope and kindness. I feel that's the way Jesus would do it; his love and kindness motivates us to change. People are more motivated by the positive influence they can have, than the negative if they do nothing. When we need to speak into the negative reality we are facing, then it is important to follow with a message of hope. Our God is a God of hope, not fear. I had an opportunity to speak at one of our church services on Creation Care, which was incredible. I felt it was important to convey the problem but also to bring a solution to follow, and not leave people in that dark space. My message was: "This is important, and part of following Jesus, but don't try to do everything at once. Pick one thing to try, and start with what you can do." I tried to make it easy, practical, and positive at the end. God wants us to feel convicted but not condemned.

When you are more passionate about something than those you're addressing it is ineffective to just yell at them to change. Everything Jesus does is through love and relationship, and we need to do things his way. It's really easy to think, "The church should change!" and point the finger at leadership: "Why haven't **they** done something about it?" Actually, we are the church, so why haven't I done something about it?

Any conversations with leadership about why sustainability is important should be respectful, with a heart to listen. I want to be a person of kindness and hope. Getting grumpy and leaving is not going to bring the change that you want, and it's going to make you feel awful in the process. Even if other leaders have an opposite view to me, I trust that they are appointed by God, and that they are doing their best with the knowledge they have.

One barrier was the perception that anything environment-friendly was going to cost more, be really inconvenient, or both! So we did a lot of work on cost savings. We showed that buying disposable stuff actually costs more long term. It took us a few years, but this year we actually saved money by doing things 'eco'. That was really cool. One of our team, who is on staff, did incredible work to achieve this.

Another barrier we encountered is the theology that 'God's going to destroy the Earth, so why should we care?' I question, is that actually what the Bible says? Does that really line up with the characteristics of a God who is about regeneration and restoration? I've found some great sermons and reading around this from the likes of Sam Harvey, who was our pastor at Grace at the time, which have been really helpful.[35]

*What inspired you?*

I was passionate about waste reduction, and wanted to see things change. How great would it be if as a church we were at the forefront of caring for the environment? Shouldn't we be the best at this, because we are connected to a God of restoration who created our world in the first place?!

When we were starting out I researched online, looking for Christian resources on caring for the environment. You can find anything on the internet, and I wanted to make sure what I was reading was biblically accurate and carefully considered. I found Ruth Valerio's work to be sensible while also calling out the need for significant change.[36] A Rocha is a non-denominational Christian organisation that I also found to have a lot of solid resources.[37]

We were also inspired by Vineyard Boise church in Idaho who did a radical turn-around on creation care issues. The senior pastor Tri Robinson was impacted by a conversation with his adult children leading up to the 2000 national election. They were frustrated that in their political climate you either had to be pro-life or pro-environment. There wasn't a Christian environmental option. This is an issue here too but in America it is quite extreme. People saw environmental issues as a very liberal thing. But they started some local environment stewardship work, and they shifted the church culture. There was no city-wide recycling, so they got a recycling truck to come to church and people could bring their recycling to drop off. They looked for fun positive approaches that were not just hard work. They encouraged people to get out in nature, go for hikes, to recognise the beauty God created for us to live in. This church is now seen as one of the leading voices in their community on environmental issues and people have come to church because of it. The local City Council actually consults the church on environmental issues!

In 2018 we worked with some other Christchurch churches on a weekend seminar on Creation Care. That was really inspiring. That Sunday I preached in our church, and it was the first time that creation care had ever been the main topic. A woman called Waveney Warth spoke in one of our other campuses that same Sunday. She had a massive influence.[38] One of our key volunteers told me how that weekend strongly impacted him. Basically his whole family changed from that service. They all started to cycle and walk to church. He started a plant-based diet. When they walk along the beach, the kids want to pick up rubbish. It was quite amazing. God really touched their hearts.

Then in 2019 we hosted an A Rocha evening, also with some great speakers.[39]

*What have you learned about going zero waste?*

Sorting rubbish is not everyone's idea of a fun job. Unless you have great motivation why would you do that? We set up waste management systems for all big church events, with recycling bins and compost bins. It is actually very satisfying when you get to the end of the day and you realise you have saved three massive bins from going to landfill. I remember what it was like before and that motivates me to keep going.

We found that the most effective way is to have people standing at the bins monitoring what goes in, rather than sorting through it afterwards. We try to be positive and friendly, rather than "the rubbish police." When someone approaches I get the team to name the item the person has and the colour bin that it needs to go in, rather than just taking the waste for them and dealing with it. That way it educates and empowers people to make change when they're at home also. And everyone thanks you as they come up to use the rubbish bins, which is lovely.

A waste system needs to be easy or people don't use it. If you have bins anywhere, make sure you have all the bins, i.e. recycling, landfill, and compost all next to each other. If you only have a recycling bin for example, people will think, "I don't know where this goes" and put other rubbish in it. Set it up so that they have the opportunity to make the right choice easily.

It is also important to work with suppliers and vendors to only serve in compostable or reusable packaging. Now we have our food vendors telling people that the plates and serviettes can go in the organics bin.

Purchasing influences the whole waste structure, so if you get the right products from the start then there's a lot less to deal with at the end when it comes through.

And you have to repeat the message over and over and over again.

In 2019 we were blown away when we won a Keeping Christchurch Beautiful community award. It was very exciting. I didn't even know the award existed, but we got an email saying that we had been nominated. We went along to the City Council event and it turned out that everyone who's nominated gets an award, which was so lovely. I see that as one of the first steps of our community recognising that the church cares about environmental issues.

*Do you see this as a calling on your life?*

I think that we are all called to be stewards. That is our first commission, right back in Genesis, being told to look after the earth.

*Comment from Chris, Angela's husband:*

I would say that for Ange it is a calling specifically to lead in this area. Her passion and involvement in church has been stronger since this has become a driving force. You can tell a calling by the fruit of it, because if you are in your calling you have the Lord's favour on it. The constant feedback around Ange's leadership is that everyone who has a conversation with Ange comes away motivated and feeling good about it. So, yes, it is a calling.

*And how do these values fit into your professional work in architectural design?*

I am always on the look out for opportunities to learn about and implement stewardship values in my work. This has been far more difficult than the opportunities I've had in our church community and home life. This is probably due to many factors: my less senior position in the work place; an industry entrenched in "the way we've always done things"; the cost of building in New Zealand; and the fact that as a designer you can only advise clients but they make the decisions in the end. This year however, I've worked on my first Passive House project, and am about to start another. I also had the opportunity recently to work for the Superhome Movement and learnt so much there.[40] Chris and I are hoping to build our own little affordable high-performance home – I'm sure there will be much learning to come from that.

**So so much greater!**

*Prayer by Angela Pennington*

Lord, we are faced with an insurmountable task.
The scale seems overwhelming,
but you are so, so much greater.
Help us to know how to do this your way.
Let our work to care for your earth
show people your love and kindness.
Let your peace and hope be at the forefront of our minds.
Lead us.
We are ready to follow your way of doing things.
We love you.
Amen.

### Action Point 7: Go Zero Waste

Significantly reduce the amount of church waste going to landfill, and inspire families to reduce waste at home.

Improve rubbish systems in your church buildings, reduce the number of landfill bins and increase recycling and green-waste bins

- Set up Zero Waste systems for church events
- Join the Eco Church Zero Waste for Churches Programme:
  www.ecochurch.org.nz/zero-waste-programme
- Para Kore: www.parakore.maori.nz
- The Story of Stuff Project, videos on Youtube:
  www.youtube.com/c/StoryofStuff

### Action Point 8: Choose what you buy

Everything we purchase reflects our values and keeps waste to a minimum.

- Don't buy junk! Choose to buy things which will last. Don't buy for the bin
- Develop a purchasing policy for your church
- Consider the life-span of what comes into your home or church
- Purchasing resources, Eco Church NZ:
  www.ecochurch.org.nz/purchasing

### Action Point 9: Social events with a creation focus

- Fun events that build friendship and community as well as inspiring sustainability.
- Movie nights with popcorn and discussion
- Church picnics or bike trips
- Home-grown food competitions and bake-off
- Celebrating enviro-friendly products such as cleaning products or skin care

# All That God Has Given: Ani Kartikasari

From Indonesia, Ani now lives in Lincoln where she is the Director of the Yunus Social Business Centre at Lincoln University.[41]

*How have you come to where you are now?*

Looking back, I see God's grace at work, and how he has used my passion and my training. I have always been curious about animals and interested in the natural world and its conservation, especially from a Christian perspective. I grew up in a small town in Indonesia. From a young age I was allowed to roam freely, to go to the rice fields or the river. My father regularly practised yoga, often by the riverside, so I would go with him and then go off exploring on my own. I was fascinated by what I saw: birds, frogs, worms, insects, butterflies and little fish darting around.

At Bogor University I did my undergraduate degree in forestry, majoring in wildlife conservation, which I'm sure was strongly influenced by those early explorations. While doing field research for my Honours I lived in the jungle for three months studying monkeys – that was my passion, I wanted to be the Indonesian Jane Goodall! In Indonesia it was compulsory to attend Religious Studies classes at all universities, and during the discussion sessions I became interested in Christian faith. By the time I left university I was committed to Christianity and wanted to work with young people.

I expected to go straight into teaching, but God had a different plan. Through mutual friends I was offered a research assistant job with a British ecologist who just completed writing *The Ecology of Sulawesi*.[42] Tony Whitten was a highly committed and internationally respected ecologist. I worked with him for 15 years, much of that time employed by the Canadian International

Development Agency. This gave me valuable first-hand experience working in the field, with Tony as well as other world-renowned ecologists, travelling all over Indonesia and then assisting with writing the resulting ecology books. Our project was to produce the *Ecology of Indonesia* series, consisting of 11 volumes and covering all the environments from the sea to the top of the mountains on the six main islands. I ended up managing and editing the translation of these books into Indonesian, a process that was to prove invaluable.

After that I headed to England on scholarship to train for cross-cultural mission work at All Nations Christian College in England. I found myself being taught by Chris Wright, who at that time was the director of studies. He was an inspirational teacher and I got very interested in the biblical ethics of caring for God's creation. Having spent so much time embedded in Indonesia's wildlife this was a natural path for me to take. Two years later I went to Cambridge University to study for my Masters in Environment and Development, learning further about the human side of conservation and development.

I then moved to New Zealand in 2003 to do my PhD in environmental management. My thesis was on the social and political dimensions of managing protected forests in Indonesia. Since then I have been at Lincoln University as a lecturer and chaplain. I have continued some work in Indonesia, including a project with three major Islamic universities, to promote the teaching of sustainability by integrating faith into the sustainability concept. Despite me not being a Muslim they invited me and it was a good opportunity to strengthen inter-faith communication.

I continue my passion for conservation, looking for opportunities to make connections with natural ecosystems. For instance, I took international students on tree planting activities around the Canterbury region, and challenge them to look at the role conservation has in improving river water quality and stopping erosion and assisting farmers in improving land quality and protecting animals and birdlife. They come to see the importance of community projects in spreading conservation knowledge and protecting local environments for all to use, particularly children – which they may not have seen the importance of before. Throughout this work I feel the guidance of God's love and encouragement. After all, it is his domain we are sharing and protecting. It also led me to reflect – which happens a lot when working amongst nature – on how God has guided me. My faith has guided and strengthened my life in very practical ways.

It is particularly important to share my passion 'one on-one' because this allows me to build a strong relationship. For me this is a priority, because these young people, with the right experience and mentorship, will be the change-makers in their own countries. I have learned so much from others, who encouraged me by sharing their knowledge and experiences, so now I can share and pass on to others, who in turn will become conservation advocates around the world.

For five years I taught a postgraduate course in international rural development, where I integrated nature conservation with economic and social development. I was recently appointed as the director of the Yunus Social Business Centre based at Lincoln University. That focuses on research and teaching social entrepreneurship: the use of business principles and practices to achieve social and environmental goals.

*What do you teach about environmentally sustainable business?*

I am passionate about promoting social business, because this is inclusive of social, environmental and economic needs: for example, a plant nursery giving work to people who are physically disabled. Some churches are developing social enterprise, and churches can support social enterprises in your area. The financial return is lower because the value is in the community investment, so they need support from customers. I keep coming back to the question of 'what can I do?' If I can be just one person, buying their product, adding to the consumer base of that social enterprise, that will help them do the good things they do.

All kinds of businesses are becoming more environmentally sustainable, which is driven by consumer demand. Green consumption is the way of the future. People realise the vulnerability of our planet – we are already exceeding the capacity of the planet, with pollution, waste and unsustainable practices. We are developing awareness, attitudes and understanding of the consequences of business behaviour. Whatever their field of commerce, our students learn to identify barriers and enablers for becoming more sustainable. The goal is to level out the price point difference for sustainable products. This can only happen by growing the consumer base, as people like you and I put our money into it.

*What can we do to make a difference?*

We need to be willing to prioritise our values. Buy things that will last for several years. Don't buy what will just end up in landfill. Pay more for items that are good for the environment. We have to think about it and not do willy nilly what we used to. If I only think about what is cheapest for me, I need to challenge myself: 'Is this how I express my worship to God?'

As consumers we can check the origins of materials we are buying, we can check the credentials of a business, both the retailer and the manufacturer. Ask: "What is your sustainability strategy?" We can make a big difference in small ways.

*Do you see God inspiring social enterprise and innovation?*

Of course he does! If you look at the book of Ruth, how Ruth met Boaz, that was a social enterprise. Boaz was very wealthy but he told his people to leave some for the poor, so that they could eat. You would be amazed to see the principles of social enterprise in the Bible! It is about integrity and values – faith is not just our beliefs but how we live and work. That is why I come back to 'How can I worship God in the way I consume things?' If I see that as part of my expression of love and obedience to God, then it will be less difficult to choose sustainable options, because we see our little things in the context of a bigger picture.

*How is sustainable social business part of global mission?*

Mission seeks to alleviate poverty and share God's love. There is a growing emphasis on training local leaders. Skills such as how to feed a goat properly involve understanding environmental, human and animal health, and can have a lasting impact, empowering a family's livelihood and reducing dependency. My church supports a mission project in Mongolia addressing food security. Most of the year it is too hot or too cold to grow vegetables, so they have built a greenhouse to extend the growing season. Then they can add value by processing their harvest, pickling gherkins. That is empowering for the local economy and a very powerful platform to serve God. The glasshouse becomes the pulpit – they can talk about Jesus while they are planting.

Strong local businesses are vital for communities to cope with climate change. It is the poorest, the most vulnerable, who can't move when the floods come, who don't have insurance or options. Climate change impacts are not distributed proportionally.

*How are you involved in creation care in the church?*

I belong to Hope Presbyterian Church in Hornby, Christchurch. I am often invited to speak about my work in conservation and the complexity of working in developing countries, juggling nature conservation and poverty. I am on the Worldwide Mission committee as well as the Care for Creation group. We were planning a 'carbon zero picnic' for the church, building on my involvement with a riparian restoration project through the City Council – before Covid interrupted our plans.

I think there is a lot of scope for churches to look at their impact on the environment. It is important to mainstream the concept of sustainability, such as how churches use energy and manage waste, so that instead of creation care being a special event it becomes part of everyday life. Practical activities embody what we believe – this is part of our mission. As a teacher I integrate conservation into my teaching, it is not an add-on. Conserving God's creation and managing the resources we have is not an optional extra – it is part of how we express our faith. There is not enough teaching on this. People think that if we have one Creation Care service each year we've done our bit. Some people choose to do conservation work outside the church, and that's OK. But there is a lot of value in doing this together as Christians; especially for children so they see that we walk our talk, and they are aware that conservation now is important for their future. Mainstreaming takes a collective effort, intentional and regular, instead of one-off occasional things.

### What is the faith dimension for you?

We have this great hope that, yes, God is renewing the earth and will create a new heaven and a new earth. But we live on this planet at breaking point, and our lives depend on the wellbeing of the planet. It is our responsibility as Christians to acknowledge God's renewing and to increase our care for the environment. I believe that this call for active involvement in conservation is not an option. It is a command from God. Our focus and our priority are to obey that command and embody it into our lives, individually and as a community. We must listen deep within us to God's command, and with strong faith and God's love walk the talk.

At a personal level, I ask myself 'What can I do with all that God has given me?' I am a new creation, and God is recreating in me and through me. An expression of that is how I manage my private life, my resources, waste, time, being ethical in my clothing and shopping; all are an expression of my faith, and I strive to do better. My faith is a major part of my conservation activism, giving me the strength to continue doing God's work and fulfill my calling.

When I was a child I didn't know it was a calling. I just enjoyed being in nature. When I was at university I was privileged to learn ecology as an academic subject, and it formed my understanding of how things are connected. I found my role in that. When I came to faith this was all bound together into a strong foundation: I have this passion, I have this training

– mission, theology as well as academic – and I have these opportunities. God has a plan for me!

*Are there particular ideas about God, theology or scripture that motivate you?*
The starting point for me is the sense of awe that I have when looking at Creation. I can look at a grasshopper, and I see God's work in there; how do the legs work in that form?

John Stott is a favourite author of mine. He teaches that you get to know God through his Word and his World. For me, it came through the world first, Creation, then through Scripture. I see the whole story of Creation, the beginning, the present, and the hope of the new Creation, as something I hold together.

One scripture that comes to mind is Psalm 24:1: "The earth is the Lord's and everything in it" – including me! I belong to God and my life belongs to God. Everything else flows from there.

*What is your hope for the world?*
Up till now, in most parts, the planet has been very resilient and did not need human beings to help it recover. But now scientific evidence shows that the earth has been damaged beyond its capability to restore itself. People have already trespassed the limits of the planet's recovery systems. We have to take intentional action to curb and repair our impact.

My hope is based on what God says, that he will recreate, renew and create a new earth. He invites a partnership with us. He can do it alone but he chooses to involve us. We live on this planet and to survive we need the sustenance that Earth provides. If we refuse to respect that provision, we are not just abusing Earth's bounty but God's creation. The more we include sustainability in our practices and lifestyle to reduce the pressure, the better the opportunity for Earth to renew itself while we are still here.

God says he will renew, through the life of people who are being renewed by the Spirit. Individually, we can't make a huge difference, but God respects even a little intention. Through our effort in putting that into action we grow our confidence to be part of a bigger entity. That is my hope for humanity. That is why the gospel is real Good News. For that to be good for me and good for the planet takes collective co-operation to make an impact. We can't do it on our own. The multiplier effect when people work together is much greater than individuals working separately. Collective co-operation, together with faith in God's plan, is my hope.

## The Serenity Prayer

The 'Serenity Prayer' was written by the American theologian Reinhold Niebuhr (1892–1971). It is commonly quoted as:

> God, grant me the serenity
> to accept the things I cannot change,
> courage to change the things I can,
> and wisdom to know the difference.

However, Niebuhr's original prayer asked for courage first, and specifically courage for changing things that **must** be changed, not things that simply can be changed. So I prefer this version:

> Father, give us courage
> to change what must be altered,
> serenity to accept what cannot be helped,
> and the insight to know the one from the other.

### Action Point 10: Talk about hope

Grow in confidence in your Biblical theology about the ultimate destiny and hope of the universe.

- Book edited by Nicola Hoggard Creegan and Andrew Shepherd, *Creation and Hope: Reflections on Ecological Anticipation and Action from Aotearoa New Zealand* (Wipf and Stock, 2018)

### Action Point 11: Support social enterprises

Thriving businesses, both here and in developing countries, that lift people out of poverty, are environmentally sustainable, and empower vulnerable communities.

Find out about social enterprises in your local area and support them

- Explore innovative 'green' church-based enterprise that can bring financial, social and environmental benefits
- Shop (and volunteer) at Trade Aid: www.tradeaid.org.nz
- Joyya (previously Freeset – Baptist fair trade mission): www.joyya.com
- The Impact Initiative, working to develop social enterprise in NZ: www.theimpactinitiative.org.nz
- Social Enterprise, Enterprise North Canterbury: www.northcanterbury.co.nz/business-support/resources/social-enterprise

### Action Point 12: Buy enviro friendly products – even if they cost more

Ani challenges us to fully commit, before God, to be part of the solution as environmentally aware consumers.

- 'Ways to buy better and shop less' GenLess: www.genless.govt.nz/for-everyone/everyday-life/shop-sustainably

## Dumb

*Poem by Ana Lisa de Jong, Living Tree Poetry*

While the earth is still breathing
I will listen to her heart beat.
She has things to share in the wind's breath,

and while the sun turns
I will pivot like the plants
towards her face.

Yes, I am aware I say too much.

But don't we each create a life
from which we preach
in pulpits of our making?

And then, step outside
struck dumb by the eloquence
of a language without speech.

We hear the birds in the trees,
their songs clear and succinct
in praise and thanks.

We sit in a short few inches,
and the grass moves with life
that we jump to our feet.

Yes, in all of our advancements
we find ourselves surpassed
yet again

by the creatures living in balance
with the earth.

# To Come Home: Anna Baird

Anna and her family are from Masterton, and are part of The Tribe church.[43]

*What was your background?*

I was born and grew up here in Masterton. I grew up quite 'outdoorsy', lots of gardening, swimming in the river and going to the beach. Hiking was a formational experience. In the forest I felt: 'Wow! Creation is good! It's exciting and it's beautiful and I love it!'

Both my parents are Pākehā. Dad's parents were born in New Zealand. Their parents came from Scotland, England and Ireland. Mum's parents came over from Holland in the 1950s and had seven children, with not much money to feed them all. Granddad Opa worked as an orderly at the hospital, and he made extra money by selling garden produce at the market. They had no lawn – the kids had to play on the street because all the space was used for growing veggies! Hard work and gardening were definitely strong Dutch influences.

Our church background was in the Reformed Church. Church was very important and faith was a big part of life. We went to church twice every Sunday and to a Christian school. It gave me a strong sense that 'I belong to God. I am part of God's family'. It was a tight-knit community. I was secure knowing I was God's child. The Reformed Church is big on systematic theology and they pass that on to the kids. The foundation is the Lordship of Christ; everything falls under his domain. It was embedded in me that faith is not just about going to church on Sunday but is everything you do.

All of your life comes under Christ's discipleship. Creation is good, and it is good to look after it, but the church did not focus on conservation.

*And as a young adult?*
I toyed with the idea of being a missionary, and went on a couple of short mission trips, to the Solomon Islands and to Japan. I saw people living together as community with a sense of shared purpose and I loved that. After high school I became a primary school teacher. My love for nature was an interest for me, there in the background. I taught the kids about birds and wildlife.

Lynton and I grew up together here in Masterton at the same church and the same school, but we didn't 'get together' until we were in our 20s. Lynton first heard about A Rocha Aotearoa when it was in its early stages, around the time we got married. We'd only been married for three weeks and we decided to go to the first A Rocha Hui in Raglan. Up till then I did not see the point of a Christian conservation group. Why don't Christians just join Forest and Bird or another conservation organisation? Wouldn't that be more missional? But I went along anyway and I fell in love with it from day one.

International A Rocha founder Peter Harris was the keynote speaker at that first A Rocha Aotearoa Hui. He taught three sessions working out the theology of creation care. He drew it out so clearly from passages such as Colossians 1: God created all things but all things have fallen, and he is restoring all things. With our Reformed background Lynton and I are geared to value solid biblical foundations. I especially valued Peter's vision of a new heaven and a new earth: God's future plan is not souls whipped up to heaven and 'burn the earth'. The Reformed Church never taught that creation is bad and will be disposed of. Creation theology was there ready inside me and Peter's teaching lit the spark. I saw the biblical reasons behind creation care and the hope that creation is included in God's redemption plan. It suddenly made perfect sense, and became a focus for our lives.

Several local groups around the country started after the Hui in 2008. At the Hui we met in regional groups and everyone said, "This is great! Let's start something." In other countries A Rocha started with a Field Centre as a hub, but in New Zealand we all wanted to get stuck in and do something around our own backyard. There was a small group from Wellington at the Hui which formed the basis of local group. Lynton and I led that until we went overseas, and for a year after we got back.

Lynton and I were born the year that A Rocha started overseas, 1983, and we were married just when it started in New Zealand. We have tracked our milestones together!

*You went overseas with A Rocha?*

Lynton and I had decided to volunteer overseas before we had kids. We muddled around with "Who do we go with?" There are so many countries, so many volunteer groups, and we're not very decisive. At the Hui we heard about Kristel going to A Rocha Kenya, so we made inquiries, found out where A Rocha needed volunteers, and thought about which countries we wanted to visit. Then in 2010 we took a year off our jobs and spent six months in Vancouver in the A Rocha centre there and then six months at A Rocha Kenya. We loved it! It was a very transformational time for us which set us on the path we have been on ever since.

We especially loved the Canada base.[44] Kingfisher Farm was a growing team, with some families living there permanently and volunteers starting to join them. We made friends with people from around the world and lived closely together as a community. Most meals were shared. The community shared agriculture scheme meant there was always gardening to do. They had various other projects and we chose which to join in, based on what we wanted to learn. I got involved with hosting visiting school groups, monitoring a threatened frog species, and creating artwork for the centre.

Food was a massive part of the Canada experience for us. In our first week we all watched a documentary called King Corn, looking at industrialised agriculture. Until then I had no concept of the scale of industrialised agriculture in America and the problems it creates. It was a huge contrast to the way we lived at Kingfisher Farm. There was a very basic pantry to cook from, and sometimes over 30 people to cook for; just beans, pasta or rice and the garden of veggies. Once a week we had some meat, from their own farm. We learned how to do everything from scratch. It was fun! I liked the challenge of it and the connection of eating straight from the land with other people.

They had the theology to go with it. We had daily prayers in the mornings. Once a week we would stop for working a few hours and spend time together: singing and prayer and unpacking a topic. We would think through theology, faith and creation care. That elevated the whole experience for me. It was important enough to stop working for half a day. There is a big influence from Regent College in Vancouver which led to great teaching. A Rocha was not closely associated with any one church. The message was not, "We are the church, stick with us." They encouraged everyone to go to different churches.

Kenya was a very different experience.[45] In Canada we slotted in straight away, found our role and were able to contribute. Kenya was amazing, living right next to a stunning white sand beach overlooking the Indian Ocean, but also much more of a culture shock. Many things felt foreign to us, such as the house servants in our guesthouse who did our washing and cooking, and met separately from the international Interns. That felt very weird. And the internet not working, the power not working, language barriers and other challenges made it hard to get things done. We learned so much from getting to know local Kenyans, whose lives were incredibly challenging. We were struck by how much they would sacrifice for their families. We are so individualistic in New Zealand by comparison. We made good friends in Kenya and Canada that we are still in touch with and we really miss them.

*Then you came back to New Zealand – what happened next?*

We felt very restless coming back from overseas. Moving back to our house, just the two of us, felt so wrong. We missed community living.

Lynton's background was in chemistry and he decided to train to be a teacher. When he finished his training he accepted a position in Masterton. That was our chance to come back home. We are small town people and our parents all live here. We had three girls and I have looked after them. The youngest starts school next year, so we are nearly through that whole preschool phase.

In moving to Masterton we wondered: "What do we do? Do we buy another house?" We don't love the system of everyone buying their own house and living in their own individual places. I felt so uninspired by that. So we looked around for what we could join. We are not pioneer types who start something new. We like to get behind what is already happening. We connected with a church with a large property. They had in the past provided supportive accommodation but they were a bit burned out and needed more team members. They invited us to come to try it out – "See what you think" – so we moved on site. We offered supportive accommodation for women and children for a few years and ran a community garden.

We wanted to develop a Christian community on that land, either with Urban Vision or A Rocha, but we struggled to find a team, and the owners didn't share our vision. We lived there for six years, trying to make it work. It was such a big disappointment when we had to leave that land. I had thought it was God's call for us to live there and live out all we had learned with A Rocha overseas. It was really confusing when that didn't work out. But actually, because we were able to buy a house just down the road, we are still able to live out our hopes. The funny thing is, it's the house my parents owned when I was a baby! We are still connected through the community garden and our church worships there. And now the stream restoration project is developing. Many of the things I had wanted to achieve are coming to fruition; the hard work we put in did not go to waste.

*What was your involvement with the community garden?*

The idea for a community garden was initiated by someone for a social work training assignment. The first week we moved in, a guy on Probation was doing community service hours putting in a garden on the property. So when we arrived, the garden was newly built, but those who had built were no longer involved. No one knew who would run it. What was the purpose of the garden? Where would the food go? Because of our time in the community garden in Canada we offered to help, so we got landed with it! We built up a solid core group of committed people who always turn up. A small group who become good friends is enough to keep something going.

*Do you agree that a faith based perspective brings together both human need and environmental need?*

Absolutely! Humans are needed for the restoration of the earth. Healing takes place in parallel. If you heal the land people heal as well. Mission brings community together and we restore the land together. They are totally interwoven, they go together.

*And now you are part of a church called The Tribe?*

The Tribe is a little pentecostal community church here in Masterton. It is affiliated with the Link NZ network of relational Spirit-led churches. I am often on the Kids team with children's church and help lead the Eco Church team. Lynton is on the preaching team, and I preach occasionally.

*How did they become part of Eco Church?*

My home group did a Tearfund bible study called 'The Good Lives Project' that got us talking about the importance of the environment. We all resonated with it and wanted to do more.

One of the church Kaitiaki (Elders) sat me down one day. She knew I was passionate about care for creation so she asked, "What would it look like if our church put this into practice?" I shared my whole vision with her and threw her lots of ideas, and she said, "OK, let's do it!" It happened for us very organically. Eco Church NZ was just getting started at that time.

*What things are emerging with that?*

Little steps, bit by bit. We have done small things like swapping the paper hand towels for reusable towels that get washed. We partnered with Para Kore to look at our waste and recycling.[46] We had a seminar and the Kaiarahi (trainer) set us up with recycling bins. We are slowly working through the Eco Church self review questionnaire, and setting a goal from each area.[47]

A local reserve restoration project has emerged, and the church has got involved. We purposely put the first planting day on a Sunday morning so our whole church could participate. Every few months our church has an Outward Sunday. Instead of meeting inside for worship we go out and connect in with local groups that need assistance in some way. So that time it was helping out with the planting of the stream. It was a fantastic opportunity for our church to get involved with a neighbourhood project.

That is the neat thing about an organic way of doing local mission. When you are committed to an area, as a family or as a church, then opportunities naturally come out of that.

*It's not so much starting with a project in mind, as looking at the place where you are?*

That's right. A commitment to the place and a commitment to the people. Mission is building local relationships and then seeing what emerges. Practical actions flow naturally when you hear what the need is.

*Specifically what does that look like?*

There is a waterway on our street – people call it a drain. It's full of weeds and rubbish, it doesn't support much life and it looks horrible. We wanted to get it replanted but it seemed too big a project. Then last year one of our team who also lives in the street decided "Yes, let's do this!" So we started having online meetings during Covid lockdown, and brought a small project group together. We had meetings with the City Council, developed a plan, talked to land owners along the waterway to get their approval. It has been a long process, a whole year of meetings! Finally we are now at the point where we have started putting trees in the ground.

*What practical things do you encourage people to do?*

I am passionate about living sustainably. How do we become producers instead of consumers? As a family we try to eat less meat, grow our own fruit and veggies, bike where possible and buy second hand. My theory is to save a lot of money by buying second hand and living simply, which we can then use to spend a bit more on quality ethically made products. We incorporate sustainability into everyday life and see that as part of worship. It counts in our Christian life, which should be consistent and make sense. My encouragement is to be thoughtful about those little things.

*What resources have you have found helpful?*

I find The Story of Stuff very inspiring – it had a huge impact. They have a series of online videos about everyday objects and the waste issues.[48] Society operates on a linear system of 'extract' and then 'make it' and then 'throw it out'. It is not the way God designed the world. Creation is circular. We have to get off that linear treadmill and start doing it differently.

Preserving fruit is one way we do that. Lynton and I grew up with preserving; both our families had jars and jars of preserves. We'd have a chain gang: someone washing the fruit, someone cutting it up, someone filling the jars. It was good fun. We have taken this on board as a family and with our friends. We preserve our stewed fruit for the year, all the pasta sauce we need as well as relish and jams. We ran some preserving workshops for the community and we are keen to do that again – though it's tricky to plan because you don't know exactly when the produce will be ready. People are definitely interested.

*Have you done workshops on other topics?*

Yes. We did pruning workshops as well, because there is a large run down orchard on-site that we can experiment on.

*How have you seen God at work along the way?*

I never feel confident to say what God is doing – that's a big call to make. I've been wrong in the past so I am hesitant to say. I think God works by making life uncomfortable sometimes! I feel God's call as a restlessness that doesn't go away. For me it is a feeling that it is not enough to be focused on saving money for retirement and providing for our children. That is just not enough for a worthwhile life. It's easy to get comfortable and self-satisfied but by God's grace we will see the urgency of the climate and ecological crisis.

I appreciate the Psalms in their negativity. Their lament realigns us, it positions us into the right posture.

I am inspired by the prophets in the Bible. They were unpopular and cranky. They speak their mind, unafraid. They say it as it is and call out injustice.

They show a vision and paint a picture of how things could be. I would like to be brave and confront people and confront corporations – but I haven't done that much. I have always wanted to show through my life that there is an alternative that is good and joyful. Living sustainably is a better way to live.

It is amazing to me that Lynton and I were able to buy this house, my family home from way back. It was a very unlikely thing that the people who owned it would sell it to us and that we had just enough money to buy at the right time. I see God's hand in that.

*What is your vision going forward? What is God saying to us as we head into this changing time?*

I would like all our eyes to be opened to the climate crisis we are facing. I think we are still in denial. We don't acknowledge how quickly we have to change. I would love for the churches to be at the forefront of that. It is scary to me how stuck in our ways we are, until change hits us in the face. I feel a lot of anxiety around climate change, and I have not been given easy answers from God. But my anxiety calls me back to God. All I can say is: "Have mercy, Lord! It's your world." I know he cares for it. "Don't let us stuff it up too much. Have mercy on us."

I think a lot about hope. Can you have hope when you don't feel hopeful? Colossians 1 talks about faith and love springing from hope. I like that; we need hope to sustain our actions.

We always thank God, the Father of our Lord Jesus Christ, when we pray for you, because we have heard of your faith in Christ Jesus and of the love you have for all God's people – the faith and love that spring from the hope stored up for you in heaven. (Colossians 1:3-5)

Hope is not a feeling, it is a belief. I believe that God will restore this earth. He does love it and he will take care of it. He does have a good plan. Don't look around or read news headlines and ask 'do I feel hopeful?' It is about trusting him. It is important to have that hope and to stay fixed on that. Otherwise you get hopeless, which leads to being fatalistic. We can think: 'Oh, we're stuffed, so let's just enjoy what we've got and not stress about it'. That's where a lot of people are at, thinking that it's too late and we can't do anything about it – just waiting for the government to do something. But I have that hope and it spurs me on. It is worth carrying on. Let's give it our best shot.

I know the ending of the book; I just don't understand how this chapter we are in at the moment will get to that conclusion!

*Prayers by Anna Baird*

## As the mountains crumble

As mountains crumble
As coastlines disappear
**We look to you, have mercy.**

As ecosystems break down
As communities unravel
**We look to you, have mercy.**

As forests burn
As species are wiped out
**We look to you, have mercy.**

Save us from ourselves, show us a new way
We are nothing, except by your grace.
**We look to you, have mercy.**

## Open our eyes

*(Based on Psalms 121 and 123)*

Our help comes from the name of the Lord,
Creator of heaven and earth.
We look to you, we need you.
Have mercy on us, forgive us.
Open our eyes to see,
open our eyes to who you want us to be.
We look to you,
as the eyes of a baby look to their mother,
as the eyes of a sheep look to their shepherd,
so our eyes look to you, our Lord our God,
until we see your favour and your mercy.

Reign, King Jesus!

From the polar ice caps to the forests of the Amazon,
from the rivers and the wetlands to the vast oceans –
Reign, King Jesus!
Then the earth will be glad, and the people will rejoice.
Reign over us, rain on us your justice and your mercy.
Reign on, rain on –
Reign, King Jesus!

### Action Point 13: Commit to a local place and people

Mission flows from a long-term commitment as you build relationships, partnerships and ways to improve the local community.

### Action Point 14: Workshops on sustainability

Host and promote practical workshops. Find people who can pass on practical skills to equip people for living sustainably. Connect with people in the community and build friendships as you learn new skills together.

- Tap into the skills of church members, especially retired folks
- Training and resources at Future Living Skills:
  www.sustainableliving.org.nz
- Host a Repair Café or Repair Fair, to help people mend clothes and toys, fix computers, small appliances, furniture etc. Find Repair Café Aotearoa NZ on Facebook, or folks like Repair Riverlution in Christchurch[49]
- Bike repairs; find folks in your community keen to help people fix their bikes[50]
- Make reusable menstrual pads; find Divine River on Facebook
- Clothing repairs and upcycling fabric; connect with community initiatives such as Stitch Kitchen in Otago: www.stitchkitchen.nz
- Talk to your local Men's Shed, e.g. making 'DIY' bird feeders or possum traps: www.menzshed.org.nz

## A Change of Heart – A Poem for the Planet

*Poem by Ana Lisa de Jong, Living Tree Poetry*

'God will take care of us'.
I know, I've said it,
meant it,
cannot not trust, somehow.

God makes a way.
Paths through the sea,
and manna heaven sent.
John in the desert, preaching,

preparing us
for one who, with his hand,
would scoop up mud
and open eyes.

We have a habit, I think,
of walking blind.
Cheerfully
stating our faith.

I wonder why then
John had to shout,
exhorting us to turn,
repent.

Are we so inclined to inaction?
Is sin so personal,
or in collusion,
is the wound deeper?

Perhaps the day has come
where a little dirt might be
the thing in the hand
to change the heart.

I wonder …

# Problem Solvers: Ava Carter, with Liz Horn and Mandy Cleave, Rolleston Christian School

Ava is 12 years old, currently in Year 7 at Rolleston Christian School, where she helps lead the Enviro Group.[51] Her father is a military chaplain at Burnham, her mother is a nurse, and she has two sisters and a brother.

*Silvia: It is lovely to be here talking with Ava at Rolleston Christian School, together with Principal Liz Horn and Enviroschool co-ordinating teacher Mandy Cleave. Tell me about how Enviroschool started here.*

Liz: I had been leading in an Enviroschool in Wellington, and so when I was asked to be the first Principal when Rolleston Christian School was getting established 7 years ago, I just said, "We are going to start an Enviroschool." So we did. It was part of the philosophy right from the get-go. Mandy has put arms and legs on it.

Ava: It is just a normal part of school.

Mandy: Our kids don't know any different – but if they went to another school, the learning and the approach and environmental focus would be quite different. So the kids here are blessed to be part of it.

Ava: I am involved with the chickens at the school.

*Silvia: You have chickens?!*

Ava: I don't think you need to have chickens to be an Enviroschool, but I really like the chickens and looking after them and their eggs. We have 5 chickens. We sell the eggs.

Mandy: Schools don't have a budget for chicken feed, so they have to earn their keep.

Ava: We made their cage ourselves – out of broken trampolines! We stacked up two round frames, put chicken wire around that, and the bouncy mat is the roof.

Mandy: Being an Enviroschool means learning through action-based enquiry. Last year our theme was all on food. We looked at food production, food waste, food nutrition and food economics. We got the chickens as a project for food production. And also ethics, because the kids discovered that how we get our food hurts a lot of animals and people and cultures along the way. Our original chickens were rescue chickens, but they were not well and sadly they died. Then a family gave us two chicks, and we bought three Brown Shavers. These ones are doing good.

Ava: They are chicken tractors! They also fertilize and dig up the ground. They dig up all the grass, so we don't need to do the hard work. So after we move the cage we use that area for planting. We plant all sorts of plants. We have just planted corn in the new round garden where the chickens were before.

*Silvia: Who does all the work?*

Ava: We have an Enviro group. If people want to do it they can join the group.

Liz: All the Year Three, Four and Five classes do what we call 'Tiaki Time' every Friday. They pull weeds from the gardens, they wash things, they water the plants, they put out mulch – lots of mulching!

Mandy: All the kids here know how to plant trees. When we started the site was just grass with pine shelter-belts. Rolleston was a rural area that is now the fastest growing town in NZ. We are blessed to have enough land to be able to expand, as well as space for garden and forest. One of the first things we did was start our own little native forest. We were donated all the plants. We worked together with Te Ara Kākāriki – The Green Pathway.[52] They are trying to get these green 'dots' and pathways from the mountains to the sea for all the native birds. And we keep adding to it.

This year we looked at biodiversity 'Kaitiakitanga in Aotearoa'. One group of kids decided plant trees especially to attract Tūī birds. We got in experts who told us all about tūī and how they will find their way across the Canterbury Plains if they have food to eat. They told us how

69

to plant trees that provide year-round food supply for tūī.[53] It will take a few years, but we're all about doing it for the future generations.

*Silvia: Have the kids found it interesting to learn about those relationships, like between the plants and the birds?*

Ava: Yes definitely! We call it LIGHTS. L is for Look. I is for Investigate. G is for 'Go for it' that's the practical project. H is 'How have things changed?' T is 'Time to share' and S is 'So what have we learned?'

Liz: We start with what our kids are interested in and then take everyone's ideas and identify a topic with enough depth to spark great projects. They identify the problems and opportunities in that area. From there they think about what the alternatives are and decide on things they can do to bring about a change in those areas of problem or opportunity. They work in groups, so we get four or five projects running. Ava's group created a video.

Ava: It was to inform people about the environment. We showed what we are doing, to inspire others. We interviewed the groups who were trapping possums and raising money for the tūī, and put it all together in a video.

Mandy: There was a tūī group and a pest control group, and an invasive species group that went to Castle Hill and pulled out wilding pines. The kids identify the problems and opportunities that they are passionate about and then do a project to fix the problem. It is an action learning cycle.

Liz: One hub looked at biodiversity and plants and animals around Aotearoa, and identified heaps of problems and opportunities. The other hub focused on our school property, our food forest and our native forest. That included science. We had soil experts come in and do testing on the soil and the kids figured out what the soil needs in order to make better so that we can look after our fruit trees better. They created a 'microbe soup' to pour onto the soil. The whole LIGHTS process takes most of the year, with several weeks for each step.

*Silvia: How do you and your friends work through this process?*

Ava: The teachers let us choose what we want to do. We can think of the different things we want to study. We talk in small groups, we brainstorm, sometimes we take a vote. We have to write down: "What are the problems?" and "How can we solve them?" Then out of these solutions we choose what we want to do. It is very interactive. At the end we write a report.

*Silvia: What is good about that process?*

Ava: It is fun. I look forward to LIGHTS in the week. I really like helping the animals and learning more about them, and our culture.

*Silvia: And it must feel good to achieve something practical. Is there something this year that you think 'Yeah, we did that!'?*

Ava: Raising enough money to buy all the trees for the tūī. That group raised a lot of money.

*Silvia: What are other aspects of what it means to be an Enviroschool?*

Liz: We are part of the Eco Store recycling program – they are doing a circular economy. Families bring their empty bottles in and we send them all in a big box back to Eco Store.

Ava: A whānau group has a compost system. They put the food waste in the freezer until it goes into the compost. We have a compost heap by the garden and worm farms. And we feed the chickens.

Mandy: There is no excuse not to compost your food waste!

Ava: Each classroom has a bin just for paper. That goes in the recycling. We have nude lunchboxes.

*Silvia: What is a nude lunchbox?!*

Ava: A lunchbox with no plastic or wrapping.

Liz: Our focus is 'Tiaki all the time'. We need to keep finding ways to induct new families into being an Enviroschool, especially our little ones. Nude lunchboxes is a good place to start.

Mandy: A local Enviro kindergarten does a challenge called No-wrap-vember every November. They run it as a competition to reduce the amount of rubbish in kids' lunchboxes. We are running that at the moment but we didn't have much reduction in rubbish, which is great because it shows that our families are already on board.

Liz: A good thing about being an Enviroschool is being connected with all the other Enviro schools, including the kindergartens.

Mandy: In another project, groups created a native and an international garden, so that all cultures would feel welcome in our school. An "expert" from Selwyn Council came to help the students design it. We help with planting at our local Council park. We did riparian planting on a dairy farm last year, as part of a theme on water.

We are still growing, and have plans for a new building. It will have a Nature Play design, to flow out from the classrooms out into the garden. It will have a theme around being involved in and connecting with nature.

Silvia: *What do you bring to being an Enviroschool which is distinctive as a Christian school? What do you think it means to be a Christian and care about the environment?*

Ava: Looking after God's land, because he gave it to us.

Silvia: *And how does it feel in your heart when you are doing that?*

Ava: Good! I find it fun. It makes me feel happy.

Mandy: Ava has a very caring nature, so she's happy to care for anything or anyone, or animal, or plant.

Silvia: *Do you think God made you to be that way?*

Ava: Yes!

Liz: Our school mission is that through our faith we 'HELP' bring light to the world: HELP stands for Hope, Excellence, Love and Peace. We see the light as Jesus, and also as positive change in the world. The environment aspect is something that kids really love, and we teach it as important because God created the world. He put us here as his stewards, we take care of it and look after it.

It is about giving the kids all those skills that they will need in the world. When they grow up they will take the skills they are learning in the Enviro programme and apply them across a whole range of issues. Our goal is for them to have the skills and the drive from knowing they can make positive change and make a difference in the world. They are able to look at a situation, think about what they can do to make a difference and actually do it! And work with other people in all of that. That is how I see it – we want our kids to grow up able to make a positive difference in the world. The environment is a great context for kids to learn these skills. And of course the environment is important in and of itself!

*Silvia: How do you help the children to connect that with faith?*

Mandy: We always talk about how we have God to help us through situations. Wellbeing ties into it as well. We use the 'Five ways to wellbeing'; one of those is 'Take notice'.[54] So sometimes we go outside, and sit there in the environment and just breathe and take notice of what's going on. We thank God for his creation. "What is he saying to you about this?" It is a really calming place.

I learn about God's character through the environment and through nature. I love walking up hills, feeling the peace and seeing the mountains: "Wow, God, this is incredible!" The Psalms come alive for me. So we try impart that to the children: God is in this place. See and learn. Get to know him here. Feel his peace. Everyone really needs peace in this day and age! They need to know where to find it.

Liz: We are also trying to encourage with our kids that everything is spiritual; you don't go to church on Sunday and then the rest of your week is separate from that. Everything is spiritual: the way you do your schoolwork is spiritual, the way you care for the environment is spiritual, the way you interact with your friends is spiritual. God is in every part of what we do. I'm not saying we do that perfectly, or that our kids have all got that, but that's what we aim for.

Mandy: 'Living Christianly' is the official teaching part of our special character as a Christian school, but it is also integrated throughout the day, with expectations of how we treat each other and behave, and our school values.

It would be good if there was a nice Christian song that talks about the environment as God's creation.

*Silvia: Do you get any push-back from parents who think that the environmental is a bit irrelevant?*

Liz: No. It has always been part of who we are. Actually, our parents are proud of being an Enviroschool.

Mandy: The kids love LIGHTS. They go home very positive about it. It brings in such a range of aspects; it is science, social studies, health, in a very integrated approach.

*Silvia: If you were talking to someone who was at a school that didn't care about the environment, what would you say to them?*

Ava: One of the good things about being an Enviroschool is there is a lot less rubbish around because people recycle. The teachers let us know about that a lot. And it's fun. If you are not an Enviroschool, you are missing out!

*Silvia: And presumably you're making the environment more beautiful. What you see around the school?*

Ava: Blossoms, you see flowers. And the trees are growing bigger. I met a boy who was here at the beginning when they first planted the food forest and he said that he really loves seeing it all grow.

Liz: We are looking forward to when our trees are big enough for the kids can use that as a space to play in and engage and be with nature. At the moment we have to be careful with them and remind the kids: "The trees might be bigger than you but they are still babies."

The kids have always had plans to give away the fruit from the fruit trees to the community. But we're not at that stage yet, there's not much fruit yet. When the trees are bigger and laden, they will enjoy giving it away, because kids are so generous. And you'll be able to pop out there and eat an apple and do your reading at the same time! Unfortunately Ava will be at high school by then.

*Silvia: Do you think you'll continue on with some of this stuff when you go to the next school?*

Ava: Yes. I hope so.

Mandy: If they don't have this you can start it!

Ava: Yes.

Mandy: Enviroschools are about creating a sustainable future. Do you think about that, how you are doing it for other people – not for now but trying to leave the earth in a good state for the people coming behind us?

Ava: Yes!

*Silvia: Are there some things about Enviroschool that you don't like or the other kids complain about?*

Ava: Lots of kids complain about being outside and digging, especially when it gets hot. But I quite like it.

*Silvia: With climate change, young people can feel quite despairing. But it sounds like the work you are doing is building a sense of agency, that we can actually do something about the problems rather than just be overwhelmed by them.*

Liz: Our kids have a sparkle in the eye, a sense of hope. We stay focused on the hope side, that you can actually address these problems, and our kids don't seem to have a doom and gloom view of the environment. They are empowered.

*Silvia: Do you get worried about the world?*

Ava: Every now and then I worry about what might happen. But it's OK. God has a plan.

*Silvia: You currently have a Silver Enviro award.*

Mandy: The kids decide whether we are there yet for each of the award levels. Enviroschools let you do the reflection process yourself when they think you are ready. Actually the students are pretty hard on themselves. Next year we will be reflecting towards Green Gold.

Ava: When we get our Green Gold award we will have a big celebration! For our Silver award we made art out of sticks – ephemeral art that goes back into nature. And we had a shared lunch!

*Ava took me for a guided tour. We walked past the pine trees …*

Ava: We will get rid of all the pines eventually, but at the moment they give good shelter from the wind. We learned about wilding pines and how the pinecone seeds come out and blow across the land and make more and more pine trees, which kill the other plants. So we make sure we pull out any baby pines.

*… the bike track …*

This area is where we ride our bikes on Wednesdays.

*… the food forest with the chickens and gardens …*

This garden has broccoli and strawberry plants. The food forest is on mounds. We started with a mound for each whānau group but now they are for everyone. That is a huge mound which we have to work on. It was a corn field but it got out of hand! Now it is all overgrown with grass.

The chicken coop gets vandalised sometimes which is quite sad. These are little apples. Little kids come and they think the apples are ripe when they are not, and they pick them.

*Silvia: That is frustrating. I guess that will be a big learning about how to do the food forest – how to not waste the fruit being picked too green.*

*… and the native forest …*

Ava: The trees are all young at the moment but they will grow bigger. There is one of our traps. We put the traps around the native forest and the food forest. We are trying to keep as many pests out as we can. We have caught a possum and a rat. Handling them is gross but some people don't mind. Here is our mulch pile, from trees or branches we cut down. And this is the compost pile.

There is another piece of land over there. It's not ready for us to go into yet. But it has lots of native trees and other things. We are thinking about which trees to cut down and which ones to keep. Lots of people cut down trees without thinking.

*Silvia: Thank you Ava, you are awesome!*

## Grow within us

*Prayer by Silvia Purdie, from Mark 4: 26-29*

Jesus said, the Kingdom of God is like a child
who plants a little tree.
She digs a hole in the dirt for it,
pours water on it
and watches it, cares for it, hopes for it.
But does the child control the tree –
make it grow, roots down, shoots up?
No, the tree will grow by the power to grow
from within itself, to be itself.

God, you plant us and you watch us grow.
You know what we are made to be,
for you placed who we are deep within us.
Jesus, grow your Kingdom where we are,
as trees grow, little by little, toward the sun,
as people grow, work and love, in your Light.
Holy Spirit, grow within us, so that all we are
and all we do gives glory to God. Amen.

## Action Point 15: Support a school's Enviro programme

Growing partnerships between churches and schools nurturing environmental projects and relationships and empowering children to be fabulous enviro problem solvers!

- Support your local school with gardening, planting and other projects
- Find an Enviroschool or kindergarten and explore ways to encourage them: www.enviroschools.org.nz

## Action Point 16: Grow native trees

A thriving network of native forest patches and corridors across Aotearoa, so that birds can travel freely.

- Get advice as to the best trees to plant to feed the birds year-round.
- Ara Kākāriki, Greenway Canterbury Trust: www.kakariki.org.nz

## Action Point 17: Use an action learning process to tackle any problem

People empowered to take positive action on difficult issues through a systematic method of reflection and action.

- 'Tools for Environmental Action' Department of Conservation, NZ[55]
- 'Creating Catalysts for Change' Waikato Enviroschools[56]
- 'Inquiry and action learning process' using the 'Rivers and Us' Science Learning Hub[57]
- 'What is Action Learning?' NSW[58]

# The Change that Love Demands: Cathy Bi-Riley

Ko Huashan te maunga, ko Huanghe te awa. Nō Haina ōku tīpuna. I tipu ake au ki Tāmaki Makaurau. Ko Cathy Bi-Riley tōku ingoa.

I live in Auckland with my husband Michael and young son Aidan in an Urban Vision community household.[59] I am the Sustainability Fieldworker for the Anglican Diocese of Auckland.

*How did your family background shape your relationship with the environment?*

I was born in Xi'an, China and moved to New Zealand when I was seven. I was raised mostly by my grandparents both in China and in New Zealand. My father's parents come from the northernmost province in China of Heilongjiang, where winters are long and bitterly cold. My grandparents grew up in very difficult times, during the political instability of China. Before the land reforms the Bi family had a small plot of land for subsistence farming. Self sufficiency was a very strong value for them.

For my grandparents the land was for cultivation: we have to look after it because if we don't then we don't eat. They had amazing skills. They understood patterns of nature, and had a connection to the natural world because it was key to survival. They had a respect that comes from a practical relationship. Even when we moved to New Zealand, they always grew food. They planted out the whole backyard as a garden, it was massive! They would have buckets everywhere catching water. They patched up blankets and clothes. They collected seeds and swapped them with others in the Chinese community. My grandma couldn't stand wasting food or wasting anything. Their value of not wasting anything has a huge influence

78

on me now, though when I was younger I thought some of their practices were a bit ridiculous!

Growing up in New Zealand I often felt more Kiwi than Chinese. My best friend was Pākehā, and her family often invited me on adventures. As a teenager I loved swimming, hiking and camping. When I return to China to visit my extended family, the dense urban environment feels so claustrophobic and the parks seemed mainly curated for photo opportunities. The younger generation in urban China seem to have lost the relationship with the land that my grandparents had.

*How did you discover a passion for caring for creation?*

At High School I especially enjoyed geography. We learnt about the realities of global inequality and environmental degradation and this sparked in me a strong sense of social justice. I got involved with my school's Enviro Group and with World Vision. I came to faith at Windsor Park Baptist. At church I felt the call to love our neighbours and care for the poor, but I never heard about care of creation. Respect for the environment came through school. Our Enviro Group went out testing the local creek for contaminants such as phosphorus and nitrates, and recorded data. We learned about climate change and I thought 'This is wrong, I have to do something'. I grew an awareness that what is good for the environment is also good for people, but that did not yet connect with my faith.

After High School I did the Intermission gap year programme at Carey Baptist College. As part of learning about mission we looked at care of creation and how that is part of our faith. That nurtured my conviction that God cares about how we treat creation. Then I moved to Wellington and lived in community with Urban Vision in the inner city. Urban Vision is a contemporary mission order with the Anglican church. Many of us share a value of living sustainably and pursuing climate justice.

After graduation I worked for Caritas, in the advocacy team, with wonderful strong Catholic social justice warriors.[60] I was in awe. Catholic social teaching is mind blowing. It articulated stewardship and God's preferential option for the poor in a language that resonated strongly for me – 'Oh my goodness!' I knew this was in the Bible, and this was the Gospel, but it connected in a fresh way as applied to current social issues. Laudato Si' was hugely inspiring for me.

In my time with Caritas I had the opportunity to visit Kiribati. Caritas was working with Kiribati women's organisations around community wellbeing and healthy eating. We also went to hear local experiences of climate change, what they were seeing. That was eye opening! They told us: "We keep having to dig new wells because our water source keeps getting salinated." We heard from people who had to move further inland and relocate their church. It used to be normal to build very close to the ocean, but that is not sustainable now. There are a number of factors: it's sea level rise, it's coastal erosion and it's changing weather patterns.

We were there during a massive storm, Cyclone Pam, in March 2015. Kiribati was hit only by the edges of the storm but that was enough to have huge impacts. It washed out a major causeway. We nearly got stuck; we crossed the causeway back to where we were staying only an hour before it collapsed. The roads turned into a mess of potholes. It was crazy!

We saw the western influence of consumer goods and all the plastic. How do you get rid of plastic waste on a tiny atoll? They can't dig landfills, so they put the rubbish into cages. But when the storm hit, the rubbish got washed out and went everywhere. The impact on the natural environment was so visual. I felt 'What are we doing to this community?!'

Another Caritas project partner was in Carteret Island in Papua New Guinea. Families were relocating from Carteret to the mainland as the sea crept closer and fertile soil became salty marshes. The Catholic church set aside land for families to relocate to. One of the people on that project visited New Zealand and shared her story. It was sobering. For me that really hit home that climate change is not just about nature, it's about human survival, especially for these vulnerable communities. They did not cause climate change but are probably going to suffer the most. That was huge for me.

*What is your role currently?*

I am now living back in Auckland working as a Sustainability Fieldworker for the Anglican Diocese.

I don't meet many people who deny climate change in the church. But I do come across people who say it should be deprioritised. Their attitude is: "Yeah OK, climate change is important but it is not up to the church to address it. It's not our role – it's up to the government or individuals or businesses." I feel quite aggrieved by that attitude. It is a real disconnect. Creation and all we have was made by God and we are treating it terribly!

We can be fixed single mindedly on the idea that the role of the church is to evangelise, to make more people become Christians. But what do we evangelise people for? What do they join the church in order to do? If people become Christians and then continue to live the exact same life, then what is the point?! What does it mean to form disciples and to be shaped by Jesus? How do we live in the radical sacrificial love that Jesus had for humanity? Living out and embodying good news means so much more than lip service. It has to be a deeper journey.

When people in the church push back against caring for creation, I sense their anxiety that the church is in decline. Creation care is an important way to re-engage our communities. People are not interested in who Jesus is and who God is if we talk about Christianity in a way that is not relevant. We have to bring the Gospel into life today, to the things that people care and worry about now. If we can't then we are not doing a great job of preaching good news.

The Gospel for me is about reconciliation of relationships. Jesus' death and resurrection is not an invisible spiritual transaction. It is tangible. Following Jesus changes the way we see ourselves and the way we live. When we live out of a place of being loved, beloved, we want to love and care for others. The Gospel is not the scarcity mindset of 'there's not enough'. It is trust and faith that God provides. I've heard Pacific community leaders say: "Yep, we've got to work hard, we've got to do our best to reduce our emissions and figure out adaptation plans. But God is so good and he is with us!"

As the church, caring for creation is part of living out good news, for ourselves, for future generations, and for all the earth.

*How do you see that from God's perspective? What is your sense of the heart of God?*

When I pray about this there can be a deep sense of grief, a deep lament.

I hear God saying: "You know what? You don't need more stuff. There's enough here, for all of you. Why do some take so much so that others can't live? Why are you obsessed with building your own kingdoms and empires, especially in the church?! You have said that I am your King, the King of your life, and yet you keep feeling that I won't provide, or it's not going to be enough."

We all struggle to change, myself included. It feels like an effort to choose to take the bus or the bike, to eat less meat, or live more locally. There is the resistance of 'I don't want to give up the way I live'. 'The way we live now' becomes an idol. What if we truly trusted in a God and a Creator who genuinely provides?! What if we made these changes together as faith communities?

I think God is calling his people back to: 'What is most loving? What is the change that love demands of me?' Let's find the willingness to step into that, knowing that our God is bigger than our fear. We'll be surprised by the joy and goodness we find on the other side.

*Can you pick a couple of practical actions that you would encourage churches to do?*

Some of our Anglican churches have incorporated the Season of Creation into the church calendar. We are very liturgical in the Anglican tradition, but any church can benefit from the Season of Creation. It creates space where we pay special attention to our relationship with creation. If every church developed a creation practice in worship, that could shift something significant. We give thanks for the way creation provides for us; we truly lament the ecological crisis; we confess our role in this crisis; we proclaim God's goodness in creation; and we intercede for climate justice. The Season of Creation is the month of September, but churches may have a creation theme around Environment Day, Earth Day, Harvest Thanksgiving, or any time really.

There are plenty of resources out there that enable a church service to have a care of creation focus. Some churches organise intergenerational services where they intentionally bring together young and old in creative ways. Some churches do the Season of Creation over several weeks, with a different theme each week, such as exploring our relationship with the forest and the river and how they provide for us. How do we see God's character reflected there?

For example, a church got the kids to make hand prints to create a river that flowed down the aisle. This was a visual action to remember that we are made up of water, and we should look after our water sources. In the Bible there is a wealth of imagery of water, images of living springs and wells. In worship we make those connections and help people of all ages to connect with them experientially. Some churches bring trees in pots into the church, and decorate the altar with nature. Some give a sprig of rosemary or another fragrant plant for people to hold, sit with and contemplate with.

After church we can take our worship into practical action; one church held a workshop on how to reduce your carbon footprint. Another church got involved with tree planting. Another built a prayer labyrinth using lavender plants. Some churches use the Season of Creation as an opportunity to kick-start a community garden. All these things add another dimension to our usual worship, a new form of spiritual practice.[61]

The second practical action I would encourage is for every church to plant food or fruit trees on church land. When I was at St Peter's Onehunga we really couldn't because the church is in a cemetery – every piece of grass had somebody buried there! So it was inappropriate to grow food. But most churches have some land and have the opportunity to grow food. One Anglican church was doing a renovation and the landscape plan only included ornamental trees. The priest asked, "Can we plant fruit trees instead?" and the landscaper said, "I don't see why not." So they did. If you have a budget for landscaping, why not plant fruit trees?

Something very exciting I have seen in the Auckland Diocese is many churches starting community gardens. It has been a great way to connect with the immediate neighbours. Every church which has started a community garden has built new friendships in their neighbourhood. They are able to be generous with that food. They have been able to connect the kids and youth and get them involved. It is a very dynamic space, with huge potential to bring people together. It is a missional venture any church can engage with. And it is very Biblical, all about bearing fruit, pruning, abundance and generosity.

## E te Atua o te Aroha

*Prayer by Cathy Bi Riley*

E te Atua o te aroha, our loving Creator,
Mountains and oceans,
mighty kauri and playful tūī,
**All** creation belongs to You.
Remind us of our role
as caretakers and gardeners.
Send your Spirit to renew our hurting world.
Give us the courage and strength
to simplify our life,
to share what we have,
to bear the cost of change and
to sow the seeds of hope for future generations.
Through Jesus Christ who is reconciling all things
through the cross.
Amen.

## Action Point 18: Creation in worship

Connect scripture and mission with faith through a focus on creation in worship.

- Have a creation theme in worship services on a regular basis and festivals such as Harvest. Visit the Season of Creation website: www.seasonofcreation.org
- Encourage intergenerational engagement in worship, including creative and experiential elements
- Preach on themes related to creation. Sustainable Preaching: www.sustainable-preaching.org. Sermons, At Your Service: www.atyourservice.arocha.org/en
- Conversations (Silvia's website) Creation worship resources: www.conversations.net.nz/worship-resources
- Iona Community worship material: www.ionabooks.com/product-category/books/care-for-creation
- Prayer resources, Eco Church NZ: www.ecochurch.org.nz/prayer

## Action Point 19: Plant fruit trees

Grow food for the community and to honour God by bearing fruit (literally!)

- Use church-owned land to plant and maintain fruit trees, especially when there are any changes to church property landscaping
- Build partnerships with the local community to grow and distribute food
- Involve children, young people and older people
- 'Growing fruit trees' Wellington City Council: www.wellington.govt. nz/climate-change-sustainability-environment/sustainable-living/ sustainable-food-initiative/how-to-grow-food-sustainably/growing-fruit-trees
- Fruit tree information, New Zealand Tree Crops Association: www.treecrops.org.nz/tree-information/fruit

# Coming Alive: Courtnay Wilson

Courtnay Wilson is Program Director for the Creation Care Study Program (CCSP) in Kaikoura.[62] She is also Priest in Charge at St Peter's Anglican Church, Kaikoura, and Creation Care Enabler for the Diocese of Nelson. Courtnay is training as a spiritual director and is involved in a range of conservation projects in Kaikōura. If you can't reach her on the phone she is probably out kayaking or sitting on a hilltop spotting whales!

*You grew up in Canada?*

My grandma's parents were from the Ukraine, and she was born on the Canadian prairie. I grew up in Southern Ontario, with my sister, in a loving family. My parents were not 'outdoorsy' – I remember camping in my cousins' backyard and that felt very new and exciting! There was a conservation area close to our house and my mother didn't want me going in there by myself, but it was one of the few ways I deliberately disobeyed her. As a teenager I spent a lot of time walking and running the trails, growing a real love for the outdoors. Getting time by myself in the woods was essential for my wellbeing during those challenging adolescent years.

Very occasionally we would go to church with my Grandpa – though my Dad would make fun of the singing – and after church we would go to Tim Horton's for chocolate milk and doughnuts! At high school my sister and I did cross country running. The coach and some of the team were Christians and they shared the gospel with us during practice. I gradually started attending a Baptist church and reading the Bible.

But well before that I had a strong sense that there was a God and that I was deeply loved. One day when I was just eight I was by myself in the living room. It was an ordinary afternoon, but suddenly I was flooded with joy! And after that experience I always knew that I was loved and known by God.

*As a teenager, what did you think God had for you?*

I wanted to be a teacher. I definitely saw myself in education in some way, but I didn't know what that would look like. At university I majored in history and political science. And then I really wanted to go to seminary. I don't use the word 'miraculous' very often, but there were a series of events that made it possible for me to go to seminary that I can't explain. God arranged for the money. So I went to McMaster Divinity College in Hamilton where I completed a Masters in Theological Studies.

While I was there I took a course called 'War and Peace in the Christian Tradition'. That put me on a Mennonite/Anabaptist path. I found a home there, and though I am now Anglican I still treasure the Mennonite peace tradition. I have never lost that peace. It is natural that an ethic of peacemaking should be extended to all of creation: peace between humans and the land.

*Where did you go after seminary?*

I was ready for a break from school. I was drawn to Japan and was accepted on the Japan Exchange and Teaching Programme.[63] JET sets up partnerships between Japanese teachers and native English speakers. I liked that team approach. Japan is one of the most beautiful countries; I had imagined concrete jungle but I fell in love with the environment, especially snorkelling at Okinawa. I was blown away by the kaleidoscope of colours and beautiful fish in the coral reefs of the South China Sea. That influenced my decision to go to Belize – to do more snorkelling!

Somehow in Japan I came across *For the Beauty of the Earth* by Steven Bouma-Prediger. Reading that book was pivotal for me. The first chapter was about a place-based model of education using Belize CCSP as an example, and he dedicated the book to his CCSP students. He described an education that connected head, heart and hands, that was interdisciplinary, that sought to connect the dots rather than get more and more specialized. I thought to myself 'Wow, I would really like to re-educate myself along these lines'. I got in touch with him and he said they were looking for somebody to join their staff in Belize.

*How does CCSP teach care for creation?*

Creation Care Study Program is an interdisciplinary study abroad program for North American university students. I loved my time in Belize: the jungles and coral reefs, and equally time in a living learning community. Then in 2008 I was appointed Program Director for the New Zealand program. I have made Kaikōura home. My best advice to students is to find a place to make home and put down deep roots. Allow yourself to be shaped by, and to help shape, particular places.

At CCSP we are all about helping students to be agents for God's shalom, especially through understanding and caring for creation. Being a residential program makes all the difference. Our students major in a range of subjects; many are already interested in what they can do to care for creation. We emphasize that more than information is required when it comes to caring for creation. Our hearts need to be engaged in a shalom model of education. What is required is the cultivation of empathy, and for that you need to get up close and personal. Sometimes we are in a classroom but often the world is our classroom, whether we are exploring tide pools or a beautiful West Coast temperate rainforest.

Students live with others, walk and bike as much as possible, linger over meals instead of rushing. They have to put down their devices and be fully present to each other. Those are things that are deeply transformative for young people, who often live in a virtual world, on their phones or in front of their computers. We want them to be more embodied when they are with us, and to do it long enough to develop new habits.

*How can churches develop some of these things in church life?*

With Covid closing New Zealand's borders our program has been on hold, and the other staff and I have become more involved with our local Anglican church. We started a small outreach group called Nourish Nights. There are a lot of people in this town who care for creation who say they are spiritual and are searching for something more. There is a longing there, but they are not likely to come to church on Sundays. So folks come for dinner: we open with prayer, we gather around food, usually very simple, homemade soup and homemade bread. We light a candle. We share with each other what has inspired us in the last week, what has nourished us. We also share insights from books we have read. And then we close with Night Prayer. Anytime people can gather around food and linger and share, that is special.

Anything that we can do to inhabit our bodies more, like walking and praying at the same time, having meals together and being attentive to what we eat – noticing the smell, the texture. Get involved in a community garden or start one on church land. Get your hands dirty in the garden, go tramping, walking around the neighbourhood, anything to get you moving and seeing what is around you. Engage your senses. Sometimes I try to slow myself down by saying to myself, "What colours can I see right now in the sky?" It helps me to better see what I am looking at.

*How is God with you when you are noticing?*
I become more aware of God's presence. "Thank you, Lord for all these colours of green, for all the colours in the sky right now. An artist cannot paint a more beautiful picture than this!" If I am kayaking I pray: "Thank you for my arms paddling, and the rhythm that connects me with my own body." Being out on the water you can feel so small but it's a good reminder that 'Yes I matter, but look at everything around me. God cares about it all!' That is what Job heard too: it's not all about you (Job 38-39). That helps me keep perspective.

*You have mentioned reading – how do books inspire your creation care?*
Reading is a default activity for me – if I have down-time you are likely to find me with a book in hand. I've always been an avid reader – from the age of 12 when I was introduced to the *Anne of Green Gables* books. Anne was a heroine for me. Those books are very rooted in place, on Prince Edward Island. That had a huge influence on my life.

*What happens when you read something that resonates?*
A coming alive! The Holy Spirit catches our attention through different ways and different means. God uses books to gain my attention. Excitement wells up within me: 'Yes, that's it! That describes what I'm feeling or what I'm thinking, or that's helping my world to grow bigger, helping me to see things'. A book can be an anchor. Authors can be mentors, friends helping me on my journey. Some writers speak to your soul. Words help me learn what it means to be in a place and to love that place, both the humans and nonhumans living there. Some authors have a way of putting things that captures exactly what I sensed but had a hard time putting my finger on.
Currently I am loving *Finding the Mother Tree* by Suzanne Simard.[64] She is a scientist from British Columbia. She describes how the different species of trees in a forest are helping each other. Trees seem to understand that it takes a village to raise a child. There is a lot of science in the book – I confess I skim over some of that so I don't get bogged down – but she also tells the story of her life. When I read this I feel excited by the ways trees are

communicating and cooperating. It expands my view of the world and my wonder at how amazing God is. God created all of this! It helps me praise God more as I learn and as I grow in appreciation for the complexity of this web of life.

One writer mentions another writer who mentions another writer and you go from there – it's limitless! I am fed by anything by Barbara Brown Taylor.[65] Her invitation is to inhabit our bodies as part of our worship, and that really speaks to me. I love Wendell Berry and how much he talks about the importance of putting down roots in a place.[66] Different books come to us at different seasons of our lives. Sometimes I get a book and think 'I'm not ready yet for this' and I put it back on the shelf.

Literature or poetry has a way of coming in through the back door and animating our emotions and imagination in ways that essays or non-fiction might not. I love Barbara Kingsolver's novels and Mary Oliver's poetry – the simplicity of her words really captures my attention. If a poem speaks to me I write it out and then I walk with it. There is something about the rhythm of walking and the rhythm of poetry read one line at a time. I memorise it, allow it to enter into me.

*You have the knack of picking out quotes and using them to inspire others.*

A line or section will stand out for me and I think: 'I can use that! I need to capture that'. I will record it somewhere, like on a 'sticky note' on my computer. Then I quote it in a sermon or an article. In my role as Creation Care Enabler for the Nelson Diocese I write articles for the newsletter each week, so I'm always pulling in great quotes. I identify poignant gems in what others have written and make them accessible to fire others.

*How do you see your students being impacted by their reading?*

It opens up new worlds for them! Literature can enlarge how they see the world and that is powerful. They see things they had not realised before. Words have great power.

At CCSP students study a range of subjects including marine ecology and terrestrial ecology. They also do a course in environmental literature where they read poetry or fiction related to creation, from a range of traditions. We have an excellent interdisciplinary library here. It is so valuable to have the literature alongside the science.

*What do you hope for the church?*

I want the church to be well known for its concern for the larger world. We are not plucking survivors out of a sinking ship. We care about God's salvation coming for all creation. That includes animals and trees and ocean. I want to Christians to be seen as full of care for this beautiful world God has made. Too often the church is viewed, in that old saying, as 'so heavenly minded they are no earthly good'! As citizens of heaven our task is to bring the life of heaven down to earth. And Jesus has shown us the way to do that. We are to be part of God's reconciling love, agents of God's reconciling life. The church has not often been seen as that in relation to the rest of creation.

*So what does that look like, to be agents of God's reconciling salvation in Kaikōura?*

We strive to be non-dualistic in worship, sermons and other aspects of church life. We want to be whole in ourselves and in how we view the world. We walk and bike to church as much as possible. We encourage home baking rather than buying pre-made stuff wrapped in plastic.

It looks like the church coming alongside and supporting good conservation work being done. Some of us from St. Peter's were involved in the Great Kaikōura Whale Count this past winter; we took shifts up on a hill, counting the whales that were going by and documenting their behaviour.[67] Some of our parishioners are involved with Kaikōura Ocean Research Institute and help with surveys of dolphins and penguins. There is a protest element also. I think back to the protests where we said no to deepwater drilling for oil; I was involved with that, along with the CCSP students.

It is important to build relationships with other conservation organisations. At a community event I am usually wearing multiple hats. I represent the Kaikōura Ocean Research Institute and now that we are an Eco Church I also say that I represent the Anglican Church. Sometimes people look a little bit surprised by that: "Oh, we have the Anglican Church at the table!"

*You have an amazing skill of developing modern parables from the lives of the creatures around you.*

There are things we can learn from the wild animals. In our Blessing of the Animals service we broaden out the worship to include the native animals that call Kaikōura home, and say a blessing for them as well as for our pets, because they bless us! We can learn from the dotterels about being faithful to their place – once they have a nest site they won't budge! As humans, we are so transient, going here there and everywhere.

The Hutton's shearwater birds breed in Kaikōura and nowhere else. They crash land in town on rainy autumn nights because of the street lights, and they can't help themselves. Unless a human helps them they will get predated upon or get run over by a car. I learn from them that we all need help sometimes, and we should not be afraid to ask for that help. God welcomes us into the family, along with other brothers and sisters, and not all of them are human!

*So you include conservation leaders in your pastoral care, as well as your local wild animals?*

This is the leading edge of mission. With so much climate anxiety, the church is missing an important opportunity if it doesn't allow its voice to be heard loud and clear right now, through words and actions.

*Nelson Diocese is known as being evangelical; how do you talk about creation care in ways that resonate in that context?*

As long as I preach from the Bible, people are very open – and that is not difficult to do, because creation care is very biblical, from Genesis to Revelation! People don't push back when the message is solidly biblically based.

*How do you approach the Bible to draw out creation themes?*

As a Baptist young person I learned to read the scriptures in a very dualistic way. It was all about believing certain things about Jesus: go to heaven, avoid hell. It has taken some unlearning for me over the years to embrace a more redemptive faith.

I now automatically apply an ecological lens to scripture. I am passionate about making those connections. As an Anglican priest I preach from the Lectionary, and I don't find it hard to find themes related to creation in Scripture. Something always stands out. We have inherited a tendency to read the scriptures in a dualistic fashion, only seeing the humans. I resist that. Ask yourself: 'How could I read this more holistically?' Look at the text from the point of view of Creation. If there are animals or natural objects mentioned, what is their perspective? As we go towards Christmas, think about the donkey or the star. I give myself permission to imagine: how would the night sky have seen this event? – and we're all made of stardust! I'm not afraid to apply some scientific insights. Words like 'all' help push us outside of our human-centric worldview. Creation as a whole becomes a partner in the process of exegesis.

I talk about reading the Book of Nature alongside the Bible as we seek to know and honour Jesus. When I look at the creation I see Jesus as the glad Creator with an affinity for feather, fur and flowers. When I look at the sun rising and setting, or winter turning into spring, it speaks to me of the Son of God who died and rose again. The pattern of death giving birth to new life is part of the warp and weft of creation, as Jesus himself was well aware. When I walk through a forest I think about what science has recently revealed: that trees can communicate and cooperate through subterranean networks of fungi. What we see as a forest is in some respects more akin to a vast single organism. This speaks to me of the Trinity, of God's preference for community and cooperation that reflects God's own inner life.

*How do you see God's call on your life?*

I see my calling as being faithful to a place and the people in that place, to know and be known by the inhabitants of that place. More recently I have felt the calling to become a spiritual director. I've been inspired by a book called *Earth, our Original Monastery* by Christine Valters Paintner.[68] She suggests that Earth is the original spiritual director. I couldn't agree more!

## Prayer for wild animals

*By Courtnay Wilson for St Francis Day service*

Most Holy One,
we thank you that we can share this corner of your world
with Hutton's shearwater, Hector's dolphins,
little blue penguins, dotterels
and so many wonderful and beautiful creatures
that call Kaikōura home.
May they receive the food, the rest and the companionship
they need to flourish.
Help us to do what we can to keep them safe,
including keeping our skies as dark as possible,
protecting their habitats,
and doing what is within our power
to keep them safe from predators.
Amen.

## The Prayer of St. Francis

Leader: Lord, make us instruments of your peace.

All: **Where there is hatred, let us sow love;**

Leader: Where there is injury, pardon;

All: **Where there is doubt, faith;**

Leader: Where there is despair, hope;

All: **Where there is darkness, light;**

Leader: Where there is sadness, joy.

Leader: O Divine Master, Grant that we may

All: **not so much seek to be consoled as to console;**

Leader: To be understood as to understand;

All: **To be loved as to love.**

Leader: For it is in giving that we receive;

All: **It is in pardoning that we are pardoned;**

Leader: And it is in dying that we are born to eternal live. Amen.

### Action Point 20: Include 'all creatures of our God and King'

Value the animals who are part of our local community, both pets and wild, and to include care for them in our mission.

Invite pets to worship (e.g. on St Francis' Day)[69]

- Learn about and pray for the animals native to your area; include photos of them in worship and church newsletters; support projects to protect their habitat.

### Action Point 21: Read

- Develop your church library with books about nature and eco-theology
- Encourage book clubs and home groups to read about creation and climate change
- BWB Texts are short books, several on climate topics, such as Living with the *Climate Crisis: Voices from Aotearoa*, Tom Doig, ed., 2020: www.bwb.co.nz/texts
- Check out the Book List at the end of this book.

### Action Point 22: Linger over food

People connecting and being present to God and each other by slowing down, eating simply, and sharing from the heart.

Hospitality-based evangelism happens when we share a meal together. Get to know people in your neighbourhood. Encourage and support those involved in conservation. Share about why we care for the world around us.

# Connected to the Earth: Diana Johnston

Diana and husband Mark help lead the Enviro Conversation group at South West Baptist Church in Christchurch,[70] together with their sons Caleb and James. They are part of the team at Adventure Specialties Trust.[71] Di is also studying early childhood education.

*What is your family background?*

I grew up in a Christian family. We lived in West Auckland on the edge of the Waitākere Ranges in Titirangi, so we grew up in the kauri forests. My dad was a Park Ranger there. His mother, my Grandma, was born in England and came to New Zealand in her late teens after the war. She was an adventurer at heart, loved the bush and was a big Forest and Bird advocate. On both sides of my family I have roots back seven generations in New Zealand, with my ancestors all coming from England originally.

*What has shaped your relationship with creation?*

I remember a moment when I was eight. Grandma took me and my sister up to the Arataki Visitor Centre when it was newly built. It is beautiful. It looks out over the Waitākere Ranges – one of my favourite places! We stood on the deck looking out over the forest and Grandma asked us a simple question: "How many shades of green can you count?" My sister and I enthusiastically started trying to count the different shades of green. Eventually Grandma said, "There's just too many isn't there?" And we said, "Yeah, there is!" I've never forgotten that question.

*What does that mean to you now?*

It is awe inspiring when you think about it, all the different shades. Her question made me notice that the forest is very diverse. When you're young it is easy to see a leaf as a leaf and a tree as a tree, and it's not until you observe that you realise that trees are all different. I am drawn to the bush. For many years I have been learning more about native plants and how they were used traditionally as medicinal or edible foods. I have started to understand more about ecology and the intricacies of how it all works together.

*As a child did you recognise a spiritual aspect to that?*

Not cognitively, but when it's the place that you play in, both at home and on holiday, it is home. I remember holidays with friends at the Kai Iwi Lakes, playing in the big pine forest. We would give names to spaces in the forest and they would become our spaces. There is a spiritual side to that sense of belonging. When a place becomes 'your place' you feel connected to it. It was also a great space for imagination. We'd make huts, climb trees and be koalas, make mud cakes, find a special place and call it Fantail Grove and sit in there telling stories. Lots of that.

*Do you remember being confronted by damage to the natural environment?*

I went to Kaurilands Primary School which is bordered by forest, with a creek running through it. We used to run all through the bush and make huts out of ponga ferns, but the teachers could see that we were killing the undergrowth and restricted us to a particular area. It made us see we were having a negative impact on the forest.

As an adult I have heard over time the stories of widespread damage. Kauri die-back is a huge issue for the Waitākere and Northland forests. Many of the tracks I used to love are now closed off. We took our children up to Northland a couple of years ago and we went to see Tāne Mahuta and Te Matua Ngahere. We stood in front of those 2,000 year-old Kauri trees, feeling the wisdom coming out of them, feeling, "How sad would it be for them to die!"

*What did you do after finishing school?*

I did drama and performing arts for two years with Excel School of Performing Arts, then got into outdoor education. I did a Diploma in Biblical Studies with a youth ministry focus at Bible College of New Zealand, as well as National Certificate of Outdoor Recreation through Adventure Specialties Trust. From there I went into outdoor instructing with Adventure

Specialties. I met Mark while I was working there and we married. Then I worked for Scripture Union for a couple of years before having James and then Caleb. I purely 'mummed' for a few years. Mark is still with Adventure Specialties Trust, and I jump in from time to time instructing, writing resources and leading family camps with the kids in tow. I am now studying part time towards a Bachelor of Teaching in Early Childhood.

*How would you describe your faith background?*

My family went to Titirangi Presbyterian church in West Auckland until my parents helped plant a small church called Titirangi Christian Fellowship which we attended before we eventually moved back to the Presbyterian church. My parents had a strong non-denominational attitude. It didn't matter what church they were at, as long as they felt connected to God in that place. My dad was always involved in youth ministry. As was common in the 1980s and 1990s I grew up with a western Christian worldview which was very centered around our individual relationship with God.

*A key question for creation care is how our theology impacts how we view the natural world. How has that shifted for you?*

That is huge! It's the same with my bicultural journey. My starting point used to be that humans are God's supreme creation. Despite loving the bush I had always assumed that God will make a new heaven and earth. I guess I had the 'pearly gates' image in my head, although I always secretly hoped he would put in a few mountains to explore! Over time that has changed. My thinking is always shifting; the more I learn, the more I reflect on different ideas. I now feel that this world is God's creation and we are part of that. It was in my early 20s that I was first confronted by this, especially by Andrew Shepherd. He articulated how we are part of creation and we are asked to care for it, not dominate it.

Over time that seed has grown in me. It has become something that happens in everyday life, not just a concept. Mark and I try to make decisions that reflect that. Not every decision we make is perfect but the way we live life matters. Sometimes it takes a while for my life to catch up with my ideas.

I personally am grappling with the possibility that a Māori worldview may be closer to a biblical worldview than Western culture. How much of the faith that I grew up with is truly biblical and how much is based on Western cultural assumptions? Te Ao Māori has had a big impact on me, especially the understanding that we are not separate from the earth.[72] Māori whakapapa (connect their genealogy) back to the earth; which to me connects with the Hebrew understanding of Adam as 'adamah'. In a sense we all come from the earth. Interweaving Biblical and Māori stories together has become important. That impacts on how I connect with creation.

*Your church's creation care group is called 'Enviro Conversations'. What is important to you about that?*

Our church is South West Baptist Church. Our values are all about the restoration that Jesus brings to our relationships: with God, with others, with ourselves and with the world. That has taken us on a bicultural journey and now we are also on a creation care journey. A few years ago a number of us were passionate about caring for the environment but there wasn't much dialogue between us. God was working away in the background, growing our desire to do something, and one day Andy started the conversation by getting us all together. Since then we meet every couple of months over kai, so there is a social aspect to it. We are an open group – anyone is welcome to come along.

We learnt a lot from the bicultural journey, especially to not form 'a group' that takes care of 'the environmental stuff'. For us it is vital to see this as a conversation, something that needs to be threaded through the life of church. Yes we have a group of people who take initiatives but the vision is bigger than that. We all use our interests and strengths to progress the conversation. And it is growing. We've seen that in the last few years. The fruit of this conversation now has a life of its own. We see great things happening in the church that others have instigated. The Regenesis planting day has become part of our church calendar and a diverse range of people in the church enjoy participating. My vision is that by growing creation care as a conversation with everyone, others feel empowered to take initiative, and as a whole church we begin to see restoring our world as a natural outworking of our faith in Christ.

*What are your faith convictions about this?*

We are part of the restoration of God's earth, of his world. We are not sitting here waiting for Jesus to come back and suddenly it will all be sorted. As humans we are a part of that healing. We are interconnected with the earth. We can't live without it. If the earth is not healthy then we are not healthy. That has been the big shift for me, away from a view that it is only humans that God is interested in restoring.

*How does that change how you relate to God?*

I was talking with a friend the other day about reading the Bible and I commented, "I'm terrible at reading the Bible." I realised that was one of those old ideas I had – that spending time with God means sitting down for half an hour a day reading a Bible. By no means am I saying that reading the Bible is not important, but that was my 'gold standard' for relating to God. Is that the only way to connect with God? I know that my faith is growing. I spend time with God when I'm in nature, when I pick up a piece of rubbish. I spend time talking with my children, considering our actions: "Why are we biking to school instead of driving, even when it's raining?" All of those things are acts of worship that grow my faith. Faith is as much practical as it is sitting down and praying. I relate to God in the every-day reminders that what we do has a wider impact.

*How do you help your children connect with that?*

Mark and I try to model sustainability with our children. It happens in little conversations. When they want a new toy I might ask: "What is going to happen to that once you finish playing with it? Is there something better that we could do?" I want to prompt them to stop and think. They also pull us up on things. When I'm walking along and step over a piece of rubbish, they say "Mum! Pick that up!" I remember during a stormy Christchurch day when James was about 5 years old, we went walking to see the river and he started picking up rubbish out of the gutter. I asked, "What are you doing?" He replied, "I'm getting all the rubbish so it doesn't go out into the ocean."

He recently did an enquiry project at school on Antarctica and he is very concerned about global warming: "How are we going to get this message out there, Mum? How am I going to get people to understand?" Children can understand very young, and it helps when they have spent time in natural places and they have had those conversations from a young age. They have the ability to notice and make a difference and they are able to encourage others too. We can empower them to be that change.

*What are you learning about helping children engage with nature?*

My current research project is around how teachers use the natural environment to enhance children's wellbeing. I am interviewing teachers working in early learning environments. Wellbeing is more than just an individual thing. It is grown through being in healthy relationship with yourself, others, the environment, and God.[73] Research shows that the more green spaces children have, the more physically healthy they are, and they are able to focus cognitively. Even within an urban environment, knowing that there are green spaces and knowing that they can access those spaces has a positive impact on wellbeing. Children are not overstimulated in natural spaces so their brains can relax, recover and focus.[74] When children are in that space they can be more aware of God moving, through them, through others and through everything around them.

[Caleb, age 8, and James, age 10, joined in the conversation]

*What do you boys think? What do you like about being outside?*

Caleb: You can play with other people, like hide and seek! I like playing outdoor games.

Di: You like climbing trees and making huts.

Caleb: I look for sticks, good long walking sticks.

Di: We found some flax one day and did some weaving.

*How would you encourage a church children's program to include more natural environments and elements?*

We have to spend time outdoors in order to connect with it and appreciate it. If you're growing a relationship with another person you spend time with them; to grow a relationship with the land you need to spend time in it. That can be a spiritual space for growing faith. Take children outside, in any weather. Just play in nature, observe nature. Connect that with the Bible. I find that children fight less in the outdoors. Being in natural places is more peaceful than being inside man-made environments with a finite number of toys. There are open ended possibilities in an outdoor environment.

Children's programmes often use a lot of stuff which is not great for the environment, lots of plasticy things. The outside can be bought in. Choose to use natural resources. They may not last as long, but if they are biodegradable they can be composted. Use resources that will eventually go back into the earth, rather than plastic which will take a long, long, long time to decompose.

At church we include the children in activities like Cycle Sundays and planting days. Children are able to have a big impact in this. They're not just passively waiting until they grow up. They can motivate their parents. They can have a voice now.

*How have the kids been involved in creation care?*

James: We bike to church for Biketober. And tree planting.

Di: We help with an area of regenerating bush managed by Banks Peninsula Conservation Trust; the owners covenanted that part of the valley. We provide the manpower. We got involved after it was destroyed in the Christchurch Port Hills fires.

Caleb: The fire burned their house down. The humans and their dog got out, but the house didn't make it.

*What happens at a planting day?*

James: We plant. We carry a big box with baby plants in.

Di: The ecological restoration team put stakes in the ground, colour coded so we know what to plant where.

James: We use a shovel to dig holes.

Caleb: We put two fertiliser scoops in and then the plant in. God helps by watering with the rain. He always looks after nature.

Di: Being winter, the ground is usually a bit wetter too.

*What do you like about planting days?*

Caleb: There are lots of other children there. And we have a barbeque!

James: You get to see it growing the next year and the next year and the next year. One tree I planted was about that big (1/2 metre) and now it's about that big (2m)!

Di: That would have been one of the original ones planted four years ago. The property is part of a forest corridor between the Port Hills and green parts of Christchurch. Eventually the birds will take over the regeneration.

Caleb: We get oxygen from trees!

Manaaki whenua. Manaaki tāngata. Haere whakamua.

Care for the land. Care for the people. Move forward.

### Action Point 23: Restore beauty

Be involved over time with a local place, planting and tending native trees.

- Grow a partnership with your local Council or a conservation group.
- Plan a planting day in the winter time, or a weeding or watering day in the summer time.
- Practical Conservation resources, Eco Church NZ: www.ecochurch.org.nz/practical-conservation

## Action Point 24: Nature-based children's ministry

Nurture children's faith, wellbeing and leadership through including natural spaces and materials and conversations about sustainability.

- Children's ministry Curriculum resources, Eco Church NZ: www.ecochurch.org.nz/curriculum
- 'What a Wildly Wonderful World' resource for children, A Rocha UK: www.atyourservice.arocha.org/en/wildly-wonderful-world-2010-resource-pack
- Check out other groups doing outdoor programmes with kids, such as Conscious Kids: www.consciouskids.co.nz

## Action Point 25: Encourage outdoor adventure

Young people growing in fitness, confidence, knowledge, wellbeing, faith and relationships in outdoor environments.

- Adventure Specialties Trust works alongside schools and community groups using outdoor adventure and adventure therapy programmes to nurture growth: www.adventurespecialties.co.nz
- Scripture Union run camps for children, youth and young adults, including E3 which is an expedition journey in ecology, faith and leadership run in partnership with Arocha and Adventure Specialties Trust. Scripture Union also work with churches in numerous ways including facilitating children and young people to experience creation: www.sunz.org.nz

## Action Point 26: Form a Creation Care team

An active group of eco champions in every church.

- Start an enviro team in your church by forming relationships, inviting people to talk, and giving things a try. This is important to sustain momentum and lead the church in practical action.

## Mustard Seeds

*Poem by Ana Lisa de Jong, Living Tree Poetry*

Teach your children to plant trees.
Teach them to open their hands,
scatter seeds.

The world which would squeeze them to its mould,
would have them hold on tight,
bury them under its avalanche
of consumption.

Whereas breathing, living,
is found in breaking open,
pouring ourselves out.
Scattering the seed
which without there isn't fruit.

Teach your children the beauty of creation.
That what we do makes a difference,
just in the act of doing.

The war for our children's souls is quiet,
quiet as the drug that lulls them to sleep.
Open their hands, give them seeds.

# From a Mother's Heart: Eliala Fihaki

Eliala Fihaki recently moved with her family to Auckland. She works with Tearfund New Zealand as Senior Programme Specialist.[75] Eliala is also doing a PhD through the University of the South Pacific.

*What was it like growing up in Tuvalu?*

Tuvalu and its natural environment constitute a simple life. Much of what you do revolves around food production for your loved ones which includes extended families and community. It is a homogeneous society – daily activities are predictable and uniform across families. There was no chemist or furniture shop or a cafeteria to go to when I was a child, only one hotel, a handful of shops, and a grass airfield with a narrow strip of concrete for the wheels of the plane.

In my childhood days we interacted with nature a lot; all our games happened outside, in the day and nights too. Riding bikes was a new thing. A few families had a TV and we would sit outside and watch through the windows. Our favourites were the *Grease* movie – I watched it so many times I know all the songs and words – and WWE wrestling – Hulk Hogan in his yellow outfit and famous entrance act, calling up the crowd and flexing his muscles! These were glimpses of another world.

Raising children in that time was an extended family affair where all the aunties, grand aunts and uncles care for you. I spent very little time with my parents. My father was away studying in England to be an accountant (1983-1988) and my mum was busy with work and other siblings. I was the eldest of five and the favourite niece and grandchild for both my maternal and paternal families. I'm very fortunate to have had much love and affection.

My childhood engrained in me the duty to serve others, particularly my family. It's a satisfying feeling to be able to serve and touch people's lives – this is a reason I do well working in the development sector. I grew up in a communal framework. However my exposure to the outside world and education curriculum opened my eyes to see the ugly side of life in other situations. I learnt about individualism. The idea of individual human rights conflicted with the values I learnt growing up and I didn't see its validity. I was not in any disadvantaged situations to yearn for recognition or escape from hardship.

I am now at a crossroad, having different worldviews on each side. I have to find ways to integrate the two, but I always view situations from my communal framework first. I believe it is biblical, abiding in the two great commandments in the New Testament: first and foremost we should love God with all our heart, then we should love our neighbour as we love ourselves. It's very simple: we are made in God's image, so loving and considering others is equally loving God. This is the foundation of the communal perspective.

## What did you love about Tuvalu?

I love everything about Tuvalu: the people, the sun, the food and the scents of the flowers, the governing systems, the traditions and community activities. It's amazing how you don't fully appreciate these things when you are living in it. I left when I was 17 for further studies in New Zealand and then Fiji. Being away from Tuvalu created this deep appreciation.

I love the simplicity – life is very basic. Needs and wants are a few compared to life here in New Zealand: food on table, a thatched roof over your head, you can walk anywhere. There are not many things to worry about.

I love the kinship values that keep people connected. There is a concept of 'tama tuagane' cross-cousins "siblings or cousins who are different sexes."[76] The children of your cross-cousin are as important as your own children, or even more important. It is reciprocal relationship. This is shown very much during the festive Christmas holidays. Families are reunited with loved ones who travelled to other islands or overseas for work and school. A lot of alofa (love) is exchanged between families – food and parties to celebrate being alive and returning after a year's hard work. Those who live overseas work and send money back, then when you get home you take a break from chores and you are treated as a prince or princess! It's an example of reciprocity and investment of good faith. The families in the islands not only receive the money, they never miss a day praying for you.

*How did you relate to the natural world?*

Tuvalu's physical environment is a very fragile place. There are nine islands, eight of which are inhabited, nowhere is more than a few metres high. The atolls are very narrow, on Funafuti the widest part of the island is 800m. The lagoon is your front yard and the ocean is your backyard. Tourists spend a lot money to visit a place like my home, I got it free every day! Having that environment as a backdrop to my life, intrigued me to know more about the relationships and interactions within natural systems. Despite the fragility of the environment I see complex networks that have sustained my people for a very long time.

From one perspective, Tuvalu is a very poor country. It does not have unique flora and fauna. It is very vulnerable to disasters. To me it's unique in that my ancestors tolerated its environment limitations with little food and water resources. My people are resilient and very positive thinking by nature. As good navigators they could have migrated to bigger islands with better biodiversity but they chose to make their homes on those tiny atolls. So from another perspective, Tuvalu is a rich country, looking at its sea area; the Tuvalu Exclusive Economic Zone area is around 900,000 square km,[77] and its people are spread around the globe!

Moving to New Zealand does not make me forget my first home. I carry it with me and I hope to transfer that to my children. That natural world of Tuvalu will continue to shape and influence my worldview and how I relate to others and the environment. It's my baseline.

*How do you see God in relation to creation?*

John 1:1 is very clear for us who believe in the existence of the Almighty. He spoke nature into existence. He created the earth and all the living things including human beings through spoken words and breathing life. Science has a different view, but doing a degree in Environment did not challenge my belief in God the creator of all things. I'm sure God had it in his plans for humankind to explore science to study his marvellous works. There will be a time when he will unveil the mystery when we see him face to face.

In my work I rely very much on God. I used to rely on my intellectual capacity to solve things, but for me today and moving forward, God will lead the way. He will show me how to carry out my work. I know that what I learned in science will be instrumental – God wouldn't let me waste my time acquiring those qualifications for nothing. We are his children: "for I have redeemed thee, I have called thee by name: thou art mine" (Isaiah 43:1).

*How did you first become concerned about climate change?*

Growing up in Tuvalu, its unique geography and climate vulnerabilities convicted me to pursue a degree in environmental studies and eventually a Masters in Governance. I needed to understand the vulnerabilities of my home and figure out ways to mitigate them. Climate change has surfaced as a major issue for the international community.[78] It exacerbates the current vulnerabilities of Tuvalu. For my PhD thesis I explore the concept of adaptation, both in the islands and for Tuvalu people living in other countries. How do we adapt to the tides and storms and cultural changes? I look at how adaptation is managed within the context of Tuvalu, both the land and the diaspora people.

*How did God call you into aid and development work?*

With God nothing is a coincidence. My life journey is immersed in and around aspects of development. I hail from a family where my grandfather and father served as members of Parliament. My grandfather was Minister for Transport and Communication, my dad was Minister for Finance and Economic Development. So development is in my DNA! At our dining table my father would talk about his day and I learned how systems in governments are connected internally and externally.

My husband for twenty-three years and counting has also contributed a lot to my career. I treasure having an educated and receptive partner. My husband is my sounding board. I wouldn't be so confident to speak my mind if it wasn't for him.

I did a degree in Environmental Management at the University of the South Pacific, and worked in fisheries and integrated water sectors, which provided a good background. I went on to do a Masters and I taught sociology, history, politics and geography.

Doing a Masters in Governance helped solidify my understanding of development and the dynamics of public financial management and ethics with different institutional arrangements and civilizations at play (geopolitics). I then was a project coordinator in the United Nations Development Programme (UNDP), based in Fiji. Working for UNDP was a privilege that taught me a lot – at times stressful as you have to be 150% efficient! Bits from different parts of my life enabled me to slowly piece together the development puzzle, and I'm still collecting pieces. I like to make things connected. In all of these, God's hand was there, and still is. The experiences, values and learnings I've gained over the years is amazing.

Last year I moved to Auckland to join the team at Tearfund New Zealand. Working for Tearfund is truly a blessing, not only for my family as new immigrants but for my professional walk too. Tearfund is my first permanent position after 20 years of short-term contracts and consultancies. It is my first experience working for a Non-Government Organisation, and a faith-based one, and my first job in New Zealand. Initially there was some culture shock but it's my new norm now and I am very grateful. It is marvellous to integrate development and faith.

*How does Tearfund see environmental issues as part of poverty and development?*

There is a growing focus in Tearfund on environmental protection. We are realizing the impacts of climate change on our projects, and our partners on the ground are witnessing the extreme changes like flooding and droughts. The positive side is helping communities to adapt and figure things out, integrating science and traditional knowledge and practices.[79]

*What are you hearing from around the world about the effects of climate change?*

Our partners in Ethiopia are going through long droughts. In Nepal there is a lot of flooding, which makes it difficult to cross the rivers to reach to communities. The Philippines are having both droughts and floods! The Pacific islands face worsening tropical cyclones and typhoons. The climate is changing and this exacerbates current climate conditions. During the dry season it becomes drier for longer. In the wet season the intensity of rainwater is extreme. That's what I am learning about climate change: it increases the intensity and the frequency of harsh events.

Originally, Tearfund's main focus was on disaster response. But after they responded to disasters they realised that to strengthen the communities they needed to foster an enabling environment to improve livelihoods. Economic and social resilience is built into the journey. So we still to respond to disasters and build local capacity to survive future disasters, and we also focus on modern slavery, farming enterprise and children's development.

For example, I am currently reviewing a project in the Philippines, in the Western Samar area. They used to be dependent on the ocean. After a big typhoon in 2009 Tearfund responded, and we heard the need to shift their livelihood inland. They still fish but no longer rely totally on that; now they have ventured into farming vegetables with contracts to supply to big markets. In our project we look at irrigation, increasing skills, and sourcing seeds, as part of climate change resilience.

Over the years our partners have learned how to incorporate science and traditional knowledge. A good example is mulching to keep the moisture in the ground so that during drought the land does not dry out so much. In Vanuatu we are developing coffee and vanilla. They have droughts and then hurricanes, so as they set up farms they look at those issues before they construct their greenhouses, to build resilience. In the Philippines our goal is to make them ready for any disaster. They have a disaster management plan for each community, so that they know how to respond to different disasters – not just hurricane or typhoon, but also pandemics. I think that is the ideal thinking for Tearfund. Going forward we want to engage in the climate change sector in order to climate-proof all our programmes.

*Why is governance training important?*
Governance is an integral aspect of life and community development. For a group (whether a community organisation or business) to access development aid it has to have good sound governance to ensure accountability and transparency. Sadly, corruption is very common in the world. One of our partners faces corruption everyday as officials ask to be paid for many things. Our partner rejects all of that and maintains a stand against it, even if it means delays. So we focus not only on developing a farming enterprise but we look at the whole picture of governance in the community. Tearfund's initiatives build resilience in governance in a holistic perspective to strengthen and improve organisations. This is a good approach and a learning curve.

*What issues do you see in climate change and development?*
My role in Tearfund is monitoring and evaluation, so I've been looking at all our projects. I am recommending ways to make all of our projects disaster-proof and adapt to climate change. We need a climate change lens for every approach we implement. In my opinion a lot of development projects are too short term. There should be more focus on the long term. To save Tuvalu from sea level rise you would have to build up the land – that's a long term adaptation.

Food security is an important part of climate change adaptation. We need to report to donors that we have addressed food security. Most donors want to see immediate results, so we plant things like tomatoes and cucumbers because they are a short term success. Within the time of the project you can see them come to fruition. But that is not enough. The food that the people ask for is breadfruit – that sustains them forever – but a breadfruit tree takes longer to grow than a 2-year project.[80] So we need to educate our donors that some measures need be longer term to see real fruit.

Another focus is water security, by having more water tanks. But the more water you have, the more water you use. Consumption leads to asking for more resources. It is our human weakness as consumers. When I was young, we only had one water tank; we had droughts and we managed with that one 10,000 litre water tank. Now there are six 10,000 litre water tanks, some families have two or three, and there is still not enough water! I worry that adaptation projects can make people more dependent and complacent so they consume more than they need to. We are mindful of these complexities at Tearfund.

Something I value about Tearfund is the partnership approach; our relationship with partners extends beyond project cycles. And it is not all about the money, we support people in need morally and spiritually also.

### Do churches have a role in a disaster?

In New Zealand, Tearfund works with the National Disaster Management Agency and the CID Humanitarian Network.[81] I believe it is very important for churches to work together and in partnership with agencies, including Civil Defence. When there is a disaster, churches need to know how to mobilise. For our international partners, we are introducing a process to develop a profile of their local communities;[82] a baseline survey covers things like building structure and roof type, water sources, health facilities, resource mapping, rivers, plantations, and churches. It is a powerful tool for communities, partners and Tearfund to be aware of the assets and risks present in every context.[83] The hope is that during a hurricane, for instance, the community has already identified which churches or buildings are safe places. It would be a good thing for churches in Aotearoa too to build up a profile of the community and have good networks. Churches are a vital community unit and they should be ready to mobilise in case of emergency.

### How do Pacific Island churches in Aotearoa support those in the islands?

One very practical way is that we fill shipping containers that go back to the islands. Anyone who wants to send stuff for their family can put things in. Churches always organise containers during disasters, and throughout the year there is a lot of alofa – gifts, food, clothing, shoes – sent to our families back home. That's one way the church here shows ongoing connection and care.

*Where do you see God in climate change and mission?*

As I started work in the environment sector, I thought about Genesis 1:28-29: "Go ye therefore ..." to multiply. As I look at those words, it does not say for us to exploit the earth. It says for us to nurture it and replenish it, not subdue and dominate. We have dominion but with care. Just like how you care over your kids, as a mother. You have dominion over your kids but you don't exploit it. You nurture them properly. In the islands, because we are very Christian and strong in our faith, that is the approach I take as an environment person working with government, to link with the Bible. We can't be seen be pushing a Christian agenda so we don't say it often but we say it in our prayers. Everything in the islands starts with a prayer. We bring in stewardship from the Bible. That guides my work and how I do things in the environment sector. It is stewardship from a mother's heart.

*How are women part of climate change adaptation?*

Gender is an important ingredient. Tearfund is expanding a cross-sector focus on climate change and gender. In the Pacific we encourage women to be involved in conservation projects, because of their mothering nature. It is becoming obvious that women are leading in water harvesting, cooking, gathering firewood, so they are good agents for both adaptation and mitigation for climate change. A colleague and I did a report for Oxfam on climate finance and women, and these are the findings we came up with. Women are important in implementing things. They are engaged with all these activities that can adapt to climate change. But women are missing from the equation of decision making.

We ask the women: "Why don't you go to the meetings?" They say: "We are invited, but when we get there our male cousins are in the meeting hall and we can't face them." It's a taboo relationship so they don't speak. They keep themselves quiet. And also they get very tired from their day's work. They are too busy with housework to sit in a meeting hall for five hours, and fatigue lowers their participation in discussions. You have to talk to the women to hear their reasons for not being in the meetings. We need to take those into account so that women's voices can be heard.

For people in the Pacific, for my people, I believe that we have the solution within ourselves. We don't have to copy or do what others are telling us to do; don't jump on new initiatives imported from the other side of the world. We should focus on what we can do within our own context, based on what we value. We have always looked after the environment because Tuvalu is very limited in many ways. My ancestors on the island knew how to make

AWHI MAI AWHI ATU

a piece of soap last for many months. Nowadays my kids just throw soap away.

Climate change survival has to do with behaviour, attitudes and values – things deeper than we can measure. In development, we can't do projects to change people's attitudes because you can't measure that; outcomes have to be tangible. I think the church has a role here, to strengthen faith in action, to address the consumer attitude, so that we learn to respect and replenish the earth. It means going back to Genesis.

*What are the faith convictions that ring true for Pacific women?*

Many Tuvaluan people, especially the elderly people, think that God's promise to Noah will hold forever. There is not going to be another flood. They cannot accept that there is sea level rise.

*So talk about climate change is a lack of faith?*

Yes, that's how they see it. They tell us that if we do right in how we live, God will not punish us. That's a strong belief. They do know that the droughts are impacting their livelihoods and making it harder to grow food. They know about the increasing storm surges during hurricanes. We hear the scientists saying that Tuvalu will go underwater in a few years time, maybe 50 years and we will be submerged. But the old people do not believe that; they will not think about climate change. For them, God cannot flood the earth because of his promise to Noah.

For me, God has given us the earth to replenish, but we have over-dominated and over-subdued it, and climate change is the cost of not looking after the world. People in Tuvalu think 'it's not our doing' and that God will save them because we didn't cause it. For them it is a test of faith. Perhaps my faith is not strong enough. I believe in God, I believe that he won't harm us, I believe that I am a child of God. But I also think that we have to be wise.

Those with education see things differently. I could have stayed in the islands, not knowing about these issues and never thinking of leaving. But on my journey God has put me in university, gave me knowledge and so I come to use it. I exercise what wisdom I can find. Coming to New Zealand is for my children and for their future. I don't want to put them through the ordeal of living in the islands and facing all the impacts of climate change. I have brought my family away from the islands, but I hope we do not cut off our connection to our home.

*How can Pacific people sustain that connection through climate change?*

My PhD thesis is on climate change adaptation and cultural identity. I use Roy Rappaport's book, *Ritual and Religion in the Making of Humanity*.[84] He defines adaptation as how a human being, a living organism or living system will adapt but core features of the person or the system will remain. I am investigating what makes us Tuvaluan, comparing people living in Tuvalu with people who live away from Tuvalu. I found that even though you are away from your country, your values and cultural systems are still with you. It is ingrained in you from birth.

In light of climate change and sea level rising I say that atoll islands like Tuvalu and Kiribati should channel resources into maintaining their identity, learning and recording our cultural traits, as a central way of adapting. Science and natural phenomena are pointing towards these islands becoming submerged. Building seawalls and improving food and water security will be futile when the island is underwater. The people can be saved by relocating them, but Tuvalu as a people will drown with the island if we don't treasure our identity. It will be a worthwhile investment to record and strengthen identity traits such as the language, the art of dancing, the making of food, the relationships, the values of families, and so much more that is distinctive to Tuvaluan people. They remain with you wherever you are. If our identity is strengthened then there is hope for Tuvaluan culture, faith and identity, as a diaspora when the inevitable happens.

I hope countries around the world will allow space and recognise us as a people even when we are relocated and living in other countries. New Zealand is heading that direction by celebrating languages and recognising the uniqueness of different Pacific cultures and identity.

I try to do this with my kids, the engrained traits of myself as a Tuvaluan: eating raw fish, respecting and serving elders, valuing extended families, visiting them to share a meal with families, especially those coming to New Zealand – or Fiji in our previous home. One thing is having devotions in the evening. Having devotions is a traditional practice in Tuvalu and makes us feel like Tuvaluans. We don't do it every day but whenever we do I feel very much at home. It is an identity as well as a faith thing; I link to God and at the same time I link to my identity.

*What is a Biblical view of a people forced from their land?*

If I think about the Israelites; they were dispersed all over the world. If that happened to the people of God, whom God proclaimed as his people, it can happened to anybody. But their faith in God remained. Their faith is their identity.

I still hope that Tuvalu can survive as a nation. There is hope that the world can limit global warming to 1.5 degrees. I look for God's hand in all of this. But if Tuvalu does go underwater, I believe that our country is the people not the land.[85]

And I know that one day we will go to a better home where we are all at home.

*How do you find time for everything?*

Yes, that's an issue! I love my work with Tearfund. I will take some leave to finish my PhD. I've been nominated as a Board member for the Council for International Development – the umbrella body for all the NGOs in New Zealand doing international work. Last year was challenging, getting used to all the change. A lot is going on for me and my family, but I believe that God has plans for me. He will be there for me. So I'm not worried.

## E Tavaegina koe: A Pacific Prayer

*Written by Silvia Purdie and translated into Tuvaluan by Rev. Sila Tepapauoatua, Ekalesia Kelisiano, Tuvalu Presbyterian Church, Auckland*

God of all creation,
thank you for the beautiful islands of the Pacific.

We praise you for the delicate balance of land and sea,
the delights of colourful flowers, tropical fruits and fish.

Te Atua ote fuafuaga o mea katoa,
fakafetai atu mote gali o fenua ote Pasefika.

E tavaegina koe ne matou ona kote matagali
nofogamalie te laukele mote moana,
Te gali o lanu kesekese o pulalakau, fuataga o lakau mo Ika.

God of grace, thank you for the peace of island life.
We praise you for families and communities
living in harmony with nature and with each other.

Te Atua ote Alofa tauanoa, fakafetai atu mote
filemu ote olaga ite fenua.
E tavaegina koe ne matou ona ko kaiga mo fakapotopotoga a matou
E oola mote manuia fakatasi mo meaola pena
foki mo nisi tino ake foki.

God of mercy, thank you for the vibrant cultures of the Pacific.
We praise you for Pacific people living in other lands:
May they continue strong in who they are.

Te Atua ote Alofa atafai,
fakafetai atu mo te katoatoa ote olaga mai aganu faka te Pasefika.
E tavaegina koe ne matou, ona ko tino Pasefika
ko oola i nisi laukele.
Ke fakatumau te malosi ia latou e iloga ai a latou.

God of all goodness,
Protect your people affected by sea level rise.
Deepen our faith through the storms.
Hold us close as we trust in you.
Give us wisdom to make good decisions.
Speak your truth to us, we pray,
in the name of our Father Creator God,
our Lord Jesus Christ,
with the Holy Spirit, amen.

Te Atua o mea lelei katoa,
Ke puipui ou tino mai pokotiaga ote tai fanake.
Ke fakamalosi omotou fakatuanaki i matagi malosi.
Puke ke pili atu matou me talitonu matou kia koe.
Tuku mai te poto ke fai ne matou a filifiliga lelei,
Tavili mai te meatonu kia matou, A matou e tinoga atu,
Ite igoa ote tou Atua te Tamana ote fuafuaga,
Te tou Aliki ko Iesu Keliso
Mote Agaga Tapu, Amene.

*Action Point 27: Support global mission partners addressing climate change*

Resource communities around the world to respond to climate change with resilience and capacity.

- Fund an environmental project in a developing country.
- Share stories of mission work around the world connecting poverty and environmental action.
- Pray for mission partners.

*Action Point 28: Think further ahead*

Climate change preparedness involves long term climate adaptation planning. Eliala is challenging mission agencies to think beyond a short-term mindset of what can be achieved in a couple of years. The people want breadfruit! This is also a great challenge for churches. In pandemic times, we don't know what next month will be like, let alone next year or next decade. But what are we building towards? What breadfruit trees are we planting, that we won't see fruit from this year, or maybe not even in our life-time?

*Action Point 29: Use less water*

- Do an audit on your church's water use.
- Water resources, Eco Church NZ: www.ecochurch.org.nz/water
- 'What you can do' Water For Life: www.waterforlife.org.nz

# Keep Showing Up: Elise Ranck

Elise is on the Advocacy team of the Anglican Diocese of Wellington, and a member of Berrigan House, a Catholic Worker Movement community in Kelburn, Wellington. She is also a volunteer farmer for Urban Kai[86] at Riverside/Umu i te Mamaku farm in Te Awa Kairangi (Lower Hutt), part of Common Unity.[87]

*What is your family background?*

My family is largely based in the USA, spread out across different states. My parents raised me and my two older in Santa Barbara, California, which in my unbiased opinion is one of the most beautiful places in the world. My parents moved there after getting married and finishing studies so my dad could take a job as a youth pastor at the local Free Methodist Church. Brave of them to move so far from both their families with an indefinite timeline – it's a three-hour time difference between SB and the states where their families live. They have always been very encouraging of us kids to get out into the world and find our place and they've set a pretty amazing example when it comes to doing that well.

*Was the natural environment part of faith?*

As I mentioned, the beauty of Santa Barbara (SB) is undeniable! Not too dissimilar to many coastal places in Aotearoa, the mountains gently hug the sea providing a vast diversity of flora and fauna in a tight radius. An acknowledgment of such beauty was instilled in us from an early age, not only from my family, who made sure trips to the beach were a regular part of the weekend routine, but also from the church pulpit came recognition of the privilege to live among such natural beauty. The scale weighed much more heavily on the distant appreciation rather than active preservation. This distant appreciation meant that our perceived relationship with the natural world was quite disconnected from our faith practices and rhythms of our daily lives. At that point in life I was not one to question the church's preaching on the character of God, and was content to rest in the knowledge that there was a Creator God who made beautiful things and who would look after their wellbeing with or without us.

*What did you particularly love?*

Thankfully I loved going to the beach. Unlike Wellington, the sea temperature in SB is pleasantly tolerable – so much so that we could spend hours splashing around, delighting in the rhythmic movement of rolling waves. When the waves died down and the tide receded, tidal reef ecosystems were revealed, welcoming the curious to explore life in the mysterious sea. There was never a dull moment at the beach and I always felt safe to play and explore. I particularly loved to be in the water – immersion is the purest form of serenity, feeling completely held. The ocean is quite mysterious and can be terrifying at times. The sea isn't as clear in SB and large cuttings of kelp forests are often swirling about, so I suppose it's less enticing in that sense. I'm grateful that fear of a violent and dangerous sea never settled in my mind as a child.

*What do you think of your upbringing looking back?*

It's easy for me to be critical of the past, knowing what I know now about systemic injustices and rampant inequality. I can wish I had eyes to see it then, but I didn't and that's OK. We were very privileged to live in SB, to frequent the beach and other similar places on family vacations, and to have a very loving and encouraging community surrounding us. I am increasingly grateful for each experience life has thrown me, as each adds shape to my ever-deepening faith and understanding of what it means to be a Jesus following, all creation loving, human being on this earth.

*What did you study at university?*

The first time I left home was to study at Seattle Pacific University in Seattle, Washington. In my first year I took a class entitled 'Faith, Sustainability and Creativity' which sparked an unearthed passion in creation care. The readings really got me thinking. I found Wendell Berry's reflections particularly eye-opening and exciting. His rural agrarian background and his approach to a faith embedded in and present to creation couldn't be more different from the approach and positionality of my evangelical home church. Yet it felt so familiar and made so much sense to me. From then on I knew I wanted to pursue environmental studies.

I was able to do a composite degree in Geo-Political Environmental Studies. There was no official degree programme but we pulled in papers from different disciplines like theology, political science, sociology, and economics. In my third year I learnt of the Creation Care Study Program (CCSP) and was quickly convinced to apply for the programme based in Kaikoura. So for three months in 2015 I joined several other students and staff from across North America to live communally in an old, converted convent not too far from the base of Mt. Fyffe. The entire programme was very formative for me. It is holistic not only in the teaching of a variety of topics but also in upholding relationships with the land and the surrounding community. Classroom learning was applied daily through communal living, sharing common goods, cooking from veggies grown in the backyard gardens, volunteering time with youth groups and conservation projects, self-sufficiency workshops led by various friends of the programme, etc. Immersion and practical learning really made clear what I value and how I want to participate in the world.

*How did that change your thinking about God?*

In those three months I came to love a God who is present in the neighbourhood, with the people and in the land. God is in the person we pass on the footpath or the herd of cattle migrating together from paddock to paddock. God is in the mountains hugging the sea, sheltering and standing firm. God is in the garden in abundance! That semester was the closest I'd ever felt to God. It was one of the happiest, most fulfilling times of my life.

I encountered God in a new way while travelling up to the lower North Island with the programme. We visited a variety of communities including Te Puawai o te Aroha Catholic Worker farm in Ōtaki. I was greeted with a wave of awe and a strange familiarity. Greenery wove between dwellings, all surrounding the most marvellous of centrepieces: a lush teeming veggie garden. Walking into the rustic whimsy we were greeted by rhythmic hammering of nails, smoke billowing out of chimneys, fragrance of fresh baked bread, chirpy chatter of birds and humans alike and perhaps even together. It was a collective unlike any other and yet reeking of Wendell Berry. We spent a couple of hours at the feet of Adi Leason, one of the founders of the farm, who used the opportunity to blow the socks off many a student. He shepherded us into the confronting realities of industrial farming, excessive consumerism, the American war machine, homelessness and loneliness, and many other forms of suffering lapping at our front doors. Floored by what I'd discovered that day, I took up the invitation to return to the farm during term break where I was once again struck by the tender weaving of hospitality to the stranger, companionship with the land and it's abundant gifts, daily routines steeped in prayer, and a readiness to speak truth to power. I couldn't help but wonder if this was a radiant glimpse into the kingdom of God.

When I returned to the USA to complete my degree I quickly felt the ache to know more of this tender weaving of community, creation and Christian values. Thanks to connections I had made with some outstanding Kiwis I was invited back to Aotearoa to explore this newfound ache. I moved into Berrigan House Catholic Worker community in Wellington which had been recently established by Jack and Finn Leason, two of Adi's sons. I hoped to immerse myself into a variety of communities, so before too long I was off on the next adventure, first to revisit CCSP, this time to offer a hand with the gardens. I intended to remain a couple of months but plans were shattered when the earthquake hit two weeks in.

*What happened?*

Kaikōura was close to the epicentre of a 7.8 magnitude earthquake on 16 November 2016 that devastated the town and caused 2 deaths. The earthquake shook us out of our slumbers smack in the middle of the night. Fortunately, my natural instincts kicked in straight away and I was able to escape out the nearest door, from what sounded and felt like a crumbling house. I waited helplessly and shaken for what felt like a long while until staff and students stumbled out into the darkness. There was a very fleeting moment of relief and safety as I looked up in the sky to see the blanket of dazzling stars. We gathered at the emergency point: the centre garden in which many potatoes had recently been buried. We huddled together, cold and confused, as we waited for everyone to gather. The force of the shaking was so strong that people were pushed back onto their beds, furniture was reshuffled, and glass spewed everywhere. We were witnessing what could have been an even more deadly earthquake. Before long we hopped into vans and boosted up to the base of Mt. Fyffe to escape the reach of a potential tsunami. There we camped out with most of the town for the remainder of the restless night.

We caught a second wind of the impacts of the earthquake when we returned to our home in the morning. Brick chimneys had collapsed into bedrooms or were hanging on by a thread. As I recalled the event we had all just survived I was sure we had just escaped death. The fear and trembling still shaking my core, I couldn't unsee the earthquake as anything but evil. For the first time in a long time, I felt miniscule in creation and afraid of its power. I could no longer see God in the mountains.

*What happened after the earthquake?*

Infrastructure was completely wrecked and we were cut off from the rest of the country. The event made world news yet we had a communication blackout. Eventually CCSP was able to get in touch with our families on our behalf but it was hard to not be able to connect directly.

The convent was no longer structurally sound so we were forced to seek alternative shelter. We couch-surfed at New Life Church and camped in tents, hardly sleeping as every aftershock woke us in a panic. After a few days many of us gratefully escaped on the NZ Navy ship to Lyttleton. We continued to hear reports from the news and friends on the ground. In some places the coast rose and fell, while other places were pushed a whole six meters above the sea. We were amazed to hear of a tsunami that rebounded from the coastline which rose as if in defence of the wave's arrival. The awe and bewilderment wouldn't fully sink in until several months into my recovery.

*Then what happened for you?*

All of the students were sent home to the USA, but I chose to stay here in the hopes of finding meaning and healing from the experience. I knew I needed a quiet and stable space to reflect and maintain some sort of peace amongst the building anxiety so I booked in a couple of weeks at Ngatiawa River Monastery. The team really looked after me, gently nurturing me with endless cups of tea, prayer on tap, nourishing kai, easy reading and time in solitude. The monastery itself is nestled amongst patches of dense bush and fresh, icy swimming holes along the Ngatiawa River, where overgrown tracks lead you to serene perches and intimate communion with nature. Short wanders, when I had the motivation to leave my room, were met with gentleness and the beginnings of a restored relationship to creation.

Rather than continue my pilgrimage to various communities I opted to settle at Berrigan House for a bit longer in the hopes that it would provide stability through the familiarity of the community and those surrounding. Friends and counselling helped me to grapple with: "where was God in the earthquake?" Despite the fear and anxiety consistently ringing in my ears, I felt deep down there was still a beauty to creation and also that God had never left me. I was able to trust that those dry bones of belief would one day come to life again.

After about five months I attended an Anglican young adults worship service at which Kate Day, Anglican Advocacy Enabler, did a callout looking for interns interested in climate justice in the church setting. Straight away I felt I should respond and was warmly welcomed by Kate. I soon joined the rest of the team to get working on communicating the Zero Carbon Act.

*How did you connect and engage the church in those early beginnings of climate action?*

In 2016, just before Kate started working for the Wellington diocese, Synod set Climate Catalysts (CC) in motion. The idea was that each parish would have an individual representative to lead climate action at their respective local levels. Part of Kate's role was then to gather, coordinate, and advise the direction of the CCs. Unfortunately, it proved difficult to get momentum, with individuals geographically dispersed and interested in disparate topics, and attempted gatherings weren't very successful. However, through Bishop Justin's leadership and blessing of our leadership, we were able to form a smaller working group of keen church climate leaders who would help us to mobilise churches beyond our own.

Alongside pushing for climate action, we noticed that there was widespread enthusiasm for waste reduction. We decided to lean into where God seemed to be moving, and support Anglicans to reduce waste – both as important creation care in itself and as a way to deepen relationships for future climate action. So in 2018 we launched the Rubbish Revolution, a 3-month challenge. Teams developed a goal, were offered accountability, were invited to participate in a variety of workshops to further educate and inspire, and were encouraged to speak up at a governmental level. Our mantra during the 3 months was "Grace, not guilt." We wanted participants to reflect on current societal systems, why it's so difficult for many people to continually do well by the environment. And also to remember that we are imperfect people on our own, but we can do powerful things when we join together in alignment with our loving God. To help people remember this, we gave them this statement to put on their wall!

I am an imperfect person, living in an imperfect world.
God loves me.
With God's help we can improve things together.

*How has your team been able to connect with the diversity of parishes?*

We are based in Wellington City where many parishes are already on board with the climate justice movement so it can easily feel like momentum is strong. However, over the past four years we've become increasingly aware of the rural-urban divide when it comes to taking action or speaking about climate change. At the Wellington Anglican Diocese we seek to be 'family on mission'. This takes relational work to ensure we're all on the same page and that no one, particularly our rural whānau, is feeling hurt or misunderstood. These are tricky conversations to be having at a time when many rural agrarian-based parishioners feel government has got them under the pump and is constantly asking them to change their farming practices. Combating climate change requires everyone to give their best effort and some major sacrifices will have to be made, but we need pathways forward to give people a hope and a future.

Despite this challenge to bridge a widening gap, we continue to create spaces, which allow people to "keep showing up" (a common phrase of the wise Bishop Justin). One of the main ways we've accomplished this is through 'Missions for Submissions': large-scale drives that mobilise parishes to gather submissions as part of their Sunday services. Each of these mobilisations was inspired by teams of young people who we equipped, encouraged, and prayed over at a breakfast briefing the morning of the event. From there each team would go out to a different church and speak from the front about the submission opportunity. We encouraged them to focus on why the issue was personally and spiritually meaningful. During morning tea the team would hold space for those who wished to make submissions.

For the whole process to be as accessible as possible, we resourced the teams with handy reference sheets in case of any big questions. We made child-appropriate submission forms on which children could draw their ideas of the future. We painted large colourful cutouts for people to hold and pose with for a photo, to show their support. We want parishioners to know that their voices, concerns, ideas, and hearts for justice matter, and to provide many avenues for them to confidently action this truth. We want to make it clear to the government and to the public that the church deeply cares about the suffering in the world, climate change included!

Missions for Submissions have been some of Anglican Advocacy's most successful diocesan-wide initiatives. During the first one, for the Zero Carbon Act in 2019, we managed to collect over 500 individual submissions. We delivered a massive box, including children's drawings, printed photos and written forms to the door of Parliament. The Ministry for the

Environment loved our creative submissions so much that they displayed them in their staff room for several months! How delighted we were to hear that our efforts had made a difference, even if only to ease the burden of the analysis process. In a similar manner, we were delighted to see the surge of energetic young people showing up at each briefing because they believed they had something valuable to offer to each cause. I hope others can take courage and follow suit, speaking to their church community and having a go at writing their own submission. The government can often seem like this distant, immovable machine, but all decision makers are humans and most will have the heart to relate to yours. We have the power to harness our words to tap into compassion.

*What has happened since?*

Following the Zero Carbon submissions there were massive school strikes for the climate. We recognized that marching would feel quite foreign and uncomfortable for many parishioners so we explored alternative ways of meaningful engagement. Being Anglicans we knew prayer would capture attention. In collaboration with our Auckland counterparts, Karakia for Our Climate emerged and quickly gained the support of other churches across the country. Our aim was to hold vigil in the hours leading up to the strikes, to prepare the way for what would be a powerful sight to behold. At the Wellington vigil we prayed for the strike and the wider issues and we made sure our prayers were loud and clear by painting them on fabric prayer flags. These flags were then carried into the march the next day, unifying all participants, marchers and prayer partners alike. It was truly a beautiful way to add our voices – mouthpieces of God's heart and our bodies, vessels of God's peace to a very public and politically charged scene. Although in-person public demonstrations of climate action are somewhat on hold due to Covid, Karakia for Our Climate is growing as a movement and continues to find opportunities to prayerfully intercede for all impacted by the climate crisis. Watch this space!

In addition, we've trialled another version of the Rubbish Revolution (RR), this time called the Low Carbon Challenge. We followed the same format as the RR; this time we asked teams to have at least two goals – one practical and one prayerful. We were encouraged by the number that took the challenge to heart, seriously considering the implications of their actions and what simple changes they could make to challenge the system, inspiring their comrades to push on in their own journeys.

*What else would you encourage churches to do?*

There is plenty for churches to do when it comes to taking action. There is scope for joining pre-existing campaigns, making submissions, jumping into marches, partnering through regular prayer, and getting amongst the local action in your neighbourhood. Looking at the trajectory of climate change and global pandemics, we will need resilient communities who are well connected, resourced, and equipped to hold strong against whatever comes their way. Jesus calls us to love our neighbours and the Works of Mercy tell us exactly what this looks like. This is what the church is made for and we now have the opportunity to join other community members who are prepared to do the same, whether or not they are motivated by a Christian God. Let us truly be sanctuaries in times of trouble: stocked with survival essentials, trained in pastoral care, partnering with practitioners, befriending our neighbours, warmly welcoming strangers, holding governing bodies to account, and attuned to the needs of creation.

Building local connections is as important now as it will be in the future. Community resilience means that when 'the shit hits the fan' we have strong relationships, with the earth and with each other. We are creating this web of connection, so that in the next pandemic, the next flood, the next crisis, we have got each other's back.

I love Wendell Berry's poem 'The Peace of Wild Things'.[88] It finishes:

> I come into the peace of wild things
> who do not tax their lives with forethought of grief.
>
> I come into the presence of still water.
> And I feel above me the day-blind stars
> waiting with their light. For a time
> I rest in the grace of the world, and am free.

*Watch on video by On Being:*
*www.youtube.com/watch?v=-ewB0WL3bNw*

### Action Point 30: Partner with local groups

Local churches connecting with local communities in service and mission.

- Research community and environmental groups in your area; explore on Facebook, talk to City Council staff and sustainability organisations.
- Go along to community events, get to know leaders, find out what their goals and values are.
- Report to church leadership and choose which groups to partner with.

### Action Point 31: Enable people to have a say

Local churches aware of current issues and finding easy and enjoyable ways to contribute.

- Find out about submissions processes and issues.
- Experiment with creative strategies, such as photos, signs, banners, prayers.
- Advocacy resources, Eco Church NZ: www.ecochurch.org.nz/advocacy

### Action Point 32: Prepare for times of trouble

Every church prepared for the worst, with emergency plans, supplies, and people aware of these plans and ready to respond when needed.

- Identify climate change disaster risks for your area. This information will be on your City/Regional Council website.
- Meet with your local Civil Defence group: www.civildefence.govt.nz/find-your-civil-defence-group
- Review and update your church (and home) disaster plan, e.g. stored supplies. Do people know where they are? Are they fresh? Who can open the church? What if there are no communications? Where is the nearest generator?
- Work with church leadership on disaster policies and planning.
- Have practice runs.
- Get Ready NZ: www.getready.govt.nz

## Soft Beast

*Poem by Ana Lisa de Jong, Living Tree Poetry*

The earth is a soft beast
who has lain down for long,
and let us live upon her resting hide.

A grazing animal,
moving in elegant ease
her heavy weight.

And we, insects in the noon day sun,
flying on and off
the slope of her back.

At most we have felt
the swish of her ear
as we dive too close for comfort.

But not her buck,
not her rear –
the earth known for her patience.

The hospitable space
that she makes
for a people unaware of their tenancy,

confused by the matter of ownership,
when in reality each step
is a thing precarious.

As, balanced on the back of a beast untamed,
we can be shook off
at the toss of a massive head.

Yes, the earth is a soft,
soft-hearted beast
lulling us into a dangerous complacency.

That we might need to wake,
wake up from the slumber
of days in the lazy sun.

What is it that we could do
if we were sensitive enough
to register her?

What is it that,
if we were to gently incline ourselves to her ear,
we might hear her asking for?

What is it that she needs,
to live her days out in peace?
Might we ask?

Yes, I imagine I can hear the earth's little cries
in the disturbance she makes
with her unsettled feet.

The way she shakes,
the tremors causing some
to hold tight to her restless legs.

Yet, she is too gracious to make a great
debacle.
She, a humble gentle giant.

But we,
we can feel a storm rising,
that she might yet charge to a precipice.

What can we do
to ease the frightened beast?
This soft, soft being

to whom we owe so much.

# Sure as the Sunrise: Faaolataga Misikopa-Leasi

Residing in Poneke (Wellington), Faaolataga (Ola) is currently the President of Presbyterian Women Aotearoa New Zealand (PWANZ).[89] With her husband, the late Rev. Perema Leasi QSM, they served at PIPC (Pacific Islanders Presbyterian Church) Porirua and neighbouring church communities. Faaolataga is currently completing postgraduate studies in theology through the University of Otago.

*How God has led you to where you are now?*

I was born and raised in Samoa, a descendant from the island of Savaii (Havaiki); my father comes from Vaipu'a Salega and my mother from Vailoa Palauli. The dynamic of my childhood's spiritual and cultural growth was collaboratively nurtured via indigenous and ministry upbringing. What resonates for me the most was my Mama Fualaau's nurturing and caring roles. My parents achieved formal teaching training and my father taught at a high school and Mama became a headmistress for junior syndicates. They then became theological students in 1974-1977 at Malua Theological College.[90] Fualaau continued to nourish her teaching skills as an influential input to theological and domestic studies and nurturing our young family at the same time. She would whip up new clothes, sewing patterns she developed herself. Sadly I did not capture her sewing skills.

There was a significant need to grow vegetable gardens around their house blocks; Malua students were assigned to plant maumaga (taro patches). Mama on her own became a cultivating grower. She precisely produced a veggie and herbal garden and embodied it in our spiritual and nutritional growth.

On sunny mornings she would take us outside to say a prayer before picking the ripened fruits, followed by a clean weeding. Creation stories of Eve's apple were narrated with red tomatoes. That delivered us into temptations of craving for real 'palagi' apples and thus we too committed sin by stealing Mama's tomatoes prior to harvesting. Coca cola (imported from American Samoa) was our favourite treat. In those days it came in one-litre heavy-duty glass bottles. Mama showed us how to collect empties, clean thoroughly, and wheelbarrow them back to the campus canteen.

There were times Mama was out of sight and we wandered around the humongous campus – 'the green, green grass of home'.[91] We children would roll and lie around on the lushly green grass; no wonder David the psalmist wrote, "He makes me lie down in green pastures" Psalm 23:2 (NRSV). This not only encapsulates a profound sense of nature with our wholeness of being, but also a sense of freedom – no fear, no boundaries in the realm of God's green creation.

One typical day after school we spotted some figures on the seashore of the diminishing tide, across the road or *gatai* – a cluster of faletua (students' spouses), digging and pulling up pipis and seashells. In a split second and out of curiosity the campus children sped in a 100m race, crossing the road with bare feet. Melting tar stuck to the soles of our feet! We rushed into the sea to cool them down. The joy of being saturated in the ocean became the natural embodiment of restoration to our hot feet.

Little did I know at the time, we were being grounded in science, culture and technology though informal learning. These were quality times of absorbing 'environmental sciences' knowledge and understanding, igniting our curiosity and problem-solving skills. In many ways I encountered the vast richness of Creation through the living creatures on land and sea, free from plastic 'weapons'. We would play free until the sun sank below the horizon, behind the coconut trees, caught up in vast explorations and discoveries with a cluster of living and non-living things, sights, smells, sounds and emotions. This learning was rarely explored in daily conversations, so long as we had fish and seafood for dinner!

My parents accepted a call to serve at Ekalesia Faapotopotoga Kerisiano Samoa church in Fasitootai; once the home of Ioane Viliamu (John Williams the LMS missionary). Adjacent with pastoral, schooling and domesticity duties, Mama mandated more cultivation: growing manioca, sugar cane, pineapples, taro and veggies in a fine fertile patch, with a few poultry and pigs. After school on Wednesdays the village children and young people brought taulua-popo (coconuts in pairs) and got to work weaving and planting in the 20 acres backyard farm. This was usually followed by a typical feast of cooked umu-hangi with a size 3 roast, whipped with coconut soup of eleni (herrings), to celebrate a job well done!

Authentically, all these real-life encounters, in collaboration with Mama's roles in creational and relational care have flourished our embodiment with nature. Recycling the coca cola bottles taught us about sustainability with material substances. Scriptural facilitations have been intentionally embedded into this authentic tikanga from my Mama's love for God, care for creation and her children. Later on, Mama established the first Aoga Amata (Native Preschool) in the region, for preserving the mother tongue and cultural values with village and the neighbouring children. I embarked on a profound dialogue of comprehending and reinventing what it means to be a carer and user of God's creation through daily living with natural, social and cultural upbringing.

Sadly, my dearest Mama Fualaau was diagnosed with an unidentifiable sickness, and God called her Home on 23 February 1980, "*How the mighty have fallen, and the weapons of war perished – Aue! ua maliliu toa, ua maumau ai auupega o le taua.*" (2 Samuel 1:27, NRSV and Samoan Bible). Losing Mama, our fragile young lives were sorrowfully heartbroken. Never did we expect she would have left us so early and suddenly. *The green, green grass of home had dried up in the sun, the red tomatoes turned sour, and the cola bottles broken into pieces!* We missed our quality and quantity time with our mother's love and teaching of creation. Our universe of joyful living, caring and coping ended. The stiffness of death in our vulnerabilities was unbearable; we had no choice but to cling to "*The Lord is my shepherd, I shall not want.*" (Psalm 23:1, NSRV). In memory of her, I persevered to move on, in God's grace, with a profound invention of what it means to be living, caring and praising – and most of all, to continue serving God in ministry and pastoral care for the needy.

*When did you come to Aotearoa?*

In 1985 I left college in Samoa and migrated to pursue schooling at Nga Tapuwae College and Auckland Girls Grammar School (AGGS). Technology and Home Economics substituted for my village outdoor cooking and earthly umu-hangi roast, cultivation tools and cola bottle recycling. Science shadowed the nuances of seashore fishing. One of the components of PE curriculum exposed me to a strange context: so-called 'sex education' that to me appeared extremely inferior to my faith teaching, relational values, family regulations and cultural practices that are taboos. Nevertheless, the highlight I acquired was wellbeing products in regard to the menstrual cycle, which was rarely a topic of talanoa (social dialogue) with my aunts!

In the history curriculum, learning about colonial history sharpened my understanding of ancestral genealogy and political landmarks of my Samoan/Pasifika native nations. I learned how trading and land confiscation impacted tangata whenua. My current theological studies are enlightening me further, though I was saddened to discover a condemnation of missionaries' role in colonization through literacy and conversion. This aligns with what I know about the suppression of Samoan indigenous theology, culture and language through historical missional conversion. It is with hope that I venture to explore how indigenous theology underpins caring for creation. It is also important to me to value the roles of women, especially ministers' wives/spouses.

Even without our mother with us, we settled into kiwi life as part of one big aiga/whānau,[92] blessed with the tremendous support of our families, brothers and stepsisters, with tua'a sinasiana/kaumātua[93] prayers, fulfilling our ministry orientation. Grounded in the tikanga (protocol) of continuous ministry, we followed where our father was called to serve, and congregations were developed. My siblings and I assisted and supported his influential ministry, through social, cultural, educational and musical input. Before long I saw the necessity to further my education, in order to encourage young people to the next level. After graduating with a Degree and Master's in Education through Massey University, I began my teaching career, while I continued to support my father's ministry.

In 2007, Perema and I got married and together we endorsed a diverse scenario, in the lens of indigenous ministry protocol at PIPC Porirua and neighbouring churches in Wellington. Our tikanga authentically flourished in multilingual preaching, pastoral caring and embracing sorrow with congregational members. Internally and externally we embraced God's mission to the unlimited brimming of communal ministry; to name a few, we outreached to the rest homes, hospice, hospitals, funeral homes, prisons, living wage and social housing dimensions.

Sadly, his Master called Parema home in November 2019. I have lost my pillar in our shared-ministry, but I never give up hope to inherit his legacy as a profound exemplar of pastoral-caring, preaching and fulfilling God's splendorous mission. I am still part of local churches, but also have inclusive involvement with wāhine whakapono (women of faith) across faith-based, political, educational, and indigenous women's organisations.

*How has God prompted you to care for creation?*

My upbringing for practical care for creation led me to become an agent for this tikanga. Caring and loving begins at home, as we *'love one another, our neighbours, and ourselves'* (Mark 12:31). I am doing it for my family – teaching my family about compost, recycling and rubbish. I am serious in this project as it's a matter of simplicity. Sorting rubbish in our homes and churches is a duty for all. We are aiming for creation care by protecting God's beautiful creation.

My personal experience with dealing with waste started during our ministry in Porirua. I began to slowly accentuate the recycling and compost awareness in our ministry dialogue. Following numerous feasts, funerals and celebration events in church and community gatherings, a lot of food scraps, paper and plastic are unthinkingly deposited in black plastic bags. I ended up taking bags of plastics home to the manse to sort them out, and had a full-on recycling bin on collection days.

I was very conscious of the huge amount of left-over food scraps that filled up several bags. And on our way home I was very aware of beggars in the shop verandas, vulnerable children and hungry young people. The sight and weight of poverty has hit me hard with a profound sense of caring for my neighbours. If I could at least invent a saving mission, to fulfil my sense of calling, as Jesus once said, *"…just as you did it to one of the least of these who are members of my family, you did it to me"* (Matthew 25:40). I may not be able to feed them solid food, but my prayers for spiritual food I could afford.

I redirected my mission and facilitated a low-key project; a collection of coloured bottle tops as a maths resource for my son (now 12-years-old). Individuals and small groups were kindly asked to recycle their plastic at home and the church and save the bottle tops for us. My intention was to approach the local councils to provide recycling containers for the church. The children learn this at school and become great ambassadors to role model this to church families. However, my dear husband suddenly passed away, and the mission came to an end.

From my diverse ministry experiences, I am passionate to create a dialogue on climate change, recycling, and environmental impacts at our communal level. It takes time within our Pasifika churches framework, to become acquainted with composting and to take recycling seriously. I may be overreacting, but my heart hurts when I see so much rubbish. This requires an authentic whakapapa of determination, through the lens of an indigenous theology, to freely dialogue this project within our wider community. Those in my generation were brought up in a plastic-free, green and natural atmosphere in our island nations. And currently we now growing awareness of climate impact and the vital importance of being reusable and sustainable.

I see and admire families who can designate some land for plantations, to grow veggie gardens and taro patches. These are publicly underfunded, but a sense of perseverance is indicated with whānau's voluntary maintenance. Interestingly, the lengthy Covid isolations enabled families to re-plant, engage and feel the herbal leaves of their gardens for healing purposes.

*How do you see women leading in creation care?*

I ventured into my duty as a faletua (minister's wife/spouse) being inspired by my late mother, a former faletua, in pastoral caregiving for God's creation and His flock the Ekalesia (churches). I know my call is to nourish the sense of nurturing, healing and sustaining as a dimension of hope to save our planet, islands, homes, families and Ekalesia.

I have been honoured to act with other wonderful women of faith as ecumenical agents for a sustainable creation. I have been blessed to encounter the prayers, fasting and the spiritual blends of Māori wāhine whakapono (Te Aka Puaho), our very own PWANZ (Presbyterian Women Aotearoa New Zealand), NZMWF (Methodist Women's Fellowship), PCC (Pacific Council of Churches) Women's and Gender Desk in Fiji and Oceania, the AEWA (Asian Ecumenical Women Assembly) in Taiwan and the various Pacific Islanders Presbyterian Church (PIC) churches Women's Fellowships. Together with our sisters with disabilities – I love you all! You boldly "care 'cos you dare to care" for God's fragmented Creation.

*What do you see as ways forward?*

I would love to give way to our tamariki/children and young people. As they gain wisdom about the climate and the sciences this may steer our way forward. They need training in relational and sustainable strategies that are authentic, through Sunday Schools and youth-oriented activities. God has gifted us with the aspiration of caring for his Creation and younger generations, since they are God's chosen ones for a mission. As apostle Paul's letter to the Romans states, *"We know that all things work together for good for those who love God, who are called according to his purpose"* (Romans 8:28). It is my hope that advances in our young people's wananga (training) will make clear the need for and encourage the next level of mission outreach, to save our people, whenua, and our island nations. *"Lota nuu ua ou fanau ai. Ua lelei Oe i le Vasa e,... Samoana, ala mai."*[94]

I have written 'Talosia le Afuafu o le Foafoaga' as my lament of hope. It is a blend of scripture verses harmonised as a prayer for forgiveness for the broken patterns we made to the Creation. I hope to transform our humanly unsustainability into prayer dialogue. God's grace is manifest in forgiveness.

*"If my people who are called by my name humble themselves, pray, seek my face, and turn from their wicked ways, then I will hear from heaven, and will forgive their sin and heal their land"*

(2 Chronicles 7:14, NRSV)

*"Heoi ki te whakaiti tāku iwi i a rātou, kua karangatia nei hoki tōku ingoa ki a rātou, ki te inoi, ā, ka rapu i tōku mata, ka tahuri mai i ō rātou ara hē; ka whakarongo mai ahau i te rangi, ka muru i tō rātou hara, ka whakaora i te mate o tō rātou whenua."*

(2 Nga Whakapapa 7:14)[95]

## Talosia le Afuafu o le Foafoaga: Hope for Creation

*Prayer by Faaolataga Leasi*[96]

*I wish to acknowledge the Māori translation of my poetic prayer translation by Ruawhaitiri Ngatai Mahue, Te Rau Theological College, Tūranga-nui-a-Kiwa (Gisborne).*

| English | Samoan |
|---|---|
| *The word from the Creator God* | *O le Malelega mai le Atua o le Foafoaga* |
| I will take the top of the tall cedar, | Ou te fa'ia le tumutumu o le arasi, |
| break off a tender sprout | ma 'oto mai lona moemoe |
| and plant it on a high mountain. | e totō i luga o le mauga maualugā. |
| It will grow branches and bear seed. | O le a totogo mai ona lalā. |
| The small seed shall grow tall. | ma fatu, e fua fetii mai ai. |
| Birds of every kind will live there | E ofaga ai manufelelei i ona lala mafalā |
| and find shelter in its shade. | Ma lona paolo, e toomaga iai manulele. |
| **All native trees will know,** | **Aua ua iloa e laau afu uma o le vao** |
| **I am God.** | **O a'u o le Atua.** |
| | |
| *Lamentation...* | *Po ua tagisā ea...* |
| When we suffer, we should sit alone | Afai ua tatou sa'i, ina saō ia. |
| In silence and with patience | Ma nofoi loa i ata lafoia o le filemu |
| Not even to walk the streets, it's nil | Ua oo lava i se laa i magā-ala ua leai |
| Because of covid impact. | Ona ua faamata'u mai le faamai-koviti. |
| **All suffering knows,** | **Ua leva a na iloa e tagisā,** |
| **I am God.** | **O a'u o le Atua.** |

*God's unfailing love*
And mercy will continue
Fresh as the morning
**Sure as the sunrise**
**The sunrise and sunset know**
**I am God.**

*Do not be anxious about anything*
Seek me with your heart

In that broken creation! Alas!
You will find me ready to help.
**The earth cries, the land sobs,**

**Because they know, I am God.**

*Oh God, give me a spirit not of fear*

In the hope
you will restore your creation.

Let the ways of the righteous
prevail,
so we and all creation may live.
**All creation knows**

**that God is God**
**Amen!**

*A ua aapa mai le Atua ma opo atu oe*
Ma faafuata a'u i lona alofa
O loo agiga mai i le sau o le vaveao
**ma 'ave o le la i le segisegi.**
**Aua na itea lava e laoso ma lagoto**
**O a'u o le Atua.**

*Aisea la e atu ai fua i le laumeavale*
Ae le saili mai a'u mai le taele o lou fatu,
mai lena falute ua solo! Aue!
Lea ou te faatali i sau alaga mai.
**Aua ua oia le fatu ma tagi mai le eleele**
**Aua ua iloa, o a'u o le Aua.**

*To maia mo a'u lou agalelei nei o'u fefe*
ma le faamoemoe naua,e te
talia i matou, pe a toe autalu lau Foafoaga
ua sosofa, ona o le tagata ma le agasala,

Ina ia soifua Tuna, ae ola Fata.
**Aua na itea lava e lagimaina ma tapuafanua**
**O le Atua lava Ia o Atua**
**Amene!**

**Māori**

*Ngā kupu ā te Kaihanga:*

Ka tangohia e au te puru o te hīta kaweka nei
whatingia he pihi pūhou
whakatōhia ki runga māunga teitei
kia tipu mātoro he kaupeka kā hua he kākano.
Ka tipu ake ngā kākano kaweka nei
me te pūkahu manu ka noho ki reira
hei whakaruruhou i roto i tōna marumaru.
**Kia mārama anō ngā rākau whēnua**
**Ko ahau a Ihowa.**

*Apakurahia...*
I ā tātau e whakamamae ana, me noho tahanga
i roto i te ngū me te manawanui
kīhai ngā tiriti e hikoia
nā te mate korona.
**Ko te whakamamae e mōhio nei,**
**Ko au a Ihowa.**

*Te aroha pūmau a Ihowa*
Me tana mahi tohu ka hāere tonu
pēnei i te ata hāpara
rite tonu i te whitinga o te rā.
**E mōhio nei te whitinga rā me te tōngā o te rā**
**Ko au a Ihowa.**

*Kaua e mānukanuka ki ngā mea katoa*
rapa noa ahau mā tō ngākau
I roto i te whatinga o te hanganga! Auē!
Tērā au ka hāpai ake.
Ka hotuhotu ake te whēnua, ka maringi roimata te āo
I te mea e mārama ana rātau, ko ahau a Ihowa.

*E Ihowa, hōmai te wairua wehi kore*
I roto anō i te tūmanako
māhau te hanganga e whakahoki
kia mārama ai te huarahi e tika ana
kia whai oranga anō, ngā mea o te ora.
**Kia mārama anō te katoa**
**Ko Ihowa tonu a Ihowa.**
**Amene!**

us. Sadly the boy left and went back to his mother. I felt that if only he had stayed on our street we could have helped him.

We are in a Māori community so those involved are mostly Māori. But the events that we hold at the garden bring lots of different nationalities. It is really good for our people to learn from others. A co-ordinator from the Thames gardens came to take a workshop. He was from Israel. Our people were mesmerised by him and the knowledge that he had. It has opened our people's hearts and minds to learn different things.

One thing that made a huge difference to the project was putting in the Pataka, the food cupboard. That gave a real sense of belonging for the community.

*That is different from a food bank, isn't it? How does a Pataka work?*

People put food in the Pataka. Then we take photos and put them on our local Facebook page, and people go and gather. It became the centre of the community during Covid the lockdown in 2020 with people bringing food to the cupboard to share. We had gloves and disinfectant for safety. It was a giving and taking time for the whole community.

The garden has elderly neighbours who watch it like hawks. They know when people take too much, and they tell me and I just say, "It's OK, the food will be eaten." They are lovely Kaitiaki. Every time I go to the garden one of them will come over to talk to me.

*How did you set up the space to make it work well?*

Right from the beginning I said that our children must be involved in the planning, and that it had to be easy for our elderly people. I think the reason the other gardens failed was that they were not set up for the community. So we decided at the start that no ground had to be turned: all our gardens would be raised gardens. It has to be easy and friendly so people enjoy it. Our elderly can sit at the gardens and weed and tidy. We don't have big problems with heavy work. I have had two hip replacements so the last thing I wanted was being down on the ground!

This year we decided to allocate garden boxes to different groups in Taneatua, including Corrections and sports groups. Two of the churches have taken on two boxes each and have planted plants to grow food for the community. One of the pastors said, "I never have to weed!" I said, "How great is that!" You don't have to be there all day to tidy it up. We have lawnmower teams who maintain the grass.

We were in the garden one day and one of the mothers said, "We really need an entertainment area." She wanted it in the centre of the garden, where people can relax under cover – with a pizza oven. So we prayed about it. Then two days later I was in Bunnings and one of the managers came up to me and said, "Do you want a carport?" And I said: "Yeah! Oh my God, you would not believe it. We have been praying for a carport for an entertainment area." And she said, "Well, it's yours."

We had to take it away whole; it was fully constructed, built for a display. I got the measurements and drove to the concrete place and asked if they could make us a concrete slab. When he heard that it was for the community garden the guy said, "If you bake me a Rewana cake, you can have your slab"! I thought, "Oh my goodness, Lord, you are amazing!" Then we had a trucking company offer to transport it. Honestly, it was just amazing.

So two months later the truck came and loaded up the car port. It was very wide so it had to have a police escort. When they came into Taneatua the cops missed the turn and the truck went all through the main street. The whole town saw it come in, and we had trails of people following the carport! Lots of guys were ready to lift it off the truck, as it had to be moved onto the base with just muscle strength. It was all done in one day. One of our local City Councillors came up to me and said, "Honey, when I want something, can I come to you and we can pray about it?"! I said, "Yes, but you can pray about it yourself, you know."

One lady came who really wanted to start a community garden and asked me to help. I said: "Do it, if this is your desire. If this is what God is calling you to do, do it!" We can't do it for everybody. Go and do a community garden in your own area. We can only share our story."

*What are you learning about God's call?*

The more we talked about steps we took in the project, the more I just fell in love with God and fell in love with his Creation! The world is looking pretty dark at the moment and our environment is suffering. I see the world shifting. I truly believe they God is calling us to go back to the basics, making us go back to the land, to be able to survive in these struggling times. You have to do it with the community – because you will struggle on your own. We have to be community.

We have now moved down to Ruatoki, to my husband's family land. When we arrived we found our neighbours struggling with living so we have been teaching them new ways. We have recently got more chickens and I said to one of the nannies down the road: "Our mokos are going to be entrepreneurs. They are going to be egg sellers. We are going to teach them to clean their eggs and count them, so that they have a little business to mind." She said, "Really?!" and I said, "They can do it!" Our mokos are still young, but let's see how it goes. We can only journey and see where God takes us.

*How does God inspire these ideas in your head?!*

I ask myself that every time! We'll be at the garden and I'd say, "Oooh! Why don't we do this …?" And I wonder 'Where do these ideas come from?!' These things pop up, and I have to say them.

*How else does God use you?*

We have had community meetings in Taneatua lately about the methamphetamine problem and the home invasions and robbery that comes with it. The evening of the second meeting I was not feeling the greatest so I decided not to go. But on the way home I thought 'No, I can do this'. So I turned up at the meeting, just wanting to sit quiet and listen. But God said to me: "You are not going to sit there. You are going to get that energy to get up and say what you have to say." Passion for community – God gives me that drive. And I'm OK with it. I'm OK that he uses me as his vessel.

There are so many incredible stories that have come out of the five years we have been doing the garden. These are stories you cannot hide. I can't not tell them. I love it!

One last story. We had a meth addict who came to the garden to do his Corrections community work. When he arrived one day I stopped to talk with him. He talked about the various things on his mind, and how he and his brother were having problems trying to give up the meth. After a while I said, "OK boy, grab a shovel and go do some work." So off he went and started digging in the garden. After a while I looked up and he was crying. I could hear somebody behind me so I looked around. It was his brother, coming down the street, and he was crying too! He was led to the garden. And so they met in the garden and they embraced each other. They made a stand that day. Because their Koro had shown them how to garden, that was for them the start of their journey to give up meth. That was two years ago, and they have both been meth-free. Now they tell the stories, share and help people. We supported them through it. We say: "Oh my goodness, thank you God! Thank you, my Lord." And they ended up digging over all the gardens!

## Nau mai e ngā hua

*Traditional karakia*

Nau mai e ngā hua
o te wao, o te ngakina,
o te wai tai, o te wai māori –
nā Tāne, nā Rongo, nā Haumia,
nā Tangaroa, nā Maru.
Ko Ranginui e tū iho nei,
Ko Papatūānuku e takoto ake nei.
Tūturu whakamaua kia tina, tina!
Haumi e, hui e,
Tāiki e!

*We welcome the gifts of food*
*from forest and garden and wild plants,*
*from ocean and fresh waters –*
*gifts of the guardians:*
*Tāne and Rongo, Tangaroa and Maru.*
*Above us stands sky father, Ranginui,*
*below us rests earth mother, Papatūānuku.*
*We give thanks and hold strong,*
*our commitment to each other*
*and to all that is.*

## Whakapaingia ēnei kai

*Traditional Christian blessing for a meal*

E te Atua
whakapainga ēnei kai
hei oranga mō ō mātou tinana.
Whāngaia hoki ō mātou wairua
ki te taro o te ora,
ko Ihu Karaiti tō mātou Ariki
āke, ake, ake.
Amine.

*God bless this food,*
*giving life to our bodies,*
*as you feed our souls*
*with the bread of life,*
*Jesus Christ our Lord,*
*now and forever, Amen*

## Action Point 33: Do a community garden

Be part of a community garden to grow skills in growing food, build relationships, and help connect people with the land.

Many communities already have community gardens that your church could assist with. If your church has land, or if there is some unused land nearby, explore developing this as a community garden.

- Community Gardens resources, Eco Church:
  www.ecochurch.org.nz/community-gardens
- Sustainable Food Initiative, Wellington City Council:
  www.wellington.govt.nz/climate-change-sustainability-environment/
  sustainable-living/sustainable-food-initiative

## Action Point 34: Set up a community food cupboard

A way for people in our communities to share surplus food and to receive extra food when our cupboards at home are bare.

Taneatua has a 'Pataka'. Rakaia has a 'Sharing Shed'. The Mamaku Centre church runs the 'Inglewood Community Fridge'. Churches put a food sharing box out on the footpath, and it is an open-access, no-questions asked. During Covid lockdowns these cupboards found a whole new place and importance. Mamaku pastor Jen Ferry explained that these pantries work because, "It takes out the stigma ... people saying we need to see community. You can't do life outside of community."[99]

- Pātaka Kai open 'street pantry' movement: www.patakai.co.nz

## Action Point 35: Pray into every plan

Prayer is a natural normal part of our creation care as we rely on God's guidance, surrender our hopes and plans, uphold each other, and return praise and thanks for God.

## Turning Point

*Poem by Ana Lisa de Jong, Living Tree Poetry*

Do you ever feel the world is at a turning point,
tipping at its axis?

It will take 26,000 years for a full shift
as this spinning top,

moving upon its turning axis,
orients itself to another North.

And the pole stars we now hold on to for direction
too will change

as summer becomes winter
and winter blooms again.

Do you ever feel this world is ever turning?
That at some point

we may not recognise ourselves,
or maybe find ourselves returned

to the place we once began,
as though time had not progressed.

Yes, Polaris now due North of us
will one day be succeeded,

that they say
there is nothing new under heaven's roof.

But, do you ever feel the world is at a turning point,
some days more than others?

That 'today' is the pivotal moment
for change.

No gradual evolution responding to gravity
or stars and moon

but something like a full movement
of humanity

from one side of the planet
to the other.

Do you ever feel spiritually
that something is happening?

Not only slowly and in season
but something like a tipping,

a humanity at the verge
wanting something different.

And that the God
who speaks in a thousand tongues

is readying her voice
for a time like this.

# Receive the Gift: Ira Schelp

Ira lives in Christchurch with her family. She leads Advivia gGmbH, a German NGO working internationally, including supporting a school and vocational training programme in Zimbabwe.[100] Ira has previously studied up to her doctorate in Germany, UK, Austria, Italy and New Zealand and been trained and admitted as a lawyer in both Germany and New Zealand. Beside her legal work, she also worked for several family businesses which her husband ran. Currently she is concentrating on conservation work, developing Te Pōhue Reserve on the Banks Peninsula.

*What shaped the way you feel about the natural world?*

I grew up with little connection to nature. I was raised first in Bangkok, a city of 12 million, and then for most of my life in cold war West Berlin, surrounded by a wall with only basic parks to walk in. No real nature, everywhere people, you couldn't get lost or be by yourself. Nature for me was places full of people with trees around. The couple of times we visited the mountains or the sea, it felt like a trip to the museum – something outlandish to look at and then return to 'real' life.

My family origins are German and Korean. My parents were not involved in church and at times opposed my faith. I became a Christian at a young age by following my best friend to church. I always felt comforted by God's presence but also pushed by his love to perform at my best, to change the world to the better and at least to try to carry God's light into it. I studied law, married, had four kids, always trying to make things happen, to be engaged wherever I was – to the point that where my husband said that if I took on yet another membership or commitment, he would ban me from going to meetings!

I never felt this as a burden but something flowing from God's love and commitment to me. My focus was always on how to live a life in the light of God's compassion. To make an impact, to change the world for the better, at least in the part around me. It was always about people, to help our community, to take my responsibility as a student in my school, at university, to create a better workplace, to take up cases with my law firm – fighting for the underdog, to help refugees and the poor in Africa and to engage with others in a positive way. But nature never had a part in this.

When we travelled the world with our children, the natural wonders were always something to 'tick the box' and take the beautiful family photo. But not only this – I began to look at nature as one of countless wonders in life which God has made. I would tell my kids to look closely, but somehow I couldn't point out what they should actually look at. I wanted to show them as much diversity as possible and open their minds and perception to the beauty and richness of life. So nature was one of the many things I introduced them to: music, different cultures, art, church, languages, engaging with friends and society. I hoped that by seeing the diversity they would see the greatness of God and the beauty of the gift of life and take up their own part to positively contribute to this world.

I remember during a very busy time of my life I got some advice on how to enhance myself – make-up, communication skills and healthy lifestyle – to become even more efficient. I remember my coach looking at me, stressed out as I was, and saying: "You need to look into the green. Watch nature!" He was passionate about helping me but I didn't get it. It felt like some secret I did not understand, but I never forgot his advice (or how to shape my eyebrows!).

We moved to New Zealand in 2017, and after all the hassle around immigration, container packing and getting a family of six plus dog resettled – my world broke down. I felt that everything collapsed. I did not know what to do with myself.

And that was where nature kicked in for me. In New Zealand I found time and space to experience nature and … I found the secret! Walking the tracks around the hills, wandering along beaches and through the bush, made me truly see the wonders.

Nature now touches me deeply. It is probably the same way young children see, when they admire the beauty of a butterfly and ask themselves how great the one who thought of this must be. To look at the details of a tiny flower or waterfall or the majesty of the mountain peaks draws me to God. I feel in awe and comforted by his love which is reflected by this greatness. Surely there must be a God who made this! And he is so close and so approachable. Can you believe this has taken me over four decades to discover?!

I feel overwhelmed knowing that someone who created all of this loves tiny little me as well. The wonder of nature consoles me – I am not that important. And it doesn't matter if I can't change the world or whether I am right or wrong. I can let it be. Just being, like a thousand-year-old tree, is beauty enough for God – and looking at it I can nearly understand why. But at the same time it assures me that I am so deeply loved, because all of this just can't be an accident or coincidence. Looking at the miracles of nature tells me that there is so much more to life than what I can see and understand. There is so much beauty in the natural world; how could its Creator not be good?

Even better, there is an invitation here too. God trusts us to be part of this miracle world and allows us to enjoy it. My first steps to care for creation felt quite selfish in the beginning. Could it really be true that I might be permitted to care for something that fills me with so much joy, that feels so good and is fun all the way through?!

*How you think God feels about Creation?*

That was one of the questions I asked myself. It is clearly stated in Genesis 1:31: "And God saw everything that he had made, and behold, it was very good." God definitely must like what he created! God has given us this world as a gift. How awesome is that! He has worked hard to create earth with all its beauty, has put a lot of effort and thought in it and done something he is really fond of – just to give it to us.

When my girls were young my sister-in-law crafted a wonderful game of fishing with magnets. She created many beautiful crabs, muscles, snails and fish, all drawn herself, coloured, cut out and laminated. It was a masterpiece. And she gave it to my preschool kids! I was petrified that it would not survive long. And behold, I was right – though we have re-fixed it and tried to save it, this beautiful piece of art did suffer a lot. Their aunt wanted to give my girls the joy of receiving a special gift, to show they were special to her.

I feel it is the same with God's creation. He has given it to us as a present. He has put a lot of love in it and made a treasure he liked himself. And he probably knew that we would mess it up.

God loves to see us enjoy what he has made. I am sure he appreciates when we respect his gift and care for it. I feel it is paying him tribute to acknowledge the beauty of it all and to keep it in a good condition, so not only we can enjoy it but also the generations after us. I am sure he delights to just wander around in it together with us. God invites us to spend special time with him out in his natural world. And I guess he wants to talk to us through it.

I love Matthew 6:28-30 ("consider the lilies"), Job 12:7-9 ("ask the beasts, and they will teach you"), and Romans 1:20 ("God's invisible qualities have been clearly seen").

*Tell us about your reforestation project. How was God part of that?*

After a few years living in Christchurch, as I was discovering nature, we sold an asset in Germany and found ourselves, by God's grace, with some cash. It was not a fortune but enough to purchase some land – better that than feeding my husband's passion for car racing! I came across a piece of bare land on the Banks Peninsula. We went out to have a look and found a steep 50-hectare block with an eroding farm track. Previous owners had tried it work as a farm but to no avail. I was totally daunted by the amount of work it would take and told the vendor I was not interested. But I kept thinking about the beauty of the stream and the majesty of the cliffs. I kept looking at the photos I took on that first walk. The vendor continued to negotiate, and lowered the price, and I started dreaming, no longer of a farm but of forest. How beautiful would it be to give nature the space to reclaim it?! How awesome would it look once people stopped trying to use it as a farm and how much better for this rugged place to be given back to the birds? How much would I love to be in such a place!!

I knew nothing about conservation. I had few friends to help me. It did not seem very logical. Surely I would be better to invest my time and energy in the community or my children's school? But deep inside I just knew 'this is it' – I must say yes or I would regret it all my life. God had planted a new dream in me. Could it be true? Might God want to give this to me? Might I be allowed to take it?

I felt God saying: "Just take it, I put it there for you, why take so long to grasp it?" I was asking: "God, but how? Will I get it right?" And somehow I got the reply: "I love you. Just trust me and go, I will care for the rest." It was quite a fight with a lot of 'buts'. Then on the other side, a constant re-assurance coming up from deep down in my heart. That inspiring feeling got so clear that I accepted the vendor's offer, and put all my faith into this new direction my life was now to take – and never regretted since.

*What have been the challenges and the joys so far?*

Actually, the only thing really to overcome was my own self doubt. Everything else mostly fell in place and God gave all I needed: friends, advice, financing, love, joy, help and support where I never expected it. This project has been a solid source of blessings, miracles and joy.

My brain sometimes takes over and I try to rush things or to get things 'right'. But the land has slowly taught me how to go with the flow. Through this project God has shown me so much. One of the things was to accept his time frame and to acknowledge that nature's understanding of short and long is completely different to mine – a tree might live a hundred years so what does it matter if I fence it one year earlier or later? Rush is not a concept of nature. But on the other hand, there are 'right' times and you need to follow them – if you plant in the heat of summer, young plants will die. And if you miss a sunset, it's gone.

Another learning is how God talks to me; there are now so many different ways in which I can hear him and how I perceive him. God continues to teach me about love: his unconditional love to me. I still can't really believe that I am allowed to enjoy all of this!

*What is your dream for that land?*

My dream is to open it as a public reserve. I would love to see people come to visit this place and find something special. I hope that we will soon finish the process of covenanting and fencing, so I can start planting more trees. The local Māori iwi gifted me the name 'Te Pōhue' for the reserve. This is their name for the high knob on the ridgeline above the property and the stream that gushes down the gully, and also the name of the native convolvulus vine with delicate heart-shaped leaves that blooms small brilliant white flowers in the summer.

It would be great to have a cottage in the valley, so that I can stay there and care for the land, to establish walking tracks, plant trees, maintain fences, trap pests etc. Resource consent has also been granted for a little farm-stay in one corner, with a fabulous view out toward the Pacific Ocean, so people might stay overnight to get some rest and enjoy the place. I desire for this to be a place where people can relax, experience nature and meet God, or at least get a feel for that other sphere of reality. I hope it will be a place to encourage children to love this planet because they will see the beauty in it – a quiet place of peace.

We hope to connect it to the other reserves around, to enable tramping around the network of walks on the Banks Peninsula. There are some funny ideas in the back of my mind too, maybe some signs to educate about the wonders of nature, a "silent track," a partnership with mental health programs or a little community garden around the farm-stay.

This will be one of the many reforested sections of Bank Peninsula, which will re-establish the very unique nature of this special place. But my deepest wish is that by being there I may fulfill a bit of what God has dreamed for my life, and that he will take over and make it good.

*Can you share about your son's baptism in the stream?*

The most special day so far at Te Pōhue was Vin's baptism. Silvia can tell the story:

Silvia: What a magnificent day! It was late summer, with brilliant sunshine. Ira arranged everything with amazing attention to detail, preparing a sumptuous picnic lunch, and tying strong rope between trees for a handrail. People drove out after church and walked down the track to the stream. Our husbands were on hand to help out, mine with his Land Rover and hers with his Gator! Heaps of people came, and managed to scramble down and find a spot to sit under the trees each side of the stream. Ira's minister, Hamish Galloway, said some lovely appropriate words and then he rolled up his trousers and stepped into the pool, fed from a small waterfall. Vin slipped on the mossy rocks, falling into the pool with a splash, but no harm done! Hamish carefully dropped Vin backwards into the pool, which was quite cold despite the dappled sunshine. An older lady also chose to be baptised, which she managed very elegantly. It was breath-takingly beautiful, with bellbirds singing and the sound of the flowing water. The Holy Spirit was so present I hardly dared to breathe!

## Großer Gott, wir loben dich

*Hymn by Ignaz Franz[101]*

Großer Gott, wir loben dich,
Herr, wir preisen deine Stärke.
Vor dir neigt die Erde sich
und bewundert deine Werke.
Wie du warst vor aller Zeit,
so bleibst du in Ewigkeit.

Great God, we praise you,
Lord we praise your might.
The earth bows before you
and admires your creation.
Who you were before all times,
you will be forever.

### Action Point 36: Regenerate bush and wetlands on farmland

Most farms and lifestyle blocks have some areas of unproductive land, especially in gullies where bush can quickly regenerate. Keeping stock out, removing invasive weeds, and local native planting restores the quality of streams and promotes diversity of life.

Churches can celebrate and support these actions in a range of ways.

### Action Point 37: Get out and about together

Church life and family life that gets us out into nature, for our physical, emotional, mental, spiritual and communal wellbeing.

- Church picnics
- Worship services outside
- Community walking groups
- Book by Catherine Knight: *Nature and Wellbeing in Aotearoa New Zealand: Exploring the connection* (Totara Press, 2020)

### Action Point 38: Baptism outside

In the Bible, baptism was outdoors event, originally in the River Jordan. The early church starting meeting indoors or underground to hide from persecution, and found ways to create channels of flowing water for baptism. The medieval church invented the font inside the church, but this is more a 'temple' model of infant dedication than the New Testament practice of baptism. Let's experience again the richness of baptism, with birds swooping and trees waving and the wind blowing. Let's baptise our kids (and grown-ups!) into the wildness and wonder of God's church including creation.

# The Trees Are Our Neighbours:
## Iris Lee Fountain

Iris is the national administrator for A Rocha Aotearoa New Zealand, and works on the Eco Church NZ project, as well as the Karioi Project. She lives in Whanganui-a-tara Wellington with her husband Philip and their two boys, Jeffrey and Samuel.

Ko Iris tōku ingoa.
I tipu ake au ki Marehia.
E noho ana au ki Whanganui-a-tara.
Kei A Rocha Aotearoa New Zealand ahau e mahi ana.
Nō reira, tēnā koutou katoa.

I grew up in a diverse multi-cultural environment in Malaysia. I attended schools where Malay was the medium of instruction, but my home language was a version of English colloquially known as Manglish – an English-based creole used in Malaysia that is heavily influenced by Malay and Chinese dialects like Hokkien and Cantonese. Many of my extended whānau practise Taoist-Confucianist traditions. My path to the Christian faith began as a child when my parents embarked on a spiritual search and came to embrace Christianity.

My first few years were spent in a thoroughly urban environment. I was born near Kuala Lumpur, the capital of Malaysia. But in their 30s my parents felt that something was missing and they wanted to find a deeper sense of peace, security and meaning. They decided to move their young family away from the hustle and bustle of the city for a remote and quiet rural life.

So from the age of five I lived in a *kampung* (rural village). We called our home 'The Countryside Garden' – a thoroughly apt name.

My childhood memories of this place were of fruit trees, a stream to play in, a lush vegetable garden, large fish ponds (six of them!), goats, chickens, rabbits, dogs and even wild civet cats. Malaysia's tropical climate meant that we were surrounded by green. It was a wonderful place to grow up. I remember as a child at school my teacher once asked the class to write about our neighbours and neighbourhood. But because we didn't have any neighbours nearby I wrote about the different types of trees around our home instead. Many years later I look back on this memory with a smile; the call to "love your neighbour as yourself" takes on another meaning.

Living in the countryside was not all idyllic, of course. It involved the occasional snake, and lots and lots of chores. I had a strong sense of smell, and looking after the chickens was my least favourite activity. I would often cajole my younger siblings to do that work instead.

While living at The Countryside Garden my parents began their journey to Christianity. In this place of 'wilderness' as a family we grew closer to God. We witnessed healing and many miracles and my parents were called to church ministry. But we were also tested. We faced persecution and challenges because of our new faith. We spent 10 years in this rural space, with our 'wilderness' home frequently used for Christian camps, retreats and as a place of refuge.

Despite finding God in the wilderness and experiencing God through nature, my church community at that time lacked a rich and deep theology of creation. Faith was anthropocentric. The church we attended was intensely focused on people's salvation alongside personal holiness and spirituality. Acts of service, mission activities, and ministry in general were all directed to other people. God's good creation, wilderness and nature were considered merely as places of retreat and refreshing in order to return to ministry for people. This human-centred theology was the dominant message that I heard in churches and Christian communities.

*So how did that worldview change?*

I left Malaysia in my late teens to study in Singapore and then moved to Aotearoa New Zealand to study at Victoria University of Wellington. It was at university that I met my husband. Both Philip and I were involved in Tertiary Students Christian Fellowship (TSCF) groups on campus. I was particularly focused on ministry and support for my fellow international students. After graduating I worked in Wellington in risk management consultancy and also did postgraduate studies in international and sustainable community development. All this time I continued to hold an anthropocentric view of mission and faith. But this view was challenged and significantly reconfigured soon after Philip and I were married.

Six months after we got married Philip and I moved to Belize as programme co-directors for a university-level study abroad programme. Creation Care Study Program (CCSP) is a semester-long field school, primarily designed to cater to North American university students. It is focused on eco-theology and creation care, sustainable community development and field ecology. At the heart of this study a broad program was educating and equipping students to be a part of, and agents for, God's shalom, particularly through understanding and caring for creation. Nicholas Wolterstorff argues that shalom is about relationships – with God, with each other, and with all of creation.[102] Shalom is about peace, in a deep and profound sense. It is also concerned for justice and with flourishing and delighting in our relationships.

Each semester we hosted up to 20 students for a field-intensive education. Students and staff members lived in intentional residential community with each other, learning and journeying together, framed by communal liturgies and rhythms of worship and study. My time in Belize was formational. Even though I was helping to lead the programme I was also learning together with the students, and soaking it all in. It was an amazing experience to explore and study up-close the ecology of tropical rainforests, streams and marine ecosystems, and also to get to know Belizean, Mayan, Mennonite and other communities through homestays and fieldtrips. I got to sit in and participate in intensive courses with amazing theologians like Sylvia Keesmaat, Brian Walsh, Steven Bouma-Prediger and other Christian lecturers and ecologists who were passionate about Christian environmentalism. The study of Scripture and creation theology inspired a significant expansion of my worldview in order to embrace a larger sense of the gospel.

I had long been aware of the need to look after the environment but I had never encountered such a clear articulation of why and how this belongs in a theology of Christian discipleship. It became clear that as Jesus died on the cross to redeem **all** of creation in heaven and on earth (Colossians 1:20), part of our worship and ministry is to care for all that God has created – both human and non-human – in order to fulfil our role as gardeners or kaitiaki of creation (Genesis 1:15).

My time in Belize was transformational and shaped my worldview moving forward. It was in Belize that I first heard about Christian environmental organisations like A Rocha and Au Sable.[103] After almost three years in Belize, Philip and I moved on to various other chapters, including some years in Australia, Indonesia and Singapore. In each place of sojourn we were involved in Christian community: in Australia we lived in a home called Irene's Place, a house of discipleship, social justice and peace supported by Canberra Baptist Church; in Indonesia I worked for the Mennonite Central Committee, an international humanitarian and relief agency working for justice and peace; and in Singapore we were part of a supportive home group and started getting to know the Friends of A Rocha network that was just beginning to get active there. During these years I saw that while a theology of caring for creation was gaining ground, it was still not mainstream in the church. I found it hard to find like-minded Christian communities that located creation care as central and integral to the practice of Christian faith.

*How did you get involved with A Rocha in Aotearoa New Zealand?*

After 13 years of living outside Aotearoa New Zealand, we felt the call to return back home. We had two boys by then and we felt a strong need to connect them with their whānau. My parents and two of my siblings had migrated and settled in Aotearoa, and Philip's family is here. While the boys were young I juggled being a full-time mother and doing part-time work, including for a church in Porirua which we attended. It was at this time that my friend Andrew Shepherd told me there was a part-time vacancy with A Rocha Aotearoa New Zealand. I had already known about A Rocha internationally but had not connected with the New Zealand organisation, since I had been overseas for many years. I was excited to apply for the National Administrator position – and delighted that I was appointed to the role! It felt like a homecoming of sorts to be able to once again be involved in a community of Christians who also see care of creation, community and hospitality as integral to the life of faith.

A Rocha attracts a diverse range of people: some are super outdoorsy, others have green fingers, some are enthusiastic about ecological science or theology, and others feel passionate about climate activism. I am interested in all these but I wouldn't say I am particularly good in any of these areas. My strengths are more organisational and administrative in nature. I prefer to stay behind the scenes, working on systems and processes to make things work smoothly. I am privileged to be able to offer these skills to help grow Christian environmental mission in Aotearoa.

Through my work at A Rocha I have been able to witness, support and connect with many Christians caring for this earth as part of their faith conviction. It is heartening to see the ecological restoration work that has been happening over the years by local groups and the Karioi Project in Raglan. And now through the Eco Church NZ project I am again encouraged and blessed to share the stories of how church communities are caring for this earth and to invite other church communities to join the journey too.

### What is your hope for church communities in Aotearoa NZ?

I am thankful for the opportunity to have my worldview expanded through my time in Belize with the study aboard programme which has been so formational for me moving forward. I wish that all Christians could have similar opportunities to learn about God's creation by learning from amazing theologians and through direct experience. A Rocha has been involved in environmental education for many years. These various programmes serve this purpose – to help Christians understand that caring for creation is central to our faith. Through A Rocha's partnerships with Scripture Union and Adventure Specialties Trust camps like E3 Wilderness Journeys and Sustain Camps are able to offer learning and transformational experiences for tamariki and rangatahi, so that they can become the next generation of kaitiaki and environmental leaders in churches throughout New Zealand.[104] Many young people at church can get disheartened if they feel that there is a disconnect between their church and the whole environmental crisis we are living in. I hope that church communities will step up to be catalysts of this shift in worldview, and also to take action to be agents of hope and restoration for all of creation. How awesome would it be if churches throughout this country embarked on a journey to help their communities understand the centrality of an ecological perspective for the Christian faith![105]

Many church communities in Aotearoa New Zealand are also exploring what it means to be part of a bicultural nation. I think this is a helpful turn in many different ways. It opens opportunities for churches to learn from Te Ao Māori in understanding the interconnectedness and interrelationship of all living and non-living things. The Māori concept of kaitiakitanga is an all embracing wholistic concept. Rather than compartmentalising things, we see all of creation as related. Learning from Māori on this and in other ways may help the church focus on the bigger picture.

Through these shifts I hope that church communities will expand their understanding of mission to include caring for this earth. Many churches ensure that in their giving they give to mission overseas as well as in Aotearoa. Wouldn't it be awesome if churches also considered giving to ecological concerns as part of their work of caring for God's good and beautiful creation!

## Praise the Lord from the Earth!

*Psalm 148:7-12*

**Praise the Lord from the earth!**
You great sea creatures and all ocean depths,
lightning and hail, snow and clouds,
   stormy winds that do his bidding –

**Praise the Lord from the earth!**
You mountains and all hills,
   fruit trees and all cedars,
wild animals and all cattle,
   small creatures and flying birds –

**Praise the Lord from the earth!**
Kings of the earth and all nations,
   you princes and all rulers on earth,
young men and women,
   old men and children –

**Praise the Lord from the earth!**

## Join with all creation

*Prayer by Dave Bookless[106]*

Living God, we gather in your presence to worship you.
May our worship join with all creation's,
praising you according to its kind.
We celebrate the beauty and importance of the trees
that you have made.
May the worship of our hearts be reflected
in the worship of our lives,
So that we enable the trees of the field to clap their hands,
And the trees of the forests to sing for joy;
Through Jesus Christ our Lord. Amen.

"Let all the trees of the forest sing for joy!" *Psalm 96:12*

*Action Point 39: Share your creation care online*

Is care of creation part of your church's mission? How does your church community celebrate signs of the kingdom for all of creation? Share it on your website and celebrate the stories on your social media.

Is your church community organising events that promote care of creation in the local community? Share it! Let your local community know that your church takes seriously the call to care for people and the environment.

Do you have a creation care team? Feature the team and their work on your church's website. Give them a voice to share on social media. Grow an online community.

- A social media toolkit for nonprofits, CommunityNet Aotearoa: www.community.net.nz/resources/nz-navigator-trust/a-social-media-toolkit-template-for-nonprofits

Many Christian mission organisations like Interserve, NZCMS and OMF now embrace care of creation as part of their mission. Check out some examples of what they include on their website:

- Interserve, Loving our neighbour – care for creation: www.interserve.org.nz/stories/loving-our-neighbour-care-for-creation
- NZCMS, Integral mission: www.nzcms.org.nz
- OMF, Creation care: www.omf.org/our-ministries/creation-care/about

*Action Point 40: Give to environmental mission*

Churches give generously towards outreach; ensure that giving is also supporting environmental action.

Talk to your church's finance team about your goals and projects. Get in the budget, and explore alternative sources of funding.

- Fundraising Plan, CommunityNet Aotearoa: www.community.net.nz/resources/community-resource-kit/fundraising-plan/

free to question, lament and explore. And when we allow those colours to complement all that we do, we are empowered to "Hear what the Spirit is saying to the Church."[122]

I was reflecting recently on Job. His friends presume that Job was of less stature with God than they were; but they had no right to do that. Job chooses to use cutting sarcasm and puzzling enigmas to get his point across. Is this a workable strategy for us today? It sometimes appears that those who are not honourable prosper more, and Job attributes their prosperity to the hand of God. So why not believe that God also allows the righteous to suffer? Job knew that God had given permission for terrible things to happen to him. He accepted and declared that "nature" would have all the answers. How so?

I wrote this reflection, from the perspective of Mother Earth addressing humanity, inspired by Job 12:1-10.

> The laughter is deafening when inquiries about your responsibility of care for ME (Mother Earth) are made. I feel distant from you when you sparingly mention ME as a part of your past, present and future, when I have been yours since time began. We are growing apart. Your compassion for ME during my increased illness is somewhat absent, which upsets my whole family. Just ask them – they will tell you! You never ask ME if I am satisfied in this relationship, and you have never told ME that I matter. Some say that it is only ME that is struggling with this, and rumour has it that you have fallen for something that satisfies you more. Then members of your whānau laugh at me. Despite my equal aptitude and astute understanding of things, there is contempt toward ME.

> We have discerned that your appetite for the 'highs' in life is satisfied by another. This quest for something that flows not from my fountain of love leaves ME filled with grief and pain. How can I possibly compete? Although I give to you all that is given to ME by God, your heart has never been mine alone. It would be a comfort if you turned to the Lord and asked what was intended for ME in this relationship. The chasm in our shared designation widens daily. The encroaching estrangement leaves ME gasping for the breath that we were all to share. Submitting my whole being to the Lord, in search of what it will take for ME to go on, has rendered us with the conclusion that you love ME no more.

> My family prays in the hope that you will seek God's counsel in how to reconcile, restore, and renew your relationship with ME. Teachings, declarations and stories of ME are free to upload, and if your connection is too weak, please feel free to contact ME at anytime, anywhere.

*How have you grown in confidence and leadership, even to finding a voice in the global arena?*

Globally we must do more to 'Save our Planet'. I was brought up to appreciate the environment, abundance and seasonal sustainability, with a strong Christian background. I was given the ability to speak out boldly when words do not match action and ethic. To speak alongside many other voices as an indigenous woman is an emotional journey. My prayerful ambition is that creation's laments can be heard. The Anglican Indigenous Network released a series of webinars from Aotearoa, Africa, Amazonia, and the Arctic, in Advent 2020 titled 'Prophetic Indigenous Voices on the Planetary Crisis'.[123] This poignant collection of indigenous stories from these regions is set to powerfully move the viewer into an emotional response to open their eyes and hearts to the plight of climate, waste, pollution and economic impacts on indigenous people's traditional practices and wellbeing.

I was part of the working group on the Post-2020 Global Biodiversity Framework which brought together 2000+ government, stakeholders, organisations, companies, financiers, and ecological voices. This week-long consultation worked towards agreement on a globally binding promise.[124] It led to the UN Biodiversity Conferences in Kunming China, which I attended online. During the COP26 UN Climate Change Conference in 2021[125] I was blessed to take part in the inter-faith workshops where diverse voices were heard. These forums are still a work in progress.

I plan to contribute to the plethora of colourful perspectives and ambitions in making a difference, so that the next generation of kākano/seeds may have less to contend with when they are in the leadership decision-making seats of the future.

*What are some practical ways that churches can care for Creation?*

We might be more demonstrative in our ambitions to reduce our carbon footprint by changing the vehicles we drive. We might refuse to buy imported products where deforestation takes place to grow them. We might divest from all fossil fuel investments, and push for safer alternative sources of energy. We might reduce our waste by buying less packaged goods from our supermarkets – or better still, produce our own by growing fruit and vegetables and home baking. There are many grass-roots practical ways to restore, recycle, reuse and renew we can support. In other words, practice what we preach to 'Save the Planet'. The church needs to get loud in the public domain to help transform mindsets, seek justice and increase much more sustainable commitment! These go hand-in-hand with prayer, theology, and culturally appropriate behaviours. "Manaaki whenua, manaaki tāngata, haere whakamua" ('Care for the land, care for the people, move forward').

## Kaitiaki Karakia

*Prayer by Jacynthia Murphy*

Kaitiaki, carer of all things, we praise you
for all that we coexist with, respectfully utilise,
and enthusiastically enjoy.
We give eternal thanks for the created order
you have generously bequeathed us.
Grant us the foresight and wisdom to appreciate it, learn from it,
and leave it as pristine as when we received it.
Eternally yours in the image you have created us,
we honour you. Amen.

He kākano ahau – I am a seed.
Pushed forth from creation,
quenched by lifegiving water,
and lovingly nurtured by my ancestors before me
to live sustainably,
so that at life's end,
when I am returned to where seeds emerge,
I may give my eternal gratitude for a life well lived.
It is my responsibility, as kaitiaki,
planted in scripture and schooled in tikanga
to lovingly care for all the elements
that enhance our journey from beginning to end.

To belong to the generational seeds of life,
in harmony with all other life,
is to each flourish and prosper.
This is our blessing from the Creator.
He kākano ahau.

Nō reira, kia tau te rangimārie ki a koutou
Peace be with you.

### Action Point 41: Reduce carbon emissions

Whānau and churches choosing to live and work in ways that reduce our carbon emissions.

- Carbon Calculator resources, Eco Church NZ: www.ecochurch.org.nz/carbon-calculators
- The Aro Project for local projects and partnerships to off-set carbon emissions: www.aroproject.nz
- As individuals, most of our carbon emissions come from getting from 'A to B'. Do the 'Transport' small group study: www.ecochurch.org.nz/transport
- Do a Carbon Fast for Lent. Anglican Youth Ministry NZ: www.anglicanyouth.org.nz/resources/worship/seasonal/carbon-fast-for-lent Lent Calendar, St. Francis Xavier Environment Ministry: www.saintanastasia.org/documents/2021/2/SFX-EnvMin-Lenten-Calendar-2021.pdf
Eco Faith Recovery: www.ecofaithrecovery.org/carbonfast

### Action Point 42: Buy local

Support local farmers and businesses through a commitment to 'buy local'.

- Promote and shop at local farmers' markets.
- Identify items that your church needs on a regular basis, and find local ethically-sourced suppliers.
- Host an eco market at your church.

# Titiro Whakamuri, Kōkiri Whakamua: Jenny Campbell

*Look back and reflect, so you can move forward*

Don't be fooled by Jenny's 'sweet little old lady' appearance! Jenny Campbell has been a powerhouse of environmental action for over 50 years, part of Coal Action Network Aotearoa and Forest and Bird Southland, writing many submissions to regional and national government and leading the Anglican church's fossil fuel divestment. A natural networker, Jenny brings people together, including through the Anglican Women's Studies Centre. She has been a lay minister, and is a supervisor and trainer with Caira.[126]

Ko Oreti tōku awa
Ko Takitimu tōku maunga
Ko Takitimu tōku waka
Ko Ngāitahu tōku iwi
Ko Te Rau Aroha tōku marae
No Mossburn tōku kainga
Ko Jenny Campbell ahau

*How do you get into environmental action?*

As a child I remember riding my pony up in the bush with my cousin, finding it a special, reflective, safe place. I grew up in Pirinoa in the South Wairarapa. I then attended Victoria University of Wellington and moved south to Te Waipounamu and settled to work and raise my whānau as a single parent. After my two girls started school I was a biology and maths teacher at Lumsden District High School, later becoming Northern Southland College, for about 20 years. This was followed by about 30 years working as a family support fieldworker for mental health across much of Southland Murihiku. Dealing with my own family experiences in this field drew me to this essential mahi for whanau of those who experience often long term mental health challenges.

A highlight of teaching was taking students on learning fun camps and field trips. Southland has the most amazing places like the Catlins, Fiordland and Rakiura Stewart Island to explore. My awareness and appreciation of the environment grew hugely through those experiences.

In my 20s I joined Forest and Bird. Popping in to an annual general meeting while on a holiday shopping trip to Invercargill got me elected to the committee – any new person was snapped up! Looking back it was one of my best life decisions. Lumsden is an hour's drive away but I went down monthly, and of course got more involved.

This group tackled some big environmental issues, including the Manapōuri power scheme national protests, spear-headed in Southland.[127] They had a vast wealth of experience and knowledge of the mountains and lakes and a long history of environmental action. Most of them were people of faith. Their wisdom impressed and influenced me. It is an important part of New Zealand history, people who fought to protect natural places. Forest and Bird is the oldest environmental group in New Zealand, about to celebrate 100 years.[128] These were people who stood up to the bulldozers over the proposal to raise Lakes Manapōuri and Te Ānau. They fought alongside many people throughout Aotearoa and won!

In 2020 we celebrated the 50th anniversary of saving those lakes, acknowledging that this was the biggest national environmental campaign and success story to date. People came from all over for an amazing reminiscing weekend of telling stories and sharing lots of laughs as the memories flowed.

I remember those Forest and Bird Southland committee meetings going on for hours as people shared what they knew and argued about the wording of submissions. This was before computers, so it was all written by hand or on an old typewriter. I would be very late home! Over the years I have taken on being the treasurer, chairperson or secretary for nearly 40 years. Computers now make it much quicker, being able to send out an agenda, type notes as we go and have the minutes ready the next day.

If I see something that needs to be done I'm inclined to leap in, in spite of not actually knowing what to do! This was the case with the 2020 Manapōuri and Te Ānau celebration with a friend asking if Forest and Bird was doing anything. I found out there was nothing proposed, I got together with Sir Alan Mark (Guardians of the Lakes chair for 30 years) and we made it happen – two weeks before our first Covid lockdown: phewww!!

I became the Convenor of Te Whenua Awhi, Invercargill Environment Centre, in much the same way. A senior woman on the Forest and Bird committee kept saying, "What we need here is an Environment Centre." She said it many times until I thought, "Yes, we could do it!" So we did. It was a place anyone could go to for information about what they can do for the environment. We started in 1999 with little money, but thankfully the Green Party negotiated funding for Environment Centres with the new Government. Green Party co-leader Rod Donald came down and presented the large cheque to get us going. We had a shop in South City with cheap rent, courtesy of a supportive owner. Resources from the Ministry for the Environment were great assets.

That was the early days of the environmental movement; people knew that we had to take urgent action for the environment. Having an Environment Centre raised the profile of environmental issues and created space for other groups to form – they could meet in our rooms for free. We did many activities including selling plants, running workshops and providing answers to questions, with a wonderful team of volunteers. It led on to new opportunities such as a bike hire scheme and a community garden. It closed after 18 years, because a lot of other groups, shops and businesses have started up and are carrying the work on in new directions. We initiated many new sustainability actions which are now taken for granted, such as worm farms, Bokashi bins, recycling and interactive learning sessions in primary schools.

A Waste Busters group got the whole recycling initiative going. Before that all of Invercargill's waste went to landfill – actually it went into the estuary. I was part of that group. Anything that needs attention and is about the environment I seem to get involved in! There is so much to do, so much to think about.

I also became very involved with Coal Action Network Aotearoa, co-convening the Murihiku/Southland group.[129] Through that and Forest and Bird I have written many submissions, working to prevent climate change, stopping new and expanded coal mines and working on Just Transition projects.[130] Other justice issues which are passions of mine include stopping family violence, addressing racism, women's equality, mental health issues…

*How can we be most effective when we want to take action on an issue?*

I learned about writing submissions from experienced campaigners. I learned to not be put off by the word 'submission'. It is really just a letter to a local or national authority which is seeking the opinions of the public about a matter they have to make a decision about.

It is important to personalise it, how the issue affects you, your children, the community and future generations. This is one way you can support others who are making a stand about an issue. A general structure could include: your personal involvement and passion about this issue, a paragraph about each concern you have, and what you want them to do about it. You may well find that a group has set up a guide or draft template which you can personalise. That saves a lot of energy and they probably have more information about the topic than you do. Put your toe in the water and focus on just a few aspects while you support other people and groups.

It is important to be part of different networks as they ask their members to make submissions or carry out other helpful actions such as join others on a march, protest action or to visit a Member of Parliament. The parliamentary website gives details of current national submission topics and closing dates.[131]

*What other roles have you had in environmental action?*

Being a networker is very important to me. I love to connect people with other people who are doing a similar thing.

I have often found myself as the treasurer or secretary for community organisations, as those roles are often hard to fill. You don't have to be perfect. It is very important to keep records of your plans so people can keep their vision moving. We need good admin people.

I work a lot with women. Stopping violence is a passion because of personal experience and the impact it has in my whānau as well as the community. White Ribbon breakfasts about stopping violence, and International Women's Day events with guest speakers talking about social justice, are one way to network, support others and raise women's issues in the community. I had the opportunity to record stories of community groups; I made oral history recordings of local people's lives as a reporter for a community newspaper. I especially love to highlight the hidden work of women which is often not acknowledged or affirmed. Women do not recognise that they are doing amazing community building work as they listen, offer heartfelt advice, make scones and are there for people who need a lift-up. Women see a need and respond; such as during Covid lockdown when some undertook

and I didn't need to think about it, I just knew instantly 'Yes! I'm doing that!' I initially went for two months as a volunteer, and then I went back for a year as a resident. It was in Iona that I felt called to ministry. It was very significant for me, especially the whole Celtic spirituality that creation is good and an essential part of who we are.

*What did you absorb at Iona about the connection between faith and creation?*

There's something about the place itself; the sand seems whiter, the air feels purer. It is described as a 'thin place' where the membrane between the secular and the spiritual is thinner that other places. People often go there in transition; I was in transition, I didn't know what I was going to do next with my life. The Iona community is passionate about justice, and care of creation is part of that. It is steeped throughout their liturgy and they endeavour to be sustainable in all they do. Celtic spirituality is a sense of God being everywhere, within and around. They don't end the daily morning worship with a benediction because the whole day is worship. We either offer everything to God or nothing, you don't pick and choose. It is an expansive faith.

*How did find your way into being a Presbyterian minister?*

I experienced the call to ordained ministry while I was at Iona, then came back to Dunedin and started my theological degree at Otago. I hated systematic theology, it felt like counting angels on a pinhead! But I loved the pastoral education; for my own wellbeing I realised that I needed to work with people. I worked as a celebrant conducting weddings and funerals as well as being a pastoral worker at Highgate Church in Dunedin. When I entered the ministry internship programme through the Knox Centre in Dunedin I wanted to be a hospital chaplain, but God has called me into parish ministry to preach the gospel, and I love it. I enjoyed Biblical studies and was especially inspired by Paul and his preaching to the Gentiles. Because I came from a non-church background I connect easily outside the church; I see myself as a missionary.

I am always looking for ways to help church folk get out and meet people. One thing we did at St Andrews was to plant seeds in little pots (the seedling pots of six) and once they were grown we gave them to parishioners to give to their neighbours as a way to develop relationships and build community – and benefit their gardens.

*How do you incorporate the natural environment into church worship?*

It is wonderful to use elements from God's creation in worship. People have different ways of engaging in worship; we Presbyterians get too focussed on words! Using shells or stones or other things from nature enables people to engage with God using other senses.

Advent is a time I like to do this; we create an Advent Koru instead of an Advent wreath. A wreath reflects a northern hemisphere winter Christmas, while an Advent Koru points to the new life that Christ's birth brings here. The Koru is made up of shells which portray our kiwi summer, along with stones, bird's nests, feathers, flowers, whatever we can find. Last Advent I encouraged people to bring along natural things each week to add to the koru to reflect that particular week's theme. For 'joy' parishioners were encouraged to bring something from the natural world that had brought them joy during the week. For 'love' they were encouraged to bring a flower to remember someone whose absence they feel strongly at Christmas. On Christmas Eve, entering the church sanctuary to see the advent koru with tealight candles emphasising Christ's new life was exquisite!

### What is your theology around caring for creation?

Throughout Scripture there are echoes of the place of creation. If the church was more engaged in environmental action and proactive in sustainability we might better connect with our communities, especially younger people. My passion is the flourishing of all people. Creation comes alongside this and is not divorced from it all, but social justice is my first love. Church for me cannot be exclusive. Jesus was always reaching people on the margins and bringing them in. Isn't that what we are meant to be doing, rather than shutting people out?

### How do energy issues contribute to poverty?

When we moved to the Hawkes Bay, we noticed the huge divide between rich and poor, too often along ethnic lines. There is much wealth here and also one of the biggest poverty gaps in the country. I did a Pecha Kucha presentation where I shared our dream of building a solar farm for the community. The response has been phenomenal. There has been so much support – although one local woman saw it and came up to me to say: "You talk poverty in Hawke's Bay. I don't see it, and I've talked to my friends, and they don't see it. What do you mean?" I was stunned.

My husband Chris has worked in the electricity industry and seen first-hand how energy costs feed the poverty cycle. People on low incomes get their power cut off, then have to pay $100 to get it put back on, and they pay more for power because prepaid is more expensive and they don't get discounts. Even in my own church some families heat their houses with their dryer, which is just awful. Illness such as rheumatic fever, which can result from that kind of thing, is rife here. When their homes are well heated people are healthier, less likely to get sick and more likely to be employed.

Affordable electricity has huge benefits. The driving force behind our solar farm project is social justice in the flourishing of people; benefitting the environment is a bonus! Energy poverty is a huge issue and it's going to get harder and harder. Power costs are going to increase significantly, we estimate they will increase 3% more than inflation.

*How did the solar power project come into being?*

Hawkes Bay is very sunny, so Chris started investigating solar power. Solar panels were becoming more affordable and he thought 'We could do this!' The idea was nested in St Andrews Presbyterian Church where I am the minister and the church got on board.

The Pecha Kucha presentation was the first step in launching the project. The Pecha Kucha format gives you 20 slides and 20 seconds per slide to tell your story – it's a movement around the world. There were 500 people at that event and it sparked media interest in New Zealand.[141] We were interviewed by Kathryn Ryan on Radio New Zealand.[142] That brought a whole lot of people out of the woodwork who contacted us and wanted to help out: "I'm an engineer." "I'm a planner, I want to help you." We couldn't have orchestrated this, it was so Holy Spirit led! We were looking for land and we met a dynamic Māori couple who were equally passionate about this. They have become good friends and have partnered with us to establish Manaaki Energy.

This year the government gave us $400,000 to put solar panels on the roofs of 46 homes owned by Māori people on low incomes, in Hawkes Bay and Rotorua. This is helping build momentum. It is great for those families, but it doesn't target the people who don't own their own homes, who are right at the bottom end. That is why we need to build solar farms.

*What is distinctive about how you operate?*

The organisation we have established is called Manaaki Energy, based on the principles of manaakitanga. It is relational. When we go to a house to install the solar panels we begin with karakia, kōrero, waiata and kai.[143] It is just amazing. We are being invited into people's homes to worship. We now have a whole group of us, a travelling karakia team.

The solar installers are wonderful guys from Greener Solutions. They are absolutely loving this project and talk about how significant and meaningful it is. Up till now they have been only putting solar on the homes of the rich, generally white middle class people. Now they are going into the homes of Māori, hearing the stories, the connections with land, with people. Even though these families don't have much, they have so much to give. The tradies are learning about manaakitanga,[144] and I just love that. The Pākehā way is "8am, get started, up on the roof, get it done!" But in our Manaaki Energy kaupapa the first hour of each day is spent in prayer and just building relationships. This is an important part of our work, and as people join us they find it very life giving. It is so rich and it offers another way of doing things. It honours God and the blessing and beauty of Te Ao Māori.

One of our karakia team is Trevor. He had solar panels put on his house early on in the project. He left the church when he was a teenager, but he has discovered how good the day is when you began with karakia. So now he comes with us every time and plays the guitar. He is a beautiful hearted man who has been living the gospel all of his life, and he is now connecting with God in a new way.

This is growing a movement. It is expressing the gospel in action and relationship. I am always talking about Jesus, in the planning, in people's homes, it is a real gift. I even got to talk about Jesus on the seventh floor of the Beehive when we met with Cabinet Minister Megan Woods. There are not many places you can do that without people wanting to 'poo-hoo' you; Māori are more comfortable including the spiritual side.

*When you talk about Jesus in those contexts what resonates for people?*
We talk about what our vision is, what we're hoping for, that we want to end energy poverty. We want to create solar farms that will alleviate poverty for the 100,000 New Zealand whānau who can't afford power. It fits into the five faces of mission of the Presbyterian church; we are trying to transform society, we are caring for creation, and we are preaching the gospel. That is cool!

Salvation is about the flourishing of all people. That is what Jesus longed for, and this is about that. Throughout scripture we see that God is on the side of the poor and the oppressed, and we see here in Aotearoa with colonisation that there have been so many systems that have oppressed Māori. It is not a case of us as 'white saviours' going and trying to fix it. We are very much being led by Māori in this. I feel a real humility in the space of going there. It is beautiful, I just love it.

*How does having solar power make a difference?*

Families are excited at the possibility of having power bills that aren't so high. We are dealing with families who get $800 power bills. These are families who often have big numbers of children and mokopuna living with them.[145] The solar system cuts power costs in half! People have to change their behaviour a bit to use power during the day; while it is sunny the solar panels run everything directly. Any excess power is sold back to the grid for 12 cents a unit – they're excited about that!

*What is your vision for this work?*

We need more power generation in NZ. This is obvious from the power cuts we had here over the winter. We also need to offset the coal and fossil fuels that we still rely on as a country, about 15% of power nationally. Our vision is to use solar, wind and geothermal energy and become a social retailer supplying to those customers that the other power companies have the most trouble with.

Generally, new technology only trickles down after a long, long time to people who are poor. They are not going to get electric cars anytime soon. It is rich people who put solar on their house and the poor miss out. This is a way of changing the structure of society to make it more even. Everybody gets the same amount of sun! I love the analogy that it's the same with God; everybody gets the same amount of God's love. If we can find ways to harness the sun to enable those who are poor to maximise that, then that helps everybody.

Hamish who runs Greener Solutions told me that one day of sunshine can provide enough energy to power the world for a year! I find this profound. What a sign of the generosity of God. God gives us so much more than we could ask for. God is absolutely abundant! It is us who stuff it up, enabling some people to get a lot while others get so little.

*What would you suggest churches could do around solar energy?*

Come and talk to Manaaki Energy about how your church might partner with local communities who are struggling in energy hardship. We hope to support local communities to create small solar farms for people to link into. The process of planning and maintaining of it builds community. It is the weaving of relationships along the way that matters most to me. I don't care as much about the technology; it's what we do with it that matters.

*What about climate change?*

The climate crisis is huge. I am less bothered about recycling, it makes very little difference. There are so many other things we should be changing. One of my pet peeves is how many Presbyterian church folk head off overseas every year – though not in these Covid years obviously – and they recycle the brochures when they get back!

Our church includes many Cook Islands folk. Climate change is very real for their island home; fresh water is harder to find, it is getting so polluted, the corals are dying.

Immigration is going to be a huge issue for New Zealand because while things are OK here, people from other countries will increasingly want to come here. I am concerned about how we welcome people, especially climate change refugees.

I am very aware of greenhouse emissions and how much carbon we each use. Chris and I bought a large house so that we could have lots of visitors. But then a refugee family from Afghanistan turned up at church, a big family of four adults and three kids. They were looking for housing and could not find any. Suddenly Chris and I realised that we did not need our big house, so we rented it to them and we rented the smaller house next door! People thought we were mad. But we actually like our rental more than our own home, and we can live more efficiently. Climate change means that we have to each think about what we are doing, what we are using, and make changes.

*What do you see as potential climate change effects in Hawke's Bay?*

Drought is going to be huge here, with the drying of the East coast. We are already seeing sea level rise, and places here on the coast getting eroded. And there are still new housing developments there – I can't believe it! They have raised the houses on a higher platform, but it is just stupid. They keep asking the Council to spend lots of money to keep the sea at bay. You cannot keep the sea at bay! There's no way I would build or buy anywhere near the coast.

*What have you learned about being Pākehā in partnership with Māori?*

My family is a 100-year Kiwi farming family. I used to feel very proud that there's a place in the Catlins named after my great grandmother. Now I know that that land was taken in illegitimate ways by Pākehā a few decades before my family purchased it. Knowing the history is personally challenging.

My grandfather's best friend was Māori, and he took Grandad back to his home in Wairoa to meet his people. As a result, growing up we were connected with his whanau. My parents' friends were freezing workers and possum hunters 'salt of the earth' type people. I'm so grateful for that. That's how I am too, I'm used to relating to all sorts. I find common ground.

I always open prayers in Te Reo, even though I'm not very good at it. One of the Rotorua home owners was later having a beer with the install guys, and he told them that he really appreciated that: "Who was that woman who prayed in Te Reo? Because she did that and engaged with my culture she is welcome in my home anytime." I feel really blessed. I am in awe as we get to do this.

*You would encourage churches to connect with Māori and Pacific people?*

Absolutely, yes. What I love about the solar project is that it has provided a focus for us to be connected. Environmental projects can help grow a good partnership. We need reasons to be in relationship.

We did this when we were in Oamaru, where there is a high Tongan population. We noticed that the Tongans and the Palagi were not mixing much. So we developed a mission project to install some water tanks in Tonga. While that was great for the villages in Tonga, the actual mahi was about the building of relationships for the people in Oamaru. People got to know each other as they fundraised, figured out how to do this and as they went on the trip. That worked really well. I am a big believer in finding ways for people to work alongside each other; that is when the magic happens!

### Action Point 47: Explore solar power

Find out about solar power generation in your area.

- Energy resources, Eco Church NZ: www.ecochurch.org.nz/energy
- Find Manaaki Energy on Facebook

### Action Point 48: Use less electricity

Review and reduce power consumption, at church and at home.

- EnergyMate is a free consultancy service: www.energymate.nz
- Consider switching power companies for more renewable energy provider.
- Energy Efficiency and Conservation Authority, NZ Government (EECA runs the GenLess website): www.eeca.govt.nz

### Action Point 49: Find out about local poverty

How do whānau in your area experience poverty, including energy poverty?

- Explore projects with low-income families to build relationships and support creative solutions.
- Talk to a local Christian social service agency in your area about working together on an environmental project to benefit the community.

### Action Point 50:

Praise God with creativity and bring creation in to church and home.

- Expand beyond traditional floral arrangements (and ban plastic flowers!) to use plants, fruits and flowers.
- Celebrate festivals with natural elements: festivals of the seasons, e.g. Spring flowers or Harvest; traditional festivals such Christmas and Easter and Pentecost; and personal celebrations such as weddings.
- Use symbols in tangible ways in worship and prayer, with children and all ages, e.g. stones, sand, water, seeds.
- Encourage creativity with natural objects, photography and art work.

## Absence

*Poem by Ana Lisa de Jong, Living Tree Poetry*

Darkness is simply an absence of light.
Everything is still here.

The bed with its hard corner
to be felt around.
The soft chair that takes all our weight.

The lounge and the kitchen,
the switch of the kettle.
The warmth of cup in hand.

Darkness is a blanket,
filled sometimes with false premonitions
and fears that need darkness to survive.

But light is like the lamp
that illuminates the circle where we sit
holding out for dawn.

That darkness has no prophetic gifting
is what the sun keeps saying
arriving as she does,

not a moment late,
wearing her golden robes,
casting her net of grace.

# It Matters to Me: Kristel van Houte

Kristel is the national director for A Rocha Aotearoa New Zealand, and co-ordinates the Karioi Project, based in Whāingaroa, Raglan.

*Where did you come from?*

I was an immigrant kid, we moved to New Zealand when I was 11 years old from the Netherlands. I am from Flemish/Dutch parents. We were from a province bordering Belgium with many peninsula and estuaries called "Zeeland" by the North Sea, which means sea-land. This is what "New Zealand" was named after by Abel Tasman. Both my parents came from fairly large families so we grew up surrounded by grandparents, aunties, uncles and cousins.

As a kid, it didn't really matter to me if the sun was shining or if it was raining or snowing, I loved being out playing in nature. Back then we could still make a snowman in the backyard and ice skate on a lake every year. I loved the sea: swimming, playing in the mud in local estuaries and collecting crabs. One of my favourite things was playing or looking at the animals at my grandparents' or a friend's farm, and riding horses. I loved being able to touch, care for and experience animals. Nature was my playground.

Nature was and will always be my place to play, relax, adventure and reconnect. This has especially been true when times get tough. Nature was there – a place I gained clarity and insight and a sense of peace when I needed it most. My first God moments were in nature. That connection to nature, feeling part of it has always felt very natural. I remember wanting to care for nature and feeling drawn to it; a physical sensation within me, deeper than words. From my earliest memories I wanted to immerse myself in nature, on my grandparents farm, in water, streams, at the beach, or in the forests.

I also had a strong sense about caring for people, especially the poor. From a young age I wanted to go to Africa – the wild animals of Africa fascinated me. I was drawn to the idea of travelling and exploring wild places and wanting to make the world a better place.

New Zealand to my brothers and me was the Promised Land. Our first home here had a huge quarter acre section with a stream down the back of our garden. The outdoor space gave us the opportunity to have animals, so we had cats, chickens, rabbits; we even had a sheep at one stage, in our backyard in South Auckland! My brothers and I played for hours in that stream, looking for eels and exploring. It went into a massive underground storm water tunnel, easy enough for us to walk through; we'd pop up in people's backyards and pick fruit when we were hungry! We were in love with what New Zealand had to offer, an outdoor lifestyle beyond what we had experienced in The Netherlands.

I got into digging the garden as a child, although I am not sure I ever produced much to actually eat. I did horticulture and biology at school and somehow decided to become a farmer; likely it was in the genes, because my grandparents were farmers and my mum too was very nature loving. When I finished high school I went to Massey University and embarked on an agriculture degree. My classmates struggled to comprehend a townie from Auckland (and female!) wanting to study agriculture.

*How was faith part of your life?*

I had an interesting faith upbringing. My family were Catholic but not particularly religious. When I was seven my parents divorced. My mum remarried – a Protestant! It raised a few eyebrows, as my grandmother was brought up by nuns. My stepdad would pray before meals and at night he would read from the Bible. I found the biblical stories fascinating and they became my foundation. We went to a Baptist Church in Manurewa, where I learned more about God and felt a real love for God.

I recognised early on that we all have a God centre. Every human, whether they acknowledge it or not, has within them that ability to recognise and connect with God. God is there, inviting connection. For me that invitation came through nature and a biblical faith. God is integral to my life and work. Faith just feels normal.

I loved the message of Jesus. His love for people, and this beautiful way of seeing the world and explaining things, that brings hope. His ability to break down and challenge the rules and regulations and thinking of the time – that appealed to my rebel nature.

I also remember feeling conflicted. Heaven was described as a place we're going to end up in, and it was nothing like Earth. I was told it would be all gold and full of precious stones, and I thought: "But I'm not into gold! I'm into trees and nature and animals. Why would God make a heaven that doesn't have trees, and all the things he created in the first place that he so obviously loves?!" This made no sense to me. People said, "It's all going to eventually burn anyway." We were taught that animals don't go to heaven, that I could not take my pets to heaven. I took that very personally: I decided I didn't want to go there either! That theology never felt right; it created a level of discomfort and lots of questions.

As a young adult I found it increasingly difficult to hold together my love for nature with my faith. I could no longer tolerate teaching on the after-life that treated creation as 'left overs' that would be discarded in due course. In church people talked a lot about not polluting the Temple of Christ, meaning how we treat our bodies and care for ourselves, especially to do with sexuality. But for me it was much bigger than that. I kept wondering 'Why doesn't this message extend to and include nature?'

I became increasingly conscious of a call to take care of the environment. I stepped away from my faith for some years as I struggled to reconcile my faith with my life's passion, a love and concern for what I can only see as "God's mystical created world." Most Christians I knew did not relate to this or understand it. At church few identified with my love of nature. At university few identified with faith. I was torn between two different worlds.

But God so loved the *cosmos* – the whole universe – that God gave his only son! (John 3:16). For me, when we pray, "on earth as it is in heaven" we see how heaven and earth mirror one another. Heaven is like earth, only even better. And earth contains hints of heaven everywhere! It made perfect sense to me to care for this created world.

### What did you do as a young adult?

I worked five years as a dairy farmer while raising my son. I qualified as a veterinary nurse and dabbled in surf lifesaving and other outdoors pursuits. I then went back to university to complete my degree. I changed direction to major in biology and completed a Masters in Marine and Freshwater Ecology. For my thesis I examined seagrass habitats in estuaries. I recall getting covered in mud collecting samples, not unlike what I had done as a child, and laughing to myself at the irony.

I spent a year working for the Apostolic Church in Hamilton as Events Coordinator for their large youth group, between my undergraduate and graduate degrees. I created a whole bunch of activities including nature based camps, enthusiastically encouraging the predominantly city kids to explore the outdoors.

*What did you do after university?*

As I came to the end of my Masters my desire to go to Africa resurfaced. I wanted to use the skills I had gained in biology to address issues in environment and poverty. So I started looking at working abroad programmes and mission agencies. I spent ages online searching, until one day A Rocha popped up. I was completely blown away: 'Wow, a Christian environmental organisation! I had never seen or heard of this before'. On the A Rocha website I clicked on a map of the world and where they worked. Because I wanted to go to Africa I was thrilled to see that they had a field study centre in Africa; and because I had studied marine ecology, I want to be on the coast. I saw that A Rocha was in Kenya, which is on the coast. So I clicked on the A Rocha Kenya website and right there on the home page it said, "We are looking for a marine ecologist!"

To say that this created some excitement is an understatement; it truly was an extraordinary moment. I emailed straight away and got a quick response from Colin Jackson the National Director. I told him what I had been doing, that I want to come, and can I bring my family. He emailed me straight back: "Yes! Come! Bring your son!"

It didn't happen immediately; we first went to American Samoa for two years, living on the island of Tutuila. I worked for American Samoa Community College in water quality research. I learned a huge amount from living in such a different culture. I loved the delights of living on a small tropical island. But there were challenges as well, especially with worsening environmental issues.

We saw the negative impacts of damage to the Pacific Ocean and the Islands. It was terrible after a big rain. American Samoa is very steep and has some of the highest rainfall in the world, which flushes every stream on the island out into the harbour. They had no effective systems to get rid of household rubbish. Traditionally all their waste would decompose, but with imported food and packaging, waste has nowhere to go. A large proportion of it is thrown into backyards and stream catchments that wash out into the ocean. One day there was so much plastic pollution at the boat ramp in the harbour we could not launch our boat. And I remember dolphins swimming around our boat while we tried desperately to catch floating plastic buckets and rubbish. It was very, very confronting for me. A lot of the work my team was doing was raising awareness of the links between water quality and human health. Polluted waterways make people sick; local people were dying from Leptospirosis (from animal waste in streams). And pollution also impacts on coral reefs due to sedimentation and degrading water quality.

Most of us have this idea of paradise when they think about the Pacific Islands, but it can be quite different living there. We would visit areas that were cleaned up for the tourists to enjoy, shielded from the realities of what life is actually like. I was frustrated by the issues and the ignorance around it. Nevertheless my time there was unforgettable, and for several years I returned to Upolu in Samoa to teach tropical marine ecology as a guest lecturer.

## Then A Rocha Kenya?

After two years in Samoa I was finally able to travel to the A Rocha base called Mwamba on the Kenya coast. There I was confronted by a whole other level of poverty – it felt more desperate and urgent. In Kenya much of the coastal rainforests have been chopped down, and as a result the climate changes and deserts form. People are no longer able to grow their own food, and there is devastating biodiversity loss. A Rocha is working to protect these coastal areas and improve the lives of the local communities around them. It was amazing to be a part of. It was an incredibly desperate situation, but by doing small things we could do so much good because the majority of the people had so very little. The poverty was heartbreaking.

My contribution was researching the Sabaki River mouth, one of the most important bird habitats on the Kenyan coast. It was identified as a 'globally important site' under the category 'congregations' of the Important Bird Areas criteria. Degradation of the estuary threatens the bird populations there, and the livelihood of communities around the river and estuary who rely on its resources for food and water.

We loved being part of the community on the A Rocha base. Staff, volunteers and students, local Kenyans and visitors live together, eat and work together cross culturally, with all the challenges and delights that come with that. A Rocha is Christian but is very open, welcoming people of all backgrounds and faiths. I loved the informal worship gatherings and discussions including both Christians, non Christians and even Muslims. I really felt I had come home. These were my people. Being there healed the disconnect and struggle I had experienced between faith and caring for creation.

In 2014 my daughter Kanika was born. She is now nearly 8 years old and has been very much a daughter of the Karioi Project, involved with everything. I climbed to the summit of Karioi with her when she was 3 months old. She has this incredible heart for nature and God. She is inspiring me!

Young people and environmental education are an important component in everything we have done, right from the start. We encourage whole families to get involved. We started an after-school environmental education programme (Karioi Kids and Rangers) for local kids and grew a partnership with Raglan Area School (Manaaki Ao programme).[150] Things developed because we build relationships – we would start doing something together and enjoy doing it, which then grew into a bigger programme. I guess we just got on and did it, and then figured out how we would keep doing it, by finding the funding to do it and eventually pay people to do it. It is a highly relational way of doing things – I call it 'organic'. We also have partnerships with Scripture Union and Adventure Specialities Trust, which incorporate a stronger faith component. All our programmes, whether secular or faith based, connect people to nature and inspire them to care for it.

*How would you describe the Christian foundation of the Karioi Project?*

Right from the start we had a mix of faiths; believers and non believers involved. Some people questioned that but I am okay with it. To me it is a missional part of the work, seeing where God was leading us and wondering where doors might open. Walking in the bush some volunteers say, "I used to go to church, you know, but ..." And then they tell me their story about how they felt hurt or misunderstood and left the church. People want to share their story. Others say: "We need as many people in conservation as possible – so if the Christians want to get on board – the more the better." Both Christians and non-Christians question us and wonder what on earth we are doing addressing environmental issues as part of a faith response.

It inspires me that the Karioi Project is very much a community project. A Rocha has been able to partner with the community and provide a unique and effective model. We are all about working with people to empower them and meet a need, and this resonates with people. Malibu told me how in the past he had been discouraged that Christians did not seem to care about the environment, but working with A Rocha restored his faith in Christians. Back in those early days we were seen as very marginal, but now I'd say we are just about mainstream!

*How has your relationship with local Māori developed?*

Through the work we have done we have seen reconciliation. The project brought people together who had previously been in conflict. Our values are about participation and being inclusive, inviting people to come on a journey. Joining together we become part of the solution. People who had been on opposing sides of the 1080 debate were sitting next to each other around the same table making plans together. It was really inspiring to be a part of that. They are all truly amazing people. Malibu shared with me that despite being a hard-core activist he learned something important: "Be hard on the issues but soft on the people." Another amazing person was Fiona, our fundraiser extraordinaire. When I sometimes lamented the frustrations of working through the challenges of a community led project, she reminded me: "Always leave the door open." Despite our differences, which at times led to some people choosing another path, we would not close the door on relationship and always welcome future participation.

We had plenty of struggles, challenges and sometimes misunderstandings. We work across different cultures and engage with a huge number of landowners, community aspirations as well as treaty negotiations to restore biodiversity on a maunga. It's not surprising that it throws curveballs now and then. For me that is one of the hardest parts of this job. I feel highly challenged at times and can take things too personally. A mana wahine once said to me: "Sometimes you just have to harden up and get on with the job, Kristel!" I smile at that now, but it was tough at the time. Partnering in a truly genuine way takes you well beyond partnership into friendship. Then going the hard yards together. Then there is loss when you part ways.

We worked with Sandy and Thomas and their crew, growing and learning together with mana whenua, keen to mutually support restoration of hapū land as well as DOC managed lands. Sandy insisted on autonomy and doing things in their own way and time. He liaised with Māori landowners to provide access for traps on Māori land and later his trust, Te Iwi Tahi Pest, contracted to the project to cut new tracks across Karioi and deploy the first traps together with volunteers. Sandy also build up his team of contractors to deliver predator control across the Waikato. Over the years our team has grown and we have seen young people from our in-school Manaaki Ao (earthcare) programme step up into ranger and education roles, employed by the project. Several of our paid staff identify as Māori. Malibu's vision of rangatahi working on the maunga is now a reality.

We have spent over 10 years building this conservation project. When we started the project people asked: "How do you know it will work?" And I would reply: "I don't know, I guess we will see. But if we don't try we'll never know." I'm proud that we did not let the fear of failure stop us from trying new things. Some things didn't work and others took off and were a success, and some things only for a period of time. I think of it of seasons, there is a season for everything; nothing ever stays the same. We have built a team with wonderful values and passion, we have paid staff and many truly wonderful supporters and volunteers. We now have over 50 burrows protected through an extensive seabird monitoring programme and over 130 regular volunteers. And we are seeing Ōi chicks fledge again. More than 34 chicks have fledged over the last 5 years.

And now we are putting that same kind of energy into Eco Church NZ.

*Why Eco Church NZ?*

From our early beginnings we recognised that we are part of the church but our primary calling is as a missional movement. Through practical 'hands-on' conservation we demonstrate God's care for creation, participating in God's loving restoration and transformation of the earth. By engaging in this mission we serve a unique role by reminding the broader church that God's love for creation cannot be reduced to a theological statement but is evidenced in action.

After more than 10 years focussing on practical action A Rocha is ideally placed to inspire the Christian community, at a time when the church is finally waking up and seeing that caring for the environment is integral to a life of faith – part of our call and mission. We are able to speak from the experience we have gained through our conservation work; and we also bring the theology, because we have an amazing suite of theological experts in A Rocha who have been talking eco-theology for many years. That is a powerful mix. We have done the hard yards; our local groups have achieved a lot around the country. We have build up a beautiful network of passionate people. Our aim is to be relevant to Christian communities across Aotearoa as churches incorporate care for creation in their mission.

Eco Church has come at the right time for us as an organisation. We have learned from the UK Eco Church model and are adapting this to our own context. Eco Church NZ is a vehicle that can bring people together and grow into the future; it creates opportunities to connect and re-imagine what 'church' is all about. I also feel strongly that it is not just talk; it's about inspiring practical action. People reach out to us and ask what can they do. We are promoting a zero waste philosophy, and our partnership with Para Kore is helping churches reduce waste.

*Why does waste matter to God?*

Ironically, I was not that interested in rubbish. Like with predator control, it was not my thing, but OK, we have to deal with the crap before we get to do the fun stuff, right?! We helped initiate Plastic Free July several years ago, and have been involved in the Litter Intelligence project with Sustainable Coastlines.[151]

20 years ago the Whāingaroa Raglan community took on the challenge of completely reorganising the waste systems to save our harbour from pollution.[152] That led to the formation of Para Kore, a zero waste initiative for marae, incorporating a Māori worldview.[153] Early on our Waikato A Rocha group helped implement their programme at a community centre in Hamilton. I was sure their model would make complete sense for churches too.

I met Jacqui, who leads Para Kore, at the beach for a swim one day and asked: "Would you be willing to take us on, to support a zero waste programme for churches?" She agreed, and we have been on a journey, learning about waste in churches and what we can do about it. This partnership is also an opportunity to be enriched by the Māori worldview as part of our bicultural learning.

We ran our first training in partnership with Para Kore with churches in Christchurch in April 2021, and we are starting to see results as they share what they have done to reduce waste. I love seeing measurable impact – perhaps it's the science geek in me! It is transformative and inspiring.

Waste truly is a major problem in our world. As Para Kore kaimahi Paul Murray says: "We want it, we buy it, we use it, and we throw it away – but there is no such place as 'away'!" I love the concept of a circular economy because it connects well with ecology; it is how the world works and how nature works, nothing is wasted. It resonates on many levels.

Everyone produces waste so everyone is responsible for it. A zero waste programme is a great way to get a community working together. It is meaningful and tangible. It's important to me that we offer something practical for churches to engage with – walking the talk, I guess.

*How do you see Eco Church NZ developing?*

Networks are building up between churches around the country. Cooperation generates energy, and resonates with how I work: collaborative and interdenominational. We are seeing a real diversity in the churches getting involved. Eco Church NZ resources include sermons, studies and seminars that everyone can engage with. We are so much stronger when we do things in partnership.

Eco Church is a movement. When a church community takes on this mission and commits to being an Eco Church, that's a very inspiring and brave step! It is great to hear about the awesome things that churches are doing. Those are the wins, seeing that positive transformative energy.

I think back to when I sat down with the Wilberforce Trust (one of our funders) 13 years ago, when they were first considering whether to fund A Rocha. They said: "Well, you are very much on the fringe, but we will support you for a little bit and see how it goes." Now, at our most recent meeting, current CEO Chris Clark explained that Wilberforce is planning their funding priorities in line with the five Marks of Mission.[154] The fifth is caring for environment, and A Rocha is the main faith-based organisation doing that. That shows how far we have come, when our broader community understands that creation care is integral to the church's mission. The world has changed so much – and it's encouraging to see how relevant our work is.

*What do you see God doing through Eco Church?*

I see church communities becoming environmental and social hubs where anyone can find a place to be, whoever you are. This is a chance for us to reimagine church and what our purpose is. Churches should be vibrant places on Sunday mornings, and they should be vibrant places every day – places where people can explore what it means to live sustainable and healthy lives. And collectively we can support each other in that journey. God is in that space! God is in the connections that form and the relationships that grow. In this early growth of Eco Church, despite the lockdowns, we see people stepping up. It resonates with people. It opens doors. There are beautiful relationships coming out of this work. It gives me hope.

I love the A Rocha byline 'Conservation and Hope'. We talk about a circular economy. Just like ecology, it is regenerative; things grow and give life then decay and die and new growth comes out of that. We find hope even in death and this brings new life. Hope is in each of us and every being. Being caretakers of God's creation is our ultimate calling. People are part of nature, not separate from it, so looking after God's people and creation is our purpose.

*What sustains you?*

Water is my ultimate place to be. I have my most spiritual contemplative moments emersed in water. It has a healing quality. Water is so good, so beautiful and invigorating!

When I am processing something I struggle to verbalise it immediately, but then I find myself having amazing conversations with people doing amazing things, and that not only inspires me, but brings to life the words I need to explain what I feel deep inside but could not express. I am learning to understand myself and listen more.

I definitely go through times of huge doubt. Personal challenges, self doubt and feeling inadequate have plagued me throughout this journey, as well as the environmental challenges that we face. I ask myself, "Am I still in the place where I should be?" One day I got a small but powerful word. I was surfing up north, trailing my hands through the water. I felt God saying: "It matters to me." There is so much to that; I tried to take it in. "It matters to me" – my life matters to God, what I am doing matters. But also beyond just me, this creation matters to God, and caring for it matters to God. Whether people agree or not. That word keeps me going for now.

My story is just me following my dreams and intuition. Recognising my brokenness. Feeling it in my body. Participating in the healing and reconciliation of all things. I still have so much to learn. I connect with nature. I am part of nature. In relationship with each other. And then the next step presents itself.

I love the poem 'When I was the stream' originally by Meister Eckhart:

"When I was the stream ...
there was nothing I could not love ...
I returned to the river and to the mountain.
I asked for their hand in marriage again."[155]

## Look After Karioi

*Poem by children at Raglan Area School*

Look after Karioi, respect her
Understand the signs of the environment,
as they will guide us

Karioi is from Whāingaroa
She is the mountain of the western side
She stands by the side of the sea
She is beautiful
She is an important woman
Her hair flows
She descends down to the sea
Atawhaitia Karioi ... Look after Karioi.

The waters flow from her
which are medicine for the whole world
She gives us strength to breath
There are trees on Karioi and birds which fly around
Karioi is the guardian for Tane Mahuta!
Atawhaitia Karioi ... Look after Karioi.

### *Action Point 51: Join A Rocha*

Individuals can:

- Subscribe to a range of email newsletter lists: www.arocha.org.nz/enews
- Like the A Rocha Facebook page: www.facebook.com/ARochaNZ
- Join a local group in your area: www.arocha.org.nz/contact-us
- Become a financial supporter: www.arocha.org.nz/donate
- Volunteer in Raglan with Karioi Project: www.karioiproject.co.nz
- Explore volunteering overseas with A Rocha International: www.arocha.org

Churches can:

- Invite an A Rocha speaker to preach or take a seminar: www.arocha.org.nz/people
- Connect with Eco Church: www.ecochurch.org.nz
- Sign up for the Zero Waste Programme: www.ecochurch.org.nz/zero-waste-programme

### Action Point 52: Trap predators

Work towards the goal of being predator free.

Less mammal pests means more bird life and healthy forest, which absorbs more carbon dioxide and makes a very significant contribution to achieving our greenhouse gas reductions.

- Connect with your local Predator Free group:
  www.predatorfreenz.org
- Join your local A Rocha group and learn how to set traps.
- Biodiversity resources, Eco Church NZ:
  www.ecochurch.org.nz/biodiversity

### Action Point 53: Citizen Science

Do some citizen science as a great way to observe nature and contribute to gathering important information.

- Science Learning Hub: www.sciencelearn.org.nz/citizen_science
- Department of Conservation: www.doc.govt.nz/get-involved
- For children - Educational Resources, Department of Conservation:
  www.doc.govt.nz/get-involved/conservation-education/resources/
- Biodiversity citizen science, Eco Church NZ:
  www.ecochurch.org.nz/biodiversity

# Sing About Everything: Lala Simpson

Harilalao (Lala) Simpson is a world music teacher extraordinaire, a passionate community songleader, solo performer, dancer, and worship leader.[156] From Madagascar, she now lives with her husband Stuart and three young adult children in Wainuiomata out of Wellington.

*What were the songs that you sang growing up?*

In Madagascar we sang about everything. There is no separation between the act of singing, and talking and being together. The rhythms in the songs are linked to daily activities: songs that you sing while you are pounding the rice; opening a school – write a song for that; met a beautiful girl – sing about that; I like my peach tree – I'll write a song about that. We would sing about the forest and the birds. We also have our traditional songs: some are just fun, some relate closely to our time during colonisation, and there are songs from the royal courts hundreds of years ago still passed down. Song is about everything! Singing and dancing for the Malagasy person is an everyday thing, for both men and women. I grew up singing in my local dialect and in Malagasy and in English, and French music.

Songs express all sorts of different emotions: excitement, joy, sadness, anger. Anger, definitely. Grief – we have lots of songs about grief and being sad. But even some of the funeral ones are happy, because you are remembering the person who died, rather than all about the sadness.

*And what about church songs?*

The first missionaries were Welsh; as they learned Malagasy they translated their hymns. Some hymns, people didn't like the tune so they made a different tune. Some hymns people gave new words to. The church encourages writing new hymns; like, if they are celebrating their minister being there 10 years they hold a big song writing competition about that!

*Did the songs sing about the natural world?*

When I was a child in church we would sing old hymns, about God and me rather than the world around me. But in my teenage years more choirs started, and they often chose songs inspired by Psalms that talk about nature, animals and trees. The songs come from people's experiences. My choir did lots of trips to different parts of Madagascar – and there was always someone writing a song about something! They would write about what we experienced together in nature on that trip, and that will become an anthem for the choir. On the next trip, we'll be singing that song!

These new hymns sing about how beautiful the world is that God created, how lucky that we get to live in it, and that God chose us to be part of it. Nature celebrates God, and by appreciating and respecting nature we also glorify God. Everything in itself praises God: the mountains and the sea, the stars and the trees, the birds and the valleys. A song may be inspired by a view or an encounter, or a wonderful time the composer spent with their family. I especially remember singing these songs as my family walked the 45 kilometres to see my grandparents. I can picture that wonderful landscape. And I also associate it with my family, with that time of togetherness – we would sing together as a whole bunch of people walking.

*Do you have a particular memory of singing?*

My family would squash in for long car journeys. Many many hours across long distances, we would drive through the night. I was not allowed to sleep because I was the radio! I had to sing all night long – eight hours straight – to keep the driver awake. I would sing church songs, French songs, English songs, pop, folk, anything! In the night you sing the songs about the stars. I can still see the bright brilliant stars framed by the windscreen like a painting. I remember feeling so small but still held by Someone who made all this. Then when everyone was awake I had to lead the songs that everyone knew: church songs or traditional Malagasy songs.

*When people think about Madagascar we think about the rich diversity of animals that live there – which do you love most?*

The lemurs are top. I like lemurs. They are very friendly. They love the sun – they love life! They manage to survive despite the environment they live in. Some of them have developed quite well in the rock formations in the northwest of Madagascar. Some are in the south where there's only cactus everywhere. They are beautiful animals and because they are only in Madagascar they are very, very special.

And I love chameleons. We have so many different types of chameleons – so beautiful. I love their colours. They look grumpy all the time. Their eyes can go in two different directions at once. There is a proverb in Madagascar: "Think like a chameleon, with one eye to the future and one eye to the past." We are always connected to the past but we also connected to the future. When you are acting at the present moment, you have to think beyond – not just to what you see now but to how it impacts further on.

*Were you brought up with an ethic to care for the environment?*

Malagasy people, because we are poor, recycle everything. It's not a lifestyle choice, it's out of necessity. You have to reuse everything. No food waste; if an animal was killed you ate 99% of that animal – the horn is used for making decorations or utensils. Cans are used to make decorations and toys – we made cars out of tins. Old clothes were turned into dolls. My cousins in the country would make their own rope out of flax. People would only grow what they needed to eat, only fish what they needed. Some of that ethic is lost now.

*Did you see environmental degradation?*

Yes, especially deforestation. We lost a lot of rice fields. My grandparents used to live in rice fields in central Tana, the capital city. But then factories started popping up, to make things to sell overseas. They covered all the rice fields. My grandparents lost their home. It changed so fast. Clothing factories were first, and then all sorts of factories, making phone parts and electronics. My cousins worked in the factories, assembling clothes. It didn't pay much, and the working conditions were not good.

Deforestation is obviously a big issue. Some of it is out of ignorance; people burn the forest to grow a crop but then the land loses its fertility so then they go and burn another forest. There is not much education for how to look after the land. But most of the deforestation happens for mining. People come from overseas, buy the land cheap from the government, and then burn whole villages and forests so they can mine that land. That is happening a lot.

*How do you feel when you think about those massive changes that have happened in your lifetime in Madagascar?*

Angry, very angry. I understand when local people burn the forest because they need to grow food and they don't know how to do it better. I am angry at the government for not supporting people. I am angry with the Western world for continuing to plunder the poorer countries for their own need. Mining in Madagascar is for minerals to use in mobile phones and computers. It upsets me when people chuck out an old phone and get a new one: that's child labour, that's loss of natural resources for my people. It makes me angry.

There is so much rubbish now. Waste from those factories, but also waste being exported from other countries to Madagascar. Unwanted second-hand clothes from Europe are just sent to Madagascar. They are sold to people but most of the clothes are in such a state no one can use them. So they just fill the place – everywhere piles of these clothes. It is terrible. It's makes me feel horrible. It doesn't matter how much the people recycle things, there is now just too much waste!

It all makes me very sad. Sometimes it just feels too much. What do I do? I feel helpless. The effects of environmental degradation are so real.

My parents used to be able to provide rice for themselves for the whole year. Now they can barely produce for half a year, which means they have to buy rice, and when you lose the ability to buy rice, that's bad. Then you are below the poverty line, if you cannot buy your staple foods. That is terrible. But the people in power have become richer and richer and richer because they get paid all this money for the land. They export all the resources that they are not supposed to export, sell those illegally and make money.

I am sure there are bold new singers in Madagascar who address all of this and bring it out, calling out the politicians.

People come from overseas who are passionate about the environment. They bring money and they persuade to the government to set aside an area as a reserve. But no one talks to the locals who live close to the reserves, who used to go into that forest to find food and to hunt – and now suddenly they are told they can't go in there. They won't get onboard with the reserve if there is no alternative for them. It is much better when people look after the nature that is close to them because it brings benefits to the community. They get tourists to come, they have work, and they can grow food alongside keeping the nature. But sadly these are only small projects.

*How did you come to Aotearoa?*

I met a Kiwi boy on a programme for Training In Mission run by Council for World Mission. He was the New Zealand representative and I was the Malagasy representative. We lived in Madagascar for four years and then we came to live in New Zealand. Our daughter was born in Madagascar and two boys in Christchurch. Stuart trained as a Presbyterian minister, so we lived in Dunedin then parish ministries in Auckland and Wellington. Now he is a mission enabler for the presbytery.

*How did you find worship in New Zealand?*

People don't sing much here. People are not very expressive – they don't connect with what their mouth is saying. I found that very hard because Malagasy people are very expressive – if a person is sad you can hear it in their voice and you can feel it in their body. I found New Zealand like a desert when it comes to singing. People are afraid to sing. Church is probably the only place where people do corporate singing – unless they're drunk in the pub – but it isn't very lively. I sing loud! What's the point otherwise?! When I first came to church I was the loudest human in the church. I got involved in the worship and music in each of the churches we have been part of. In Auckland that was a multi-cultural church. The Pacific people felt close to my home – they sing all the time too!

*How can worship nurture creation care?*

Many of our worship prayers and songs include references to the natural world, but often these are only symbolic. Do we honour the real world for its own sake in our worship, or do we just use it when it suits us for pretty metaphors?

There are some songs that do give voice to creation. One of my favorites is 'How great Thou art' – that I love. A chorus that comes to mind is 'We shall go out with joy ... and the trees of the fields shall clap their hands'. And there are modern hymns such as 'Creation sings the Father's song'. We need more of that; we should include this in our worship and write new hymns. The more we are aware of God's involvement in nature, and honour this in our worship, then the more we will take care of creation. How can we take care of what we are not aware of?

For me, looking after nature is very much part of worship. You don't have to go to the church every Sunday and sit on pews and close the door. Some churches worship at the beach and clean up the beach as part of Sunday morning. Especially with Covid, now is a good time to do more outdoor worship. With my choirs, we sing outdoors sometimes so we don't have to wear masks. I love being together as a group in nature. Our songs about creation make so much sense when we sing them outside!

*In your choir work, do you get people singing about the natural world? How does that resonate for people?*

One of the songs that I've done with a lot of my groups is called 'Pretty Planet'.[157]

> This pretty planet spinning through space.
> You're a garden, you're a harbor, you're a holy place.
> Golden sun going down.
> Gentle blue giant spin us around.
> All through the night, safe till the morning light.

When I teach that to children they start telling me all about the earth – it is our home. And what we need to do to look after it. The gentle blue giant – what does that mean? They talk about the ocean. They talk how the earth is important because we are safe in it, but we may not be safe anymore because there is climate change. It creates amazing conversations – we talked about this for months! The kids' choir did a concert all about animals, which led to talking about endangered animals and what can we do to help. One of the children got so into it she designed a poster and we had so much art work that we had an exhibition on the day of the concert.

Adults also love to sing these songs. We sing it in a song and then the discussion naturally comes out. People are very ready to talk about the natural world.

I teach songs from all around the world. One from Bolivia is about cutting the corn, a work song. People move together with the rhythm. And it sparkles discussion about food and the inequality of distribution of food in the world. During lockdown we went to sing in Featherston at the Japanese war memorial, because we were learning songs about justice and war. We went during the spring blossoms and it was so clear how nature brings healing, along with the music. My women's choir is learning songs about water – ocean and river – and they talk about how to look after riverbeds and resources: water as resource, water as life. One song is about people being transporting into slavery across the water. One song is: "Don't wait from the shore. There's so much more. Just edge yourself in and let the sweet water hold you." It is about how being in water helps you let go of fear – to be one with nature.

Most of the people I work with are non-Christians. In singing they experience connection with other people and also with this land, this world that we live in. Music can do that. I see God at work in people's reaction to the music. It awakens in them a deep sense of wanting to care for creation. Which makes perfect sense to me because God put us here to look after creation! After God created us he said, "Go and look after it."

*What would you love churches to do more of?*

I would love to encourage families and churches to learn songs from around the world. I don't like the phrase 'world music' because it puts everyone else in the world in a different box than our 'normal' music. When we sing a song from another culture it is important to also learn the story behind the song. There are lots of other songs we can sing. Churches include different people from different cultures; get them more involved – what songs do they have? That enriches us.

Get out of the building and go worship outside! Our Wellington church, St. John's, does 'picnic church' once a year at Otari-Wilton's Bush. Worship incorporates the stream in the worship and the activities involve the natural world. Stuart's home church in Christchurch does 'church in the park' at New Year. But we need to do that more often, not just a special occasion once in a while. Singing worship in the natural environment builds strong group memories. To worship God in the environment is good for us and it is a witness to our community. People walk past and say: "Who are these people? What are they doing?" It is another way – don't just wait for people to come and see us in our building.

*Is there a Bible story that connects for you about the role of music and caring for creation?*

I think of when King David was dancing in front of the Ark (2 Samuel 6). Music has that power, to connect you deeply with God. You can be you and express yourself unreservedly when you worship – which is very hard to find in church. When I lead worship I get people to clap or **do** something, especially when the song screams out for that: **"Come on everybody!"** Kiwi people are reserved in church, as though being 'proper' is the way to be. I don't think so! I think you're just meant to be you!

*How are Lala and God these days?*

Getting on very well! I have always had this feeling of God being close, especially in nature. And because I am a singer I feel closest to God when I am singing. And if I am in nature **and** I am singing, that is absolutely amazing!! Even if I am on my own I carry a sense of being with the community also. God is not just with me but with everybody else as well and in the places that we are in.

*How is God calling you, in relation to creation?*

We were recently able to buy our own home. Having my own little piece of land and garden for growing things has given me a deeper understanding of what it means to be custodian of land. It is becoming more and more important that I am a custodian of this place where I live, but also that God gave us the responsibility to look after all of this world. It is a privilege as well as a responsibility. So what does that mean? When I look after my little garden, or I recycle things, or when I go for a walk in the forest, I feel very, very close to God. I have that connection. I am part of this world and I am supposed to look after this world. I feel very privileged to be part of it. I am taking my responsibilities even more seriously than before. I know this is what God is asking me to do and what God wants all of us to do.

God, you are part of all of this and you allow me to be part of your vision for the world.

*Do you have a song that you would like to share?*

There's one song that has became my family's song. It was written for us. 'God, we praise You. We celebrate your name'. It talks about the ocean, the mountains, the rivers, the valleys, the hills. All of this shows your glory. They all say thank you and so do I, because I am part of all of this. You made me and I am in this.

## Midera Anao

*Song by Solohery*

**Midera Anao, mankalaza Anao**
*We praise you Lord, we celebrate you*

**Midera ny anaranao zahay ry Tompo ô**
*We praise and celebrate your name*

Ny tany sy ny lanitra asan'ny tananao
*Look at the beauty of the earth and sky which you made*

Ary ny tendrombohitra noforoninao
*And the mountains you created from nothing*

Ny zanak'olombelona zavaboarinao
*The humans that you have fashioned in your image*

Volana aman-kintana asan'ny tananao
*The moon and the stars, the work of your hand*

Ny ranomasindehibe kotrok'orana
*Look at the vast oceans and the mighty thunder in a storm*

Lemaka sy havoana koa nampitoerinao
*The valleys and the hills you have put in place*

Ny vorona ao an'ala injao samy mihira hoe
*All the birds in the forest singing*

Ny voninahitra ho Anao ry Tompo ô
*Glory to you our Lord and Master!*

### Action Point 54: Worship outside

Praise God in creation!

- Take chairs outside onto the lawn or in the courtyard or sit on the grass
- Children or youth only or the whole congregation
- Guitar-led acoustic-style singing
- Communion is very beautiful in natural surrounds
- Plan into periods of the year, especially the Season of Creation (in Spring), summer service and picnic.

### Action Point 55: Worship God with all creation in song

Sung worship that opens our hearts to praise, and to lament, in company with all things.

- Find songs that include references to nature in more than just symbolic ways.
- Use natural objects and images in worship.
- There are a host of worship resources online, including hymns and songs.

### Action Point 56: Celebrate a diversity of culture in worship

Grow beyond mono-cultural worship and be enriched by the insights, words and rhythms of other cultures.

- Start with those cultures represented within your congregation; work with families to enable minority cultures to find a voice in worship.
- Use new resources, e.g. video.
- Invite a choir from another church, and invite them to sing in their own language/s.

# It Will Be Spring: Marg Fern

My name is Marg Fern. A few years ago my husband and I chose a new surname together, Fern, because a fern represents new life. Ferns grow towards the light, which was important spiritually for us. We have three children and we are the Fern family.

I grew up in Christchurch. I wasn't from a Christian home but became a Christian when I was 14, at Spreydon Baptist – that is where my husband and I met. After high school he went off to Otago to study medicine and I went to America to do summer camp and then back-packed around Europe. When I got back I moved to Dunedin to study and be close to my boyfriend (who later became my husband) and did a Performance Music degree in singing.

*Are your parents both Pākehā?*

Yes. My dad is from a North Canterbury farming family. My husband's parents are Swiss immigrants. That Swiss heritage is a big influence in our family.

*How did you become interested in the environment?*

Initially it came from my husband. He's always been big on recycling and caring for the planet. Eating natural food was part of his upbringing as his father is an organic farmer. So we made small changes where possible; opting for butter over margarine, opting for less processed foods and organic grains and produce. I used to think this was a 'nice-to-have' but a big inconvenience because organic is often the more expensive option. It wasn't until my husband became unwell that growing food became truly important to me.

Early on in our marriage he was training as a Surgical Registrar. I thought I would be the wife of a successful surgeon and live in a giant white weatherboard house. It was mostly sub-conscious, I didn't say those things out loud, but that was where I thought my life was going. And that is not how it tracked out for us.

Three years ago he burned out, quit his work and became very unwell. The fast life became totally overwhelming. We went from a six-figure salary to living on the benefit – for 18 months, with two and then three kids, I lined up in the social welfare line. It was very, very tough.

*How did you cope with life not working out the way you planned?*

I started going out into the garden, just to be out of the house. Up till then I had not been interested in gardening. But when my husband became unwell I threw myself into weeding; it was physical, something I could control, I could make things look nice. Then I bought seeds and planted vegetables. When he had respite time at home he would notice how great the garden looked. He'd say, "Wow, you're doing a good job, this looks great!" I was encouraged by his compliments.

While I was out in the soil it started to make sense at a spiritual level. I kept thinking of analogies. I learned about God in a new way while weeding. Like, I learned to not pull out all of the plants that were going to seed. My husband told me about 'nursery plants'; you leave some of the old ones growing to protect the small plants. When there was so much loss and stress it helped that I didn't have to pull out everything from my past – I could try to focus on positive things that were important to me that were still alive and needed nurturing. It helped me to focus on joy that could be found in simplicity: a beautiful flower, sunshine, my children smiling. I started to love composting; I love the idea that nothing is wasted. God uses everything.

Another important insight is that nothing is perfect. I would plant 10 seeds and one grew really well, most were OK, and one seed did not come out of the ground. That's just how nature works. That helped me deal with disappointment in life. My brother struggles with addiction and my husband struggles with his health. I can get absorbed in trying to figure out 'Why?!' or agonise over why the seed didn't grow or why this plant has gone brown or caught a fungus: 'Why has that happened?!' But gardening has helped me to accept that life is not always optimal and perfect.

It is also accepting our lack of control. We don't have as much control over things as we think we do. I can work really hard, make the soil perfect and buy the best seeds, but still some won't grow, and some won't thrive – the injustice of that! I have made more peace with that in life.

Living on the benefit, we started gardening so that we had food. It's one thing to grow a garden because it's trendy and fun; it is a very different thing to have to garden in order to eat. I can look back now and know that it was empowering, but at the time it was a desperate thing. We ate all sorts of green leaves, not just lettuce – beetroot leaves, all sorts – to fill out meals, put in a smoothie, to stay healthy. We began to eat a more plant-based diet.

Our friends became very interested in what we were doing, and wanted to know: "Wow, how do you grow things?" Suddenly having less material wealth didn't matter. We were developing a richness of another kind in our lives.

*How did that burnout experience affect you spiritually?*

It is still hard. I am still catching up with the grief of it. Life is not Plan A or B or C – I'm on Plan D or even G! My life is not what I thought it would be, but I have realised how personal God is.

When things were falling apart I stopped praying because I realised that my prayers were all 'fix it' prayers. I wanted the bad things to stop, so I prayed: "Please may this not happen!" And then those things would happen and I would feel God was letting me down. That cycle went on and on. I had a wise counsellor who said, "I think you're praying the wrong prayers." She asked me to notice where Jesus showed up during the day. That was a mind-blowing concept for me.

One particularly bad day, when my husband was admitted to the Cardiology ward, I drove home terrified he would have permanent heart damage. The kids were at my Mum's. I didn't know what to do or where to go. I went out into our garden and just lay on the grass under our big tree. It was winter time. I looked up at the branches.

I recently read a book by a woman who had lost a child, and her illustration of loss resonated with me. She described how she would go to the forest in winter, and it looked really scary, and Jesus said to her, "But look how far you can see." When there are no leaves in winter it gives you clarity.

That day the tree had nothing on it, and I could see clearly: 'Yes. This is life in its bareness, at the bottom'. And then the Holy Spirit planted in my mind: "But it will be spring. And it will be summer." That was all I could grasp.

*That was enough, knowing that it won't be like this forever?*

Even God was too hard a concept for me at that point. I could not see that God was in it. All I could hold onto was the tree, just the tree.

*How did you as a family find your way back from there?*

My husband used the analogy of playing soccer: you're on a team, playing on the field, then suddenly you get taken off the field and put on the bench – you're on the sideline and it's a shock. "Oh! I'm not playing anymore." You are out of the rat race. There is sadness at first but then comes relief. His trajectory in medicine was so full on. I had succumbed to a life in which I would not see my husband: he would work 100-hour weeks and I'd bring up the children alone. I was OK with that, but when that wasn't an option anymore the relief started to sink in. We wanted to create a slow life, with more moments of joy and connection.

We kept our garden going. We gradually re-landscaped the whole property, with no straight edges – my husband makes curves with everything. We slowly but surely got a routine back on track. We incorporated lots of simple things to keep that simplicity going. That was really important for us.

*How was cycling part of that?*

We sold one of our cars and bought a cargo bike so that we could live more simply. It is called a Christiania Bike. There is a big box on the front between two wheels, like a rickshaw.[158] Two kids can sit on the bench seat in the box, with a seat belt. When the baby was small I put him in his capsule in the front; now he sits on a beanbag.

I had a moment on my bike which was very empowering. One day I was riding and a lady drove past in a new Range Rover (I used to want a posh white car!). She stopped, opened her window and was so enthusiastic: "Oh, my children would have loved that! You are so amazing!" It felt such an irony; she was the one in the flash car, looking like the winner, but she was telling me how envious she was of my more 'simple' transport.

*What do you value about cycling?*

I see cargo biking as an expression of the Kingdom of God!

It makes you fully present. You have to be engaged and focused, especially with kids. It awakens the senses: smell, sight, touch, even the wind. If it's cold that can be invigorating. If it's hot that can be really fun in the sun, very joyous. Cycling gives you energy. It improves your fitness. When you arrive somewhere you feel fully alive; for the first five minutes the endorphins are excellent!

It connects you with your environment. It is very visceral, you feel the elements. I used to avoid cycling in the rain but even biking in the rain is enlivening. The cargo bike has a roof that goes over the box so we can go out in all weather.

It sparks joy in other people. I notice that a lot. When I take the kids to school many kids comment: "Oh that's so cool! I want to have a go!" It just looks fun, even for adults. They want to be sitting in the box being pushed around! Sometimes my husband and I do that, go out on a date with me in the cargo seat. It is playful and makes you feel like a kid again. Everyone needs to play. Sometimes we string up lights. We can do all sorts of things with the cargo bike!

Cycling slows life down. It takes longer, so you can't do as much. You have to plan your trips rather than rush around fitting too much in. You can't go as far so it makes you live more local. It's a way to come back to basics. It keeps me tuned in to how I am and aware of my energy levels and my limits. Some days just dropping the kids to school and back is enough. For women the menstrual cycle affects our energy; I take iron tablets and my energy can get quite low, which is a good time to hunker down and take things easy. I am more aware of these things and I am more content to stay close to home.

We still own a car, and I notice how different I am when I cycle or when I drive. I enjoy being 'Cargo Bike Marg' but as soon as I get into a car I become 'Car Marg'. I start thinking about going here or there because I can! I get hectic pretty quickly. I notice that shift in myself.

I think about Jesus and his disciples, and how they wandered around not carrying much. Their food was simple and their plans were simple. Biking slows you down to a pace that is manageable. There is so much going on and it is easy to feel overwhelmed. A biking lifestyle brings you closer to a rhythm that is sustainable and maintains joy and connection.

*How much are carbon emissions a factor for you?*

I'm not very up to date with climate science, but reducing carbon emissions is a big goal for us. The kids and I decided to travel only by bike and bus for two weeks; afterwards I called a local newspaper reporter to say: "I'm a mum of three children and we are to trying to live a more car-free life, but it is so difficult." I want to address this with the City Council. The city needs to make it easy and accessible for families with young children to get around. Christchurch buses have bike racks, which is great, but it is too hard to lift a cargo bike onto a bus when you have a toddler. I had all the energy in the world for it, but after two weeks I had to stop. I needed to use the car for my own sanity!

Being less reliant on cars is not just an individual issue; we can't solve this on our own.

We have now put a battery on our cargo bike, which makes it easier. But I feel ambivalent about that. Is the lithium ethically sourced? What will happen to it when it dies eventually? It can get overwhelming, trying to fix one problem but causing another. So I focus on what I can do.

*Has your church supported your thinking around sustainability?*

Yes, it has. Cashmere New Life regularly has a Go Week to support local mission projects.[159] Our family likes to help with the stream restoration project. Our church encourages biking, and we have cycling events. Our Pastor has supported cycling from the front in preaching; she has said that biking is a form of worship and we are caring for the planet. I think it is catching on, slow and steady, and there is scope for more.

*Thank you for your deep insights about surrender and learning how God works through reflecting on the natural world.*

It was too hard for me, trying to make sense of my grief when loved ones became unwell. I could not figure it out. But as I was able to see imperfections and restoration through nature, I could start to process it. God made it less scary. We don't know why bad things happen, but Jesus will make it right in his time. He has this – in his time, not in my time!

I had knee surgery last year, which was tough, but while I was incapacitated my husband managed the kids and our household, just as I had done previously during his period of unwellness. That experience was important for us as a family. Being completely out of action forced me to let go and trust that we are going be OK, and to trust in my husband's wellness again. God spoke to me through that experience. Balance has been brought back to our family.

### Action Point 57: Grow food

People skilled and equipped to create vegetable gardens, both at home and at church.

- Run workshops to encourage gardening, provide gardening buddies, teach kids, build planter boxes, have working bees or a veggie competition.
- Hold a Harvest Festival service and other ways to celebrate wholesome home-grown food in church life.
- Food resources, Eco Church NZ: www.ecochurch.org.nz/food

### Action Point 58: Cycle

Biking as a normal way to get around, including getting to church.

Marg: "A biking lifestyle brings you closer to a rhythm that is sustainable and maintains joy and connection."

- Have a social event on bikes.
- Install a cycle rack at church.
- Biketober and 'Bike to Church Sunday': www.biketoberchch.nz
- Cycling resources, Eco Church NZ: www.ecochurch.org.nz/cycling

### Plenty

*Poem by Ana Lisa de Jong, Living Tree Poetry*

Lack can be a good thing.
Enough in itself
when we focus on the plentiful,
the gifts still amongst us.
Do we not remember
how the fullness of bread
forms itself from yeast
and warmth
and the soft, kneading hands
of love's attentiveness?

Might we
in our lack
measure what we have,
count the things remaining
here at our disposal?
The stuff at hand
to give yet,
in ways we hadn't imagined
or considered in our plenty.

Yes, our palms might sweep across
an emptying shelf,
find an egg, flour, rice,
basics to make nourishment,

and then our hands
might find feet
to lace in shoes
in which to walk
with sole intent
to our neighbour's door.

Yes, did we ever think
the gifts we are given
were to keep?

Perhaps this is the rainy day
for which we have been hoarding our treasures.

What indeed happens to the
things we don't forfeit?
I know there is much I've thrown out
from too much excess,
and a spare shelf
might instead
clear a path for miracles.

# A Tribe of Enthusiasts: Marie Preston

Marie led a faith-based environmental group called God's Earth Our Home for many years. She lives in Pāuatahanui, north of Porirua, where she continues to find creative ways of resourcing the church for creation care, including a recent Low Carbon Cookbook.

It is a pleasure and privilege to be invited to contribute to this book of women tackling the major environmental issues that face Aotearoa New Zealand.

*What is your family background?*

I am a fifth-generation New Zealander, descended on my mother's side from James and Elizabeth Hamlin, missionaries who arrived in Kerikeri in 1826 to serve our land with their skills and Christian faith.[160] I treasure the wealth of historic research on them; it is good to know about this gallant couple who stood alongside the indigenous culture. Elizabeth is a role model for me. I look towards her for guidance and wisdom; she settled in a strange land, bore 12 children, while teaching new skills to Māori with the principles of kindness, aroha and the strength of being female.

*What formed your passion for environmental action?*

I remember a friend back in the 1970s saying to me, "Marie, we should not be using plastic bags." I've never forgotten that. She was conscious of environmental factors back then; she influenced me, and no doubt many others. 50 years later we are in this huge quagmire of the need for climate action. Plastic is one of the worst – we have stuffed up our oceans. We have kai moana in our local harbours that people can't eat.

*And your professional life?*

As a nurse and through all my work and all my care for creation I care for people. I am holistic, because we are all connected. I had three sons and we had animals galore; my job was to see that they were all properly fed and looked after. I have always had a holistic approach. I knew at age nine that I wanted to become a nurse. I remember visiting my mother in Whangarei Hospital and watching her coming down the steps hunched over with pain. I said, "Mum, stand straighter and you will find the pain easier!" I trained and worked as a nurse, then went on to become a nurse educator, with Plunket as an Early Childhood Health Lecturer, and then as a senior lecturer at the College of Education, across the Primary and Early Childhood departments. I had a particular interest in the bicultural journey, and I presented a paper on this at an international ecumenical conference in Sydney.

This career was interrupted when I began my cancer journey, age 49. I kept getting back up on my feet, but the cancer limited my nurse educating role because I was not well enough. So I re-trained in psychotherapy and massage. I was able to carry on my involvement in peace groups and supporting the Royal New Zealand Plunket Society. But I would no sooner get up on my feet and I would get another tumour and then there would be more chemotherapy or radiotherapy or more surgery, God knows what! At one point I collapsed and was basically dead for three days.

They were difficult years. My marriage ended, and it took some time for my children to understand. In 1990 I had attended a Presbyterian Women's conference. I took a workshop on the Treaty of Waitangi and another on grief and dying. At that Conference I met Anne Hadfield, a minister and spiritual director. Little did we know what would unfold from that meeting! We became good friends, and then partners seven years later. She has supported me through 18 cancers and 13 operations and has been deeply caring.

Anne is so steady in her faith and ministry, focused on God and the gift of the Spirit within her. Her wisdom is definitely of the spiritual nature, and I am the practical one. We complement each other. I am very grounded in my personhood. Some of that is because I am trained as a nurse and have healing hands – people have often told me that. But I have had to heal myself first, and then to heal others and the earth.

*What is your faith journey?*

My faith has been shaped by my forebears and many other influential men and women. I believe in a personal God who cares, loves and guides me day by day. God infiltrated my journey as early as my baptism at three months old and then my confirmation at 13 years old. I remember the laying-on of hands, baptising me with the gift of the Holy Spirit.

I started out Anglican, and am now back in an Anglican church, but I was a Presbyterian, including an Elder, for 30 years. My husband and I lived in Tawa where I was a contributing member of St. Christopher's Anglican parish. When life got quite complicated and difficult I stopped attending church for several weeks until I decided to walk just down the road to the Linden Presbyterian church. The minister and his wife supported me enormously. I especially remember one time after a service she came over to me and said, "Jesus is well pleased with you." It was so spontaneous, so beautiful. They encouraged me to do Education For Ministry and I led camps and did all sorts of things.

Over the long years there have been times when I have wavered, wondered, doubted and queried this amazing God presence in my life. However, I have not turned my back for long. Faith is a mystery, humankind is complex, and at times there are difficult situations, but my God is a loving presence in mind, body and spirit, always encouraging, supportive and gentle. Each day I maintain this personal relationship through routines of prayer and meditation, and I continue to learn. Spiritual mentoring and supervision were important too. I was in responsible positions involving people from many walks of life and it was important for me to have support, teaching and guidance. I have been blessed with family, friends, amazingly good people who have guided me, encouraged me and supported my endeavours to 'do what I do' for others. I am who I am. God has led me step by step along many stages and transitions.

My partner Anne is Presbyterian. She has worked for the Presbyterian Church of Aotearoa New Zealand in Parish Development and Mission and been a Spiritual Director and trainer, helping to found Spiritual Growth Ministries.[161] 15 years ago we made the decision to move to Pāuatahanui; which church would we join? We had deep respect for the then priest at the Pāuatahanui Anglican church. After we put an offer on a house Anne said, "If we get this house, I will join the Anglican tradition." We got the house and we joined the church here and we love it. At times like that we very much felt that God was blessing our relationship. Every time something amazing happens she will look at me and say, "We are meant to be together, aren't we!"

Both Anne and I are blessed to have children and we are very grateful for that. We came to our relationship in mid-life and of course that has not been easy. There are very, very few gay or lesbian or transgender people in the church. Most of our lesbian friends have left the church.

*Why do you stay?*

Anne and I have remained very faithful to the church. I am faithful because I have lived through 18 tumours and I am still alive, which is an absolute miracle! People have seen our strong commitment to each other and to God.

So I have come back to my Anglican roots, and Anne has been happy here. Dan Ross came to our parish last year to be our vicar. He didn't bat an eyelid about our relationship. Anne is now approaching her 82nd birthday and she is also returning to her roots; she says, "Marie, I am a mystic." We read from *Of Monks, Mystics and Martyrs* each day.[162]

*How did God's Earth Our Home (GEOH) get started?*

Anne and I would meditate together – that time of listening and being quiet and bringing the issues before God has been an important contributor. I had been reading about environmental issues. In 2006 we moved to the Pāuatahanui Parish and we were invited to share our combined gifts in ministry and mission. We chose as our priority to focus on the environment, to highlight the fifth Face of Mission, care for the integrity of creation. We embraced this fully and the parish was supportive. Our idea was to get a group to meet together regularly; so Anne and I initiated God's Earth Our Home – although I was quite ill at the time.

*How was GEOH organised?*

We put out some initial publicity. I said to Anne, "It needs to go out on the network through the churches." Yours truly is a born organiser! Right from the word 'go' between 18 to 24 people came every month, from around the region and from various churches, which was wonderful. We met monthly; alternating between one month of theological and scientific discussion then the next month getting out doing practical projects. We did a whole heap of stuff in the community! We were always open to learning, to give and receive the wisdom of the environment. The Porirua area is diverse, rich in resources as it is rich with willing people, cultural diversity and good leadership.

Sometimes Anne would lead, brought her deep understanding of scripture and the people skills she is gifted with. Sometimes I would lead and sometimes we had scientists speak: biologists, horticulturalists. Leadership changed over time. I would initiate something, do it for a while and then I'd get another flipping tumour! So somebody else would carry the baton and I would just be there to support or provide food. The movement unfolded. It was a time for healing and a time to make true friends. The group formed a close bond – a tribe of enthusiasts!

We were fully independent, which we valued. We were invited to join A Rocha and Caritas but it felt a bit overwhelming to join another group. We treasured the uniqueness of what we were doing.

We could access money if needed. Initially we each contributed an annual subscription to buy resources but then moved to fundraising as necessary for specific projects.

It was faith based, no doubt about that. St Francis of Assisi was very influential in our thinking. As a group we read, studied, learned and prayed, embracing St Francis' thought and attempting the action where possible. In 2015 Pope Francis published 'Laudato Si' the Encyclical letter on Ecology and Climate.[163] This document informed the group and undergirded the principles of GEOH.

I heard how Bishop John Bluck would call all the Christchurch priests together at the beginning of every year to do a pilgrimage. I was inspired, and decided to begin every year with a walk for the parish and GEOH. We prayed together outside and introduced people to the environment. Those walks were very well supported.

## What practical projects did you do?

We did beach clean ups. We did cockle counts. We planted trees, sometimes in difficult places. We planted out a nursery. We taught how to do composting and worm farms. Some of our conservation projects were with Forest and Bird, including on Mana Island. We supported water management, both local and regional.

We helped get a community garden started at the church, blessed and planted by the members of the Parish. Ten years ago, a young mum who came to our Noah's Ark children's ministry got involved with the community garden. Rebecca Morahan saw a real need to support new mothers with food after the birth of a baby, and she helped set up Bellyful in Porirua.[164] The Bellyful project picks the greens and other vegetables and then gives the produce to families in need. Rebecca went on to co-found the WELLfed cooking classes.[165] This is an amazing story of love, energy and good will. I revel in all that God is able to achieve through God's loved ones! Ministry outreach is always needed and God always provides. I say: "Do what you can, with what you have, and God offers the rest."

*How did you connect the practical action with worship?*

We contributed to worship in services during Lent, Advent and the Season of Creation in September. Once a year we held a combined service on the theme of Creation. We heard from Māori and from Pacific nations, weeping with them as we listened, wondering how best we could offer support and encouragement. We joined occasionally with the local Catholic community to share resources. We celebrated and commiserated what was happening to the environment. We would sing together beautiful hymns such as 'How Great Thou Art' 'Amazing Grace' and New Zealand hymns on the theme of creation.

*How did GEOH come to an end?*

God's Earth Our Home stopped meeting a couple of years ago after our previous vicar left and Covid came. The lockdowns created by Covid-19 were difficult, especially for those in retirement villages who were very shut off. It was hard to sustain the cohesion that is so much a part of Parish life. It was a fallow time, with changes in leadership and energy.

GEOH came to an end partly because of our 'aging and staging'. Most of the group are my age or older, into their 80s. Some have a greater Spirit focus, praying more; their lives are quieter now. Many live in retirement villages or have moved away. Some have died. We still see GEOH people from time to time. We continue to talk about environmental issues and how to live sustainably: what to plant, how to reduce, recycle or reuse. Transport issues change as you get older. We feel guilty when we have to drive: if the weather is too cold, wet or miserable or if we are unwell. One of the practical things that many people are doing is reducing plastic. My cookbook encourages people to avoid buying plastic and not use cling wrap.

Now Eco Church is unfolding in our parish from our GEOH roots. Our new Eco Group met earlier this year. We decided to embark on a number of actions to lower our carbon emissions: we would act, we would make a difference, we would be a witness to others by our actions! One person said, "I will reduce my use of plastic"; another said, "Let's set rat traps in the church grounds"; another said, "I will find out more about solar power"; another said, "I am making compost and looking forward to growing more vegetables." And all those things have happened! I said, "How about a cookbook?" So I embarked on collecting recipes to promote lower carbon eating, as part of the Diocese of Wellington's Low Carbon Challenge.[166] It sold out and raised over $700 for the 'Get one, give one' appeal for vaccine aid.[167] I am delighted that it is of interest to old and young alike.

*What you see as the environmental issues with food?*
Reducing waste is the biggest issue. The 158,000 tonnes of food waste in New Zealand each year is appalling.[168] Absolutely appalling. We are too spoiled. People have to learn how to cook and to use what they have got. Buy local, eat regularly, minimise waste. As an educator I'm always building up people's skills. It is a central mission principle: 'Give a man a fish and he eats for a day; teach a man how to fish and he eats for a lifetime'.

Climate change will bring challenges for our food supply, as the eastern parts of our country become drier and there are more violent storms and unpredictable weather. How we care for our fresh water is a massive issue.

*Do you promote a vegetarian diet?*
I do encourage people to not eat meat every day. Have a couple of meat-free days each week and learn more about cooking vegetables in delicious ways. From a carbon perspective we should not to be eating imported meat. And from a health perspective it is not good to eat highly processed meats. But Kiwi lamb, for instance, is very good for us.

As a nurse educator I taught a lot about diets. I would get students to write diaries of what they ate and get them to check their haemoglobin levels. We found that those who ate vegan were often very anaemic. That can have big impacts on energy levels and fertility. The Bible encourages eating some meat, particularly for festivals, feasts and celebrations; but in Biblical times they certainly would not have eaten meat every day.

The other major health thing is to not eat too much. Unless you are working on a farm or doing manual work you don't need a large quantity of food or protein. I teach cooking to create good quality food, and then you eat less. Our diets need to reflect our energy levels.

*What is your vision for Eco Church?*
The world is in crisis. Climate change is real and people need to be better informed and more involved. Transformation in ourselves and others is imperative. Christians can be involved in all sorts of ways, like signing petitions, attending workshops, looking at positive ways to support, both practically and financially. I also see the value of regular prayer and meditation.

It is exciting to see new people getting involved and more congregational members taking an enthusiastic interest. Energy and commitment is growing and we are starting to make notable progress. We value Amy's leadership and wisdom. I pray that within God's timing the principles of Eco Church will infiltrate the heart and soul of parish life. My vision is for an environmentally inclusive church embracing all the principles of Christian community.

It is marvellous that young families are involved. We now have up to 30 children at our church – that is the power of karakia! Anne would often say, "If we do not invest in youth ministry, we won't have a church."

The vision of Eco Church is for all to live a faithful life, following the leadership of Jesus. It means loving our neighbours as ourselves and sharing resources fairly. We want to reflect and protect the glory that is God in our world.

## Margaret's Mushroom Bake Recipe

*Margaret Ogilvie*

Vegetarian, quick and easy, yummy. Serves four. Good for lunch or a dinner dish with salad.

### Ingredients:

- Mushrooms (approx. 250g) – sliced
- 1 Onion – chopped finely
- Tomatoes (either a tin or ½kg fresh) – chopped
- Breadcrumbs (approx. 2 cups) – a great way to use stale bread, can be crumbed in a blender.
- Parsley (a handful) – chopped
- Lemon – zest and juice
- 75g Butter – melted
- 50g Nuts – walnuts, almonds or hazelnuts (optional)
- Salt & pepper to taste
- 125g Cheese (any kind) – grated

## Method:

- Heat oven to 180C (fan bake). Grease oven dish.
- Gently fry onion in a little oil, then add the mushrooms, fry. Then tomato and heat through. Optional: add other veggies, e.g. zucchini, silverbeet.
- Blend together the breadcrumbs, parsley, lemon juice & rind, nuts with butter, salt and pepper (preferably in a blender, or mash by hand).
- Place half of the breadcrumb mixture in the dish.
- Spread the onion, mushroom and tomato over the bread mixture.
- Cover with most of the cheese.
- Top with the rest of the breadcrumbs and grated cheese.
- Cook until golden, about 50 minutes. Serve and enjoy!

## Let's Say Grace

*Karakia to say before a meal:*

Whakapaingia ēnei kai (*Bless this food*)
Hei oranga mo ō mātou tinana (*to give life to our bodies*)
Ko Ihu Karaiti tō mātou kaiwhakaora (*through Jesus our saviour*)
Āmene. (*Amen.*)

For life and health and daily food
we give you thanks O God.
For fellowship and all things good,
we praise your name O Lord. Amen.

We thank you, God, for happy hearts,
for rain and sunny weather.
We thank you, God, for this our food,
and that we are together.

We close our eyes, we bow our heads
and offer thanks for daily bread.
For friends and family near and far,
for forests, rivers, sun and star.
For oceans, mountains, fern and stone
for all we feel, for love and home.

### Action Point 59: Eat healthy – for you and the planet

How might you use the talents of the people in your church to promote healthy eating? Maybe…

- Put together a church recipe book
- Run cooking classes for the community
- Have a vegetarian shared meal, or celebrate diverse cultures' food
- Involve all ages!
- Food resources, Eco Church NZ: www.ecochurch.org.nz/food
- More recipes and tips at Love Food Hate Waste: www.lovefoodhatewaste.co.nz
- 'Eat Low Carbon' GenLess: www.genless.govt.nz/for-everyone/everyday-life/eat-low-carbon
- Research report 'Healthy and Climate-Friendly Eating Patterns in the New Zealand Context' Environmental Health Perspectives, January 2020: https://ehp.niehs.nih.gov/doi/pdf/10.1289/EHP5996

# Tiakina te Taiao, Tiakina te Iwi: Mina Pomare-Peita

*Look after the environment and it will look after the people.*

Mina Pomare-Peita is Principal of Te Kura Taumata o Panguru, a Māori Area School in Panguru, Hokianga. Mina is a driving force behind Noho Taiao Māori youth science programme. She is embarking on a PhD on engaging Māori young people in understanding and caring for the environment.

*How was life for you growing up?*

My name is Mina Pomare-Peita. I am from Panguru which is in north Hokianga. My main tribe is Te Rarawa. I still live and work in Panguru, my kāinga – born and bred in the Hokianga.

Growing up we had a dairy farm. I have eight siblings. I'm the eldest of three girls and we have six brothers – seven born but one of the twins died young – most of them older than me. My sisters and I all became teachers.

As well as a dairy farmer our father was a hunter gatherer, up in the Warawara Forest, our ngahere. No cell phones – I don't know how Mum knew when to go and pick them up but she always did! He would go up there with the men and the boys for a few days and bring home meat and other bush delicacies. We grew up eating wood pigeons, though we knew it's illegal. I still salivate at the thought of eating kūkupa!

key understandings. First, when we live as kaitiaki we belong; what we do matters for the common good. Second, kaitiaki work together with creation to strengthen the obligation we have as children of Creator God. Third, learning about and taking action to live as a kaitiaki brings increased hauora (wellbeing) to all our relationships.

The outcome? A curriculum document called 'Te Warawara, Te Wairua o te iwi o Te Rarawa: A teacher's guide for nurturing kaitiakitanga of the Warawara Forest'.

Catholic principles underpin all the resources, and connect with the youth. As Māori we acknowledge our Creator, our relationship with Atua. We live in a relationship with Atua (God) and tāngata (people) and whenua (land). This had to be a foundational part of our curriculum; it is fundamental to who we are as Māori people.

*Does your whānau have a long story with the Catholic church? There is amazing history there, especially in the North.*

Yes indeed. I whakapapa (descend) from one of the first women to meet Bishop Pompellier when he came to New Zealand in 1838. Her name was Ana Ngapiu. She was only four years old but she vividly recalled meeting him. She was the daughter of an English blacksmith and a Māori mum, over in Paihia. She lived till she was 106.

*What is Katorika? What does it mean for you to be Catholic?*

I argue about that – I say we are not 'Roman'. We are post-Roman! We are definitely Māori and we are definitely Catholic. We are Katorika because our ancestors agreed to the faith, and I value that. We honour our heritage, with discernment. I have immense faith in the resilience and knowledge of my people.

Let's not throw everything out the window. There is an abundance of negativity around the Catholic church, worldwide as well as nationally. We can listen to that – we can sit on our laurels, and say, "Oh, those ancestors, what were they thinking, for goodness sake?!" Or we can engage and work with it, to see where we can really add value to the church. I have seen it and history shows it: our ancestors were not silly. They made these choices in the best interests of their people, for the greater good.

My relationship with Atua was enhanced by the words of Pope John Paul II. I was there in 1986 when he spoke in the Auckland Domain – that was 35 years ago but I remember it like it was yesterday. The Pope said: "It is as Māori that the Lord has called you. It is as Māori that you belong to the church, the body of Christ." I was 22, a university student, there with my parents. I had only been half listening but that stopped me in my tracks. I was ecstatic!! Kua poho kererū (my chest stood out like a wood pigeon). For me this confirmed that I was OK. As a Māori Catholic woman, who grew up in a Māori Catholic home and community, I had the right to be here and I was valued.

I thought, "Now we have permission to be right up there with the priests!" I grew up listening to priests from overseas. They had a big say in our community, like the mayor of the Catholic community, and I didn't like that. I thought to myself: "I don't know you. I would rather listen to my Papa than to you. My Papa has a lot of mana."

In the early days our parish did not have a priest and our chiefs ran our church. They would bring what they had been taught and share with the people. Our faith was whakatō (planted) by our own ancestors.

*What would you name as the pono, the key truths that you were taught as a Catholic woman?*

To be pono, faithful. We were all brought up with the guilt thing – guilt goes hand in hand with Catholicism. But far more than that I am blessed with what anyone wants: to be loved, to be valued, nothing less.

The key truth is: we are human and God is a living God. God is everywhere. The resurrection tells us that God is alive. That warms my heart, to know that's what my ancestors brought us up believing: God's not dead, God is living! Ehara tō tatou nei Atua i te Atua mate. He Atua ora!

*How do you experience that on a daily basis?*

There are miracles everywhere – you just have to look for them. They pop up and you acknowledge "That is a miracle!" A young father visited me in my office recently, feeling desperate. I hear it a lot: they can't do this and they can't do that, because of the Covid. It is a common āhua (attitude) people have these days. They turn up to the Principal's office to see if I can give them the answer. And basically my answer is this: "There are miracles everywhere. You just need to look for them and acknowledge them." This man looked at me: "What do you mean?" And I said:

"Sure, we are not getting busloads of people tuning up to this or that event because of Covid. But I see your two children at sports every Friday, and your sister's children. We are so blessed to have such beautiful young people growing up during this time. Those young children see me and run up to me, '"Hi Whaea Mina!' hug my legs, and I give them big cuddles, because

I am grateful for them. They are miracles. They are our future. So instead of hoping for somebody to come and help us, let's love those who are here." Every day I look for the miracles around me. That's not to say that I don't have bad days. Of course I do. But even in that, before I go to bed I think: 'What is something I can be grateful for?'

*How about Mary – is she central to your faith?*

Absolutely. I say the Rosary every day at 12 o'clock. Mary is a big part of my wairuatanga. I didn't understand why until I got older. I didn't realize that other hāhi (churches) did not acknowledge her, and thought that Catholics worshipped her. I remember being quite affronted – "What do you mean?!"

This takes me back to my Master's degree. For my thesis I wrote about the impact of schooling on Māori boys. I grew up with six brothers and lots of male cousins. I watched them leave home to go to school as confident bright young men. But they would come home insecure, feeling that they were failures. Their schooling made them feel they were unintelligent. I became aware of the abundance of negative images of Māori men, and the historical processes that have impacted negatively on Māori men.

When I was just getting started I was challenged by some women in a tutorial. They said to me, "Who are you to speak for Māori men?" I thought, "Oh. I don't know. OK." This was the early 1980s, a time of very strong mana-wahine (feminism), to the point of being anti-men. I felt put down. I lost all my words and motivation. I was too shy to articulate my whānau values about the important role of women in advocating for men. I got totally put off and decided I would have to find another topic. After a few weeks my mother noticed that I was not doing any writing, but it took me some time to get up the courage to tell her that I had been put down for wanting to be a mouthpiece for Māori men to help them express their views.

My mother said to me: "Men need us. As women we speak for them when they need us to. Through Mary we are liberated. Through women, men are made strong to fulfil their role, the role that has been given to them and blessed for them to fulfil. Women are part of that and you must do that!" I looked at my mother and I thought, "Yeah!!" And I wrote my thesis in six weeks!

The intercession of Mary to God and to Jesus is something I have been taught, told about and taken to heart. She has a very important role. Every day I work on understanding Mary and her role as intercessor. Mary is a way of being, building up other people; she is a pathway to God. For me it is on the level of 'the work to be done'. Every day I am learning it. It is a journey, but I get it.

One day I challenged my Dad about why Māori women can't be Katakita (Catechists, lay ministers) and he said to me, "Let the men speak, but when they cannot speak then you must speak for them." That has been a powerful message in my life. I have felt recently that the time has come for me to speak up in the church, that the men need that, so I have gone to meetings of the Archdiocese for the first time and I stood up to speak. Other women have been going to these meetings but they just make the tea!

I don't worry about what to say. I aspire to walk my talk all the time. And I also aspire for what comes out of my mouth to be transcribed into writing. I've had a number of role models that I've looked up to over the years, like Rangimarie Rose Pere, she was one of my favourites. She was very much an inspirational speaker, and when you read what she wrote – ako! You get it.

*So how do you see your role, your calling?*

There are lots of reasons why women like myself are involved in the politics of our own whānau, our communities, our iwi. For me, I am the eldest daughter in a family of 10. From as long as I can remember I was trained, taught and mentored by my parents to be the one to be spokesperson for the whānau, our community and tribe; to do the work of finding solutions. My siblings would say, hand on heart, that I am the māngai (mouthpiece) for them.

I love my people. I observe the unfairness they face, such as how the mana of Māori boys is diminished in the education system. I still see my people not living their best lives and I want to do something about this. We need to stop focusing on the inadequacies and limitations of marginalized groups in this country and start treating all as equals. We can accept that we have Te Tiriti o Waitangi and The Treaty of Waitangi, and we can rewrite our future together. My learning from this pandemic is that we can do much to improve our relationships in this country. The lockdown showed us all that we can love, show love and give love.

*How do you understand whenua and moana? What is your theology of creation?*

I know inherently, and also from having the stories around me, that we are not unto ourselves. There is a greater divinity. I have felt it. I feel it all the time. I remember as a little girl I went out to the field to find my father, and he was talking to someone but I could not see who he was talking to. I could feel the Wairua there with him. And I feel it as I have got older, the spiritual essence and the mauri of a place. Even when I was young, I knew: "Human beings didn't make this. Something greater than us created this!"

The school of thought I have been brought up with is all about the relationship between Tāngata, Whenua and Atua. You cannot have one without the others. Atua is the Creator and we must always acknowledge Atua. We are reclaiming our knowledge about the domains of the whenua. In our world we have the deity of the forest, Tāne Māhuta, and of the Moana, Tangaroa, and all of the others. In my mind and understanding, they are the kaitiaki, and Atua is the Creator of all. We respect all the tamariki of Tāne Māhuta and Tangaroa. You would be silly to think that man is the highest species. Not at all. In fact we are the pōtiki. Humans are the last ones to come along.

*What is your work as a principal, leading in environmental education?*

It is quite simple: Tiakina te taiao, tiakina te iwi. If we look after the taiao, the taiao will look after the people. This is our whakataukī, that came about when we started our Noho Taiao camps. Noho Taiao started off initially because a colleague and I could see that our students were not passing in the sciences. My colleague was a physicist. I had science in my degree and an interest and love for the environment. We paired our skills together, filled in a few application forms, none of which were funded, so we decided to just go ahead and do it anyway. That was 13 years ago, and now the programme is well established; all our costs get covered, funding is not a problem. It is supported by our iwi Te Rūnanga o Te Rarawa, and the Northland Regional Council and the Far North District Council have also got involved.

*So why is it growing?*

Because the model works. Our model is four days on a marae in the summer holidays with 50 taitamariki from 13 to 18 years old – if they're only 12 they can't come and once they turn 18 we kick them out. We had to start small. I don't like to be exclusive but I knew we had to keep it tight. It is only for our tribal children, who whakapapa to Te Rarawa. The young people come from all over the place: from the South Island, from Sydney, from America, because they whakapapa back here to the Hokianga.

There is lots of science. A really important aspect of our model is that Crown Research Institutes help us run the program and give strong science input. We work with Geographical and Natural Sciences (GNS), NIWA (National Institute of Water and Atmosphere) and Plant and Food Research. How many reports are written that they want to consult, consult, consult with Māori?! But they are insulting us by not consulting with us in our way. So we get them to come and they teach us their stuff. Crown Research Institutes advise the government on policy and they have really awesome scientists – let's get the best people!

We have set up internships. GNS never had internships before, but has now decided to continue them every year. We want our young people to go into career pathways in science fields, to become geologists, physicists, environmentalists. The research institutes wanted to connect with Māori but did not know how, so we are the best thing since sliced bread for them! It has been great. One of our own people has now been appointed to the GNS Board – he comes with a wealth of knowledge – as a result of being involved with Noho Taiao.

*What happens on the Noho?*

It is unique, marae-based. We stay on a marae (one of 23 marae in our iwi rohe, region) and travel to two others to do environmental activities. For example going up to Pukepoto or Ahipara marae to do water monitoring in their dune lakes and their awa (river), or going to Pawarenga and walking up the Warawara to look at the kauri or collect rongoā plants.

It breaks down so many barriers for Māori taitamariki. They get to learn outside, not just in a classroom. Not everything has to be written down to retain knowledge; they learn through waiata (songs) and pūrākau (stories). Matauranga Taiao is Māori knowledge of the environment from a Māori worldview. It is real, it is valid. It is validated by our people and it belongs to them.

Noho Taiao is a strategy to get our taitamariki involved in the oranga or wellbeing of our iwi. We provide role models and opportunities to look at the issues that impact on us as a hapū and iwi.

All along the way it is a deliberate act of teaching that we empower our taitamariki's confidence in their culture, that they are safe to be Māori. We want our young people to connect with their marae, embed cultural identity and learn about themselves. Not all our Māori kids know who they are or where they come from. Not all of them have our language. Not all of them have a tūrangawaewae, a place they call Home, because they have been urbanised.

In 1975 the Waitangi Tribunal was set up so that Māori iwi could present their case for why their land should come back to them. But we now have to teach our young people about the environment so that they understand the land that is being returned to them in Treaty settlements. They have to go into the land and learn to love the environment.

And from there we have to create an oranga for them, a living, economy and income. Oranga is a pathway to wellbeing. That's what we want for our rangatahi. I don't expect them all to come back and live off the land, but they can all contribute. As we contribute to the environmental infrastructure of our country there are more people at the table.

Both our Te Warawara curriculum and the Noho Taiao are contributing to the strategic goals of our iwi: that Te Rarawa people look after the environment so that it sustains their communities, and that Te Rarawa people are educated to achieve their full potential and support the development of the tribe.

*Do you see this growing into the future?*

Absolutely! Our model is now being used in other tribal groups; my colleagues and I work with them. It is meeting needs. And we have added a winter programme, where we get dirty. We plant trees, do workshops such as with rongoā. With the Covid it is even more important that they learn about rongoā (medicinal plants) and how to grow and transplant them. There are certain ways to do that.

*Young people live in this crazy world with climate change, urbanisation and poverty in all its impacts. How do you want to equip them to deal with the massive problems they face?*

They must never be impoverished in knowledge. No matter what, don't be a victim in your own head. It's as simple as that. I said to someone the other day, "Do us a favour, come home and teach your child how to read." Matauranga matters, education and knowledge matter. When our children are engaging for themselves, the world is their oyster!

*Young people struggle with a lot of anxiety about the future. How do you see that?*

At first I didn't understand it. I said to a colleague: "I was never an anxious child, so I don't understand. Can you explain it to me?" She gave me insight into what feeds anxiety in our young people. Wow. Ka aroha. I feel love for these kids. The biggest thing we have to plant in our children is resilience, to have faith.

The social media world has its positives but it has huge negatives. It has become normal, through Facebook and all other social media platforms, to give mana (kudos) to strangers and their judgements. It is very damaging to young people's mental health. I want to say to them: "Listen to those who care. Don't listen to Facebook. Listen to real people. And if you can't find any real people in your life, call us!"

Kanohi ki te kanohi (face to face) relationships is what I cry for. That's what we need to be doing, building strong relationships with our young people. That will build their resilience and build their mana.

*You were interviewed for a Caritas video on the Oceania environment and you talked about decolonisation. That is a big word – what do you mean by that?*

We have been programmed by Western frameworks of thinking, how things have to be done: Gregorian time, linear 'this, this and this'. We are trying to decolonise ourselves from some ways we have learned. We are in an age now where our people are reclaiming their knowledge around the maramataka (the calendar) for example. When you learn how the maramataka works you learn a different school of thought and that supports other ways of thinking. That is decolonisation.

It is important so that we can understand climate change. At the moment we are only touching the surface because we were not taught to observe for ourselves. Tirotiro (observation) was taken out of the education system. So our people don't understand climate change. We are told to do this, do that, pay for this, reduce this, recycle that, cut carbon emissions. But we need to understand why we should do those things. Then we will do it and do it well. If we only do what we are told to do from outside, that is just lip service. We have started to look at this in its entirety, so that we understand climate change as a whole, from who we are as Māori. Then it will be much more sustainable and impactful for the next generation.

Mauri ora i roto i te ingoa tapu o Hehu Kerito.

*Blessings in the sacred name of Jesus Christ.*

Kia ora rā.

## Whakawātea

*This is an uplifting karakia that my mother taught me for when I was afraid and needed strength.*

E te Ariki
whakawātea i ahau i te otaota
kia maranga ai ahau ki runga
whakawātea ahau i te taurekareka
kia maranga ai ahau ki runga
whakawātea ahau i te ngoikoretanga kia toa
kia mataara kia tu kaha ai ahau ki runga.
Āmene.

Dear Lord,
Clear the weeds and the clutter and lift me up
Dissolve the shame and the chains and set me free
Overcome my weakness and give me strength
Wake me up so I stand strong with you.
Amen.

## Action Point 60: Connect with young people

Take every opportunity to build relationships with young people. Send them messages to remind them that you care. Go walking or cycling together, nurture their love of nature. Encourage an interest in creation through science, art and conservation. Share with them what motivates you. But mostly, just love them!

## Action Point 61: Join Caritas

Subscribe with Caritas Aotearoa New Zealand to be part of their action for environmental justice: www.caritas.org.nz

# Unveiling Nature: Nicola Hoggard Creegan

Nicola is Co-Director for New Zealand Christians in Science and chairs the board of A Rocha Aotearoa New Zealand. She lives in Auckland and is part of All Saints Anglican Church, Ponsonby. This chapter is based on Nicola's lecture at the Wellington Theological Consortium Seminar 'Caring for Our Common Homeland'.[169]

*Where did you come from?*

I am a fifth generation New Zealander from Irish, English, Scottish and European origins. If I were choosing mountains I would choose two: Ruapehu and Mt Kaukau, because Ruapehu was visible and on fire when I was very young in Taupō, and I climbed Kaukau constantly when I was growing up in Wellington. My river, however, would be the Thames, signifying my deep and surprising resonance with the English countryside and cities. When I first visited England I felt an immediate, visceral and unexpected connection to its landscape, which has seen me returning frequently, although always as a foreigner. In these connections I have experienced how as humans we can be very drawn to nature, but political and cultural considerations can make our connection very conflicted.

Speaking of whakapapa, I would like to start with a tribute to my mother who died in August 2021, in the first week of a Covid lockdown. She was a life-long understated green activist, and a botanist by training, from a time before the environmental movement was mainstream. For many years she taught students at Marsden and then at Kāpiti College biology and mathematics, and took them on tramping trips, teaching a whole generation of students to love nature. In Waikanae she organised regular beach clean-ups and plantings on the dunes until she was well into her 80s. Her last task before her stroke was to name all the native trees in the vast Parkwood retirement complex.

*How was faith a part of your life as a child?*

My mother also features in my story because she became a Roman Catholic, and my childhood was spent navigating the boundary between Catholic and Protestant. My parents were married in the Anglican church, before my father brought her into the Catholic church and they got married again.

The dominant feature of my childhood was Roman Catholicism, brought into more vivid focus by living constantly on religious boundaries. I was an intense, religious child. I took the whole drama of salvation very seriously: who was in and who was out. I realised that all my wider family, to whom I was very close, were in jeopardy of eternal damnation. So were my parents. And so was I, because mortal sin was so easy! That meant that I experienced personally what has been one of the big deterrents to an eco approach in the Church; if we are dividing people up, one from the other, then we won't be concentrating on God's concern for nature.

But more than that – I was taught explicitly that at death the spirits of humans go up to God and those of animals go down into the ground. I loved the natural world, but that teaching was like a switch in my heart turning off – I was much less interested in animals after that.

Life like this can be exhausting. I came to a crisis of faith at the tender age of 11 when I read the story of a Muslim child who was more religious than I was. But soon afterwards I had an epiphany: I was introduced to the work of Teilhard de Chardin. I overheard a radio program on de Chardin, while I was meant to be sleeping. I was transfixed and began to read all his books. They gave me a new vision of the whole of life on earth and of evolution as swept into a spiritual continuum, with its omega point in the cosmic Christ. That vision has never left me. Even though I thought I was not a believer, in the fluidity of youth I was able to hold this together with an attraction to de Chardin.

*What influenced you as a young adult?*

At university I studied mathematics, as a form of secular theology. I was always amazed at the way in which ideas in our minds can be uncannily true to the natural world. The mathematics department at Victoria University of Wellington at that time, under Wilf Malcolm, was predominantly Christian, which was unusual, and it kept the issue of faith alive for me.

I came back to Christianity at L'Abri in England. This is a Christian community in Switzerland, England and the US which exists to allow young people to question and come to faith; to experience hospitality, to work on the land, and to dialogue together with students from around the world. Although I came back to faith somewhat cautiously, I fell totally in love with the English countryside. Since that time I have known that gardening, long walks in nature, and faith all go together.

I was drawn to the United States to study theology. I knew that persisting in faith was not going to be easy, and that I needed to study it to sustain it. I was inspired by these words from Psalm 71:18,

> Even when I am old, do not abandon me until I tell of your wonders to generations who are to come.

I did a Masters of Theology, and then completed a doctorate at Drew University in New Jersey. In the intense study of systematic theology I was plunged back into the drama of salvation, and into a complex discipline which at that time had very few edges open to science. This was the era in which theology was dominated by Karl Barth, whose 'Sola Scriptura' approach had little need for the natural world. However, a number of influences from that time would influence my future eco-theology.

One was Jonathan Edwards, known as the father of the great awakening in the 18th century, the author of *Sinners in the Hands of an Angry God*. But he had another side; he was a close observer of nature, and was overcome with the reality of love at every level of creation. Flowers and plants, and spiders and the laws of nature all reflect God, as lower forms of love manifest in harmony and symmetry. From Edwards I learned that nature is signing to us. Creation speaks. Edwards spent many hours observing the habits of small creatures, which informed his book *Images and Shadows of Divine Things*.[170]

The other was Friedrich Schleiermacher, the 19th century theologian who was first of all a Universalist, believing that everyone was elect in Christ. He also saw continuities in consciousness between levels of nature and in the animal kingdom. Human consciousness can discern nature as a whole. We are dependent on God who is beyond nature but visible within it. He talks about the, "infinite being known within the finite." He wrote that the Incarnation opens up the, "supernatural within the natural."

A third significant influence for me is process theology. This gives a vision of continuity of life, vitality and God-presence at every level of creation, from stones and atoms to humans. Even elementary particles have 'prehension'.

All things participate both in the material, which we can see, touch and hear, and also in the spiritual.

And I should not forget the voices of women and the dominance of feminism in the 1980s. Women's voices from the past were being discovered, and there has always been a deep link between feminism and eco-theology. Feminist theology has always been more inspired by the earth, more cognisant of embodiment, more aware of power dynamics and more resistant of patriarchy than the traditional Western canon.

These influences prepared me to think about nature and God together, but it was not a straight line from there to eco-theology. Theology has a way of drawing you in to its problems and complexities. American theology was very open to public issues, and I engaged with these modalities before I embraced the harder questions of science and faith. I lived for a while in the American south. My second child was born as the Gulf war was starting in January 1991. Planes were leaving for the Middle East and bombing was starting. I had an overwhelming sense that damage was being done, to people and the environment, which would never be made right. But all around me Americans were cheered by the bombing. Some welcomed Armageddon and with it the drama of salvation, dividing the saved from the unsaved, yet again!

*What roles have you had since?*

After my doctorate I taught in various roles in small liberal arts colleges in North Carolina, and at Shaw University, an African American college.

The 1990s saw a growing respect for the relationship between theology and science, prompted partly by investment from the John Templeton Foundation. I began to relate my love of theology and love of science together. In the late 1990s I taught a course 'Biology and Religion: Questions at the Interface' with students from both biology and religious studies. I remember there was a religion major, the daughter of a Washington DC pastor, who did not believe she was a mammal. I didn't have to say anything, the biology majors did it all, and the course became a long meditation on being a human animal and yet being made in the image of God. We thought deeply about that central mystery, how we partake of both the animal and the divine. My childhood turning away from animals was cured to some extent. I began to listen more openly to my children's pleas for a pet.

I returned to Aotearoa New Zealand with my family in 2000 to lecture at Laidlaw College. Teaching in an evangelical context does not necessarily make eco-theology easy. Theology's engagement with science seemed to most students and staff at Laidlaw at that time to either be wrong, eccentric or unimportant compared to the 'real stuff' of evangelism.

A very hopeful sign was the Māori renaissance in New Zealand, which had grown while I was overseas. I have always felt a strong affinity with the Māori spirit-filled holistic understanding of nature. In Aotearoa this has kept open a lifeline to more integrated and more spiritual thinking, in institutions otherwise quite hostile to faith.

What did keep me sane was a connection to a small group of Christians who formed the kernel of A Rocha Aotearoa New Zealand: Kristel van Houte, Richard Storey, John Flenley, and Andrew and Ingrid Shepherd. I was a part of the fledgling A Rocha and have journeyed with them ever since. I am currently the Board Chair. I am not the most useful tree planter, and I am positively a hindrance when it comes to traps, but every now and then I try. My contribution is trying to think theologically about creation and sustainability. For more than ten years we were seen as the left wing eccentric edge of the church, as way-out Christian 'greenies' not to be taken seriously, struggling for recognition or funds. That is beginning to change. We have now launched Eco Church NZ and this is growing rapidly as churches engage with the theological and missional challenges of our environmental crisis.

I am currently co-director of New Zealand Christians in Science/Te Kāhui Whakapono ki Nga Kaipūtaiao o Aotearoa (NZCIS), an organization with close ties to A Rocha. NZCIS seeks to support scientists and students who are Christians, and to provide venues and spaces for education and dialogue in the science/faith interface. We have a mission to those who are scientists, but also to the wider public, to be a witness to dialogue and integration between worldviews and explanatory systems that are often seen to be in conflict. At NZCIS we rejoice in the unity of all knowledge, and the way in which science uncovers more and greater mysteries and wonders and levels of interconnection all the time. Although science has been responsible for a view of the world as mechanical and reductive, it can also expand our horizons and is a kind of deference to higher realities and to the power of things unseen. In recent years we have emphasised how close this work is to eco-theology, and how necessary a science based approach is to the work of restoration and healing. In this capacity I am part of the chaplaincy team at Maclaurin Chapel at the University of Auckland.

*What have been other influences on your eco-theology?*
It has been particularly exciting to see the paradigms of biology and evolution opening up in a way that is more accessible to faith. Some of

# Pray With Hands and Feet: Olivia Yates

Olivia is a PhD student in Auckland. She co-ordinates Karakia for our Climate.

*What is your family background, where you come from?*

My first ancestors to arrive in Aotearoa New Zealand came in 1842 from England. They were part of a group of settlers who left Cornwall after a drought and famine in the very early days of Ngāmotu New Plymouth. I have other ancestors who came from Ireland and Scotland; my family has been here for a long time. I was born in Tāmaki Makaurau Auckland and raised in a small rural town called Te Puna near Tauranga, and I still consider Tauranga to be my home.

My family was drawn to rural life to escape the hustle and bustle of Auckland. My Mum was a very keen gardener, so having beautiful garden space was always part of my life. The farm we grew up on was at the base of a large park. I consider myself to be a 'free range child': I could run across the farm and walk in the bush, and I loved the beach – the joys of Tauranga! I always was able to connect to the environment.

*Was church part of the picture?*

Oh yes. I grew up in a Christian home, going to church every Sunday. Faith has been a significant part of my life for as long as I can remember.

*As a child did you connect faith and the environment?*

I did not see creation and faith as inherently linked, as I do now. Early on, I appreciated the beauty of creation as an indication that God exists;

Creation as an arrow pointing towards the Creator. I grew up holding the belief that people have 'power over' creation, according to the 'dominion' interpretation of Genesis 1:26-31. I believed that eating animals from our farm was our right, because God gave us all of creation, including all the creatures in it.

*What were significant points along the way for you?*

My university studies were a turning point in my relationship with Papatūānuku. I moved up to Tāmaki Makaurau Auckland to go to University and I studied biology and French before shifting to psychology. Biology has always been a low-level passion of mine, now superseded by psychology. I've always loved understanding how the natural world works, especially animals – when I was a child I wanted to be a vet.

Midway through my degree I started engaging in conversations about sustainability. I remember one pivotal moment at a supermarket with a friend. He was putting a bunch of bananas in the trolley and I said, "Aren't you going to put them in a plastic bag?" for that is what my mum had always done. He asserted: "No, we don't need it. Plastic is bad for the environment." My immediate response was, "That's silly." But this sparked for me an investigation into sustainability within the Christian faith, leading me to ask whether we have a responsibility as Christians to steward creation.

Despite my sustainability shift I was doubtful about the reality of climate change. I had absorbed the rhetoric of climate change being ambiguous and unproven, that Al Gore's *Inconvenient Truth* was not really true. However, I cared very deeply about God's heart for shalom, for active peace. A seminar about climate justice awoke me to how climate change is not just an environmental issue, it's also a social justice issue. It connected the injustice that people suffer from climate change to our responsibility towards our neighbours, globally as well as locally.

However, this was not a common conversation within my church or the groups I was part of at the time. Such was my environmental privilege; I could block out the thoughts about climate change which bombarded me. I could assume that it would not affect me or those immediately connected to me for many, many years.

The same thing plays out in the church generally. The more steps removed we are from a problem the easier it is to deny. People who are more disconnected from the lived experience of injustice are less likely to be engaged with it. I used to believe that Christians should be apolitical. But through the climate change conversation I realised that if you claim to be apolitical you are just upholding the status quo, which is in itself a political stance. If we take an apolitical stance on climate change we are consenting to a warmer world, to the displacement of people's lives and the loss of their ways-of-being.

*How was God part of this process?*

God was there 100%! I needed my 'environmental conversion' to be a gradual conversation because it required a lot from me. Learning about the reality of climate change was a whole-of-life experience. It was a sudden pivot point in my life, and became a platform which connected all of my diverse passions. It took firm strength to get through what I was learning, because of the extent of the environment grief – 'ecogrief' – that I felt.

I remember reading Naomi Klein's *This Changes Everything*.[176] I had a vivid dream whilst I was reading that book: I was in India on a missions trip with two friends, also Pākehā. In my dream we were working with people who lived on a dump and trying to improve their daily lives. My friends were stressing: "What they need is food and water. We've just got to give them food and water." But I pointed out that the dump was on top of a giant tar sand deposit, and the dump was there because the waste from the mining process formed the foundations of the other waste. I remember in my dream crying out, saying, "We need structural change!"

*Wow that's pretty strong stuff to be dreaming about! How did you experience God in that?*

I came to lean heavily upon God for hope. I know that hope is contentious in the climate space, even for Christians. Some say that we don't actually need hope; what we need is courage. The way that I see it now is that praying and engaging with God cultivates faith, and then faith cultivates hope and courage.

Accepting the reality of climate crisis for me also sparked a deeper love for God. I came to see the real heart of God, on the side of the oppressed and the marginalised, and on the side of Papatūānuku. It is OK to feel real pain for the way we treat the planet, because it grieves the heart of God. God invites us in, to journey towards bringing the Kingdom on Earth. I have a vision for what that looks like.

I see it as the restoration of Eden, the Garden of Eden. This is humanity living in deeper connection with God, with the environment and with each other. That is the way that things are supposed to be. My vision is the restoration of balance which has been lost, especially over the course of colonisation. My ancestors at some stage would have lived in balanced relationship with the environment, attuned to the rhythm of the seasons. This interconnected way of life was lost through poverty, colonisation and the industrial revolution, when living circumstances radically changed. Community and family systems were reordered to enhance productivity, and we lost our closeness with creation. I think God is calling everybody to find this balance again, and to listen in to Indigenous peoples who always had it. To be stewards of creation is a mutual nurturing role, not a power-over role.

*Where is Jesus in this?*

I see Jesus in the way we are called to love our neighbours (Mark 12:31). Jesus was always standing on the side of the marginalised and the oppressed. As I figure out how to respond to challenging situations I often ask myself 'What would Jesus do?' That may sound cheesy, but I genuinely find this helpful: 'What would Jesus say? Who would he critique?' He was never afraid to stand in solidarity with people pushed to the sidelines. He prayed with his voice, **and** his hands and feet.

Zechariah 8:16 reminds us that we have responsibility to render justice in the courts. Jesus did just that, seeking justice through relationship, through coming alongside people. Christians who are engaged in the climate space should follow that same story. It is not the one or the other.

I was taught as a young person in the church that mission is caring in practical ways, like giving food to the hungry, and cannot be political. But I now see that loving neighbours requires both: relational connection paired with action so that our neighbourliness is more than just lip service. It's not just a symbolic gesture – we must be willing to give our whole lives towards the restoration of this balance.

> These are the things that you shall do: Speak the truth to one another, render in your gates judgments that are true and make for peace, do not devise evil in your hearts against one another, and love no false oath; for all these are things that I hate, says the Lord.
>
> *(Zechariah 8:16-17, NRSV)*

*What has God called you to do within this framework?*

Improving the wellbeing of individuals requires improving the wellbeing of our society. We need to look at how societal structures impact people at the individual level. In my own life that means not shying away from steps that are challenging or that require sacrifice of me. I feel a keen sense of personal responsibility to act upon injustice, especially climate change injustice. I believe that God is calling the church to engage in this. I am involved in the climate movement, which was a catalyst for my awareness of all this. I am also studying community psychology, the study of how peoples' attitudes and behaviours are shaped by their communities, societies and nations.

My interest in community psychology emerged from connecting justice, climate and human behaviour together. This was a gradual process, very much due to God changing my heart. My PhD topic looks at the wellbeing implications of climate-related mobility to Aotearoa New Zealand. I am working alongside people from Tuvalu and Kiribati who have migrated to Aotearoa New Zealand pushed to the sidelines, especially for climate change-related reasons. Together with these communities we are highlighting the ways in which their lives and ability to flourish are shaped by the situations and the society and the structures that they now find themselves in.

*How can churches engage with climate change and support refugees?*

Before answering, I'd like to highlight the importance of labels. 'Climate refugees' don't actually exist; researchers, activists and NGOs do not use this terminology. International law does not recognise 'climate refugees'. Most importantly, the communities who are the most exposed to climate change reject the language of 'refugee' because it implies that they have neither autonomy nor power to resist displacement. It also implies that it is their responsibility to ameliorate their own situation as a consequence of climate change. Instead, we have to push the responsibility for climate change back onto the major emitting states who created this circumstance in the first place. I'm emphasising this point because of the implications of how narratives can make communities on the frontlines of the climate crisis more vulnerable.

I want the church to understand that the way we talk about and care for the foreigner (e.g. Psalm 146:9; Leviticus 19:34) is political. For instance, immigration creates numerous obstacles for the communities I work with. The first barrier they face is getting a visa; there's already a lack of pathways to residency for people who migrate in pursuit of new opportunities, let alone for climate-related reasons. Consequently, both now and increasingly into the future, people are forced to become 'irregular' migrants – so-called 'overstayers'. The church is called to look after its neighbours, both our Pacific neighbours across the ocean, and also our Pacific neighbours in our back yard, in Tāmaki Makaurau Auckland and throughout Aotearoa New Zealand. This requires us to recognise the political structures that shape people's lives.

We have to accompany our thirst for shalom with action to remove societal barriers in order to allow all to flourish. I heard an interesting quote: "God changes hearts, but people change laws." God can use us as a tool to change the laws which then become the foundation for changing people's hearts. Thinking about the severity of climate change in this way requires something from us. Let's not be afraid to approach the topic and have the difficult conversations. Listen to the stories of communities on the frontlines of the climate crisis, and think about our response in terms of our common humanity as created beings and children of God.

Walking in solidarity alongside our neighbours is a good place to start. Gustavo Gutierrez was a priest and theologian in Peru, who famously asked, "You say that you care for the poor; tell me, what are their names?" In the context of the climate crisis, his challenge would be thus: We say that we care about people affected by climate change – "tell me, what are their names?" We must ask ourselves whether we have a personal relationship with the people we seek to support. If not, don't be afraid to question what led to this separation. The climate movement globally is held up by racist, colonial and imperialistic ideas, which countries demonstrate in their slowness to act. Let not the church be the same.

I feel frustrated by the (Pākehā-dominant) church's sluggish response to climate change and reluctance to recognise our climate privilege. This silence about the severity of climate change stems partly from relational distance, that is, the number of relationships which separate oneself from another. Growing personal friendships, being in spaces where I am in the minority, and hearing stories from people directly affected by climate change helps to overcome the relational distance. This is an important step in speeding up our response and our commitment to creation care.

*You are also inviting the church to pray about climate change. What is Karakia for our Climate and how did that get going?*

In 2019 there was momentum building around climate action, but there was mostly silence from the church in Aotearoa New Zealand. I was in an organisation called Generation Zero, a youth-led climate advocacy group, where I met other climate-savvy Christians. We began a conversation: "How can we mobilise our churches to connect in with climate change?"

We want to create an 'on-ramp' for other Christians. My own engagement in climate action was enabled through a friend who was a Christian and also a climate activist. Through talking with him, joining the climate movement felt attainable and less terrifying. Joining a protest can feel daunting, especially for churches who believe that their place is to not get political.

Climate change affects everybody, but I understand that people are afraid of political action.

However, there's one thing that we are not afraid of – we're not afraid of prayer. Prayer is safe for us. So a small group of us decided to pray and to call the church to pray. We mobilised our networks, connected in with other Christians who cared about sustainability, and organised to meet together for prayer at the time of the September 2019 Strike for Climate. Prayer vigils in all the main centres across Aotearoa shared liturgy, intercession and worship. Then some people from those different vigils walked together in the strike, representing all Christians who care about the climate.

Karakia for our Climate (K4OC) is a growing network of people who are longing for a faith-based outlet to express their concern for our global climate. Although limited by Covid, we hope this will be a consistent space for people to express our hopes for a new creation but also to lament for what we are have already lost and what we are in the throes of losing. We pray for those making decisions, those affected by climate crisis and for our environment. We pray ultimately for God's redemption of humanity, that we will stop wrecking the planet!

*Can you share a moment in one of the Karakia vigils that stood out for you and touched your heart?*

The first time we did K4OC, we had a vigil at my home church in Mt Eden on the evening before the school strike. In preparing for this my friends and I drew a large map of the world on a sheet. However, we had been working from a printed map that was eurocentric and did not show any of Pacific countries. Pacific countries might have little land, but their oceans and lifeways are big and should not be invisible to the rest of the world. So we added them in. During the vigil we laid this world map on the ground and everyone put candles on regions where they wanted to focus their prayer. Many candles were placed on these Pacific 'Large Ocean States'. It was a powerful reminder that God sees everybody and nobody is invisible. There were many candles on the large wealthy countries, which dominate decision-making spaces, but also many candles on those who are afforded very little voice on the international stage.

In April 2021 we met again for another School Strike for Climate. I had been walking in the strike with some other members of K4OC, as well as with people from ADJust (the Anglican Diocese Youth Justice Group). As well as banners we carried a big cross. It is a tall beautiful cross with a long history, called the Melanesian Cross. At some point I was separated from my group and could not see the cross anywhere. I approached my friends from Generation Zero and asked, "Has anybody seen a giant cross?" And they were like, "What?!" I explained, "I am here with Karakia for our Climate." They asked, "What is that?" I explained that we are a Christian climate action group and we have made a protest cross. One person said, "Wow! Everything in that sentence was awesome!" This was doubly significant for me because they are a leader of the indigenous rangatahi group, Te Ara Whatu. I realise that for them, and also for many other Māori in New Zealand, the Christian witness has not always been faithful to what God has called us to. That moment in the climate strike reconnected me in to what the Christian witness can be and should be.

## God of Grace

*Prayer for Waitangi Day*[177]

God of grace, show us the way as we seek your guidance and wisdom.
From good and honest intentions gone astray
in this country and across the earth.
From the irresponsible and unjust use of natural resources,
of economic and political power.
From a narrow patriotism which ignores the needs and welfare of all
people …
**God of grace, show us your way.**

From the discrimination, prejudice and racism in our land
that hurt, wound and ruin lives.
From a preoccupation with the past
and a refusal to confront the future with faith, hope and vision.
From false pride and blindness to our nation's frailty,
from complacency and timidness in speaking the truth …
**God of grace, show us your way.**

### Action Point 64: Pray for climate action

Pray with voice, hands and feet for climate justice.

- Join Karakia for our Climate, and share in prayer vigils, either online or in person.[178]
- Include prayer about climate action in regular services of worship and intercessory prayer
- Join Anglican Advocacy Wellington on Facebook: www.facebook.com/anglicanadvocacywn
- Climate Intercessors global network: www.climateintercessors.org
- Join a climate action network such as Extinction Rebellion, 350.org, or Generation Zero.

### Action Point 65: Hear the stories of communities affected by climate change

Build genuine, mutually-beneficial relationships with people different to oneself (e.g. Māori, Pacific peoples, low-income, youth, people with disabilities or gender-diverse). Talk about the impacts of climate change.

Support the policies which influence their wellbeing; for instance, submit in support of policies that welcome people from Pacific nations affected by climate change.

- Book, edited by Helen Clark, *Climate Aotearoa: What's happening and what we can do about it* (Allen & Unwin, 2021)

# Take Jesus Out from the Church: O'Love Uluave

O'Love Uluave[179] is a community youth worker, currently working for the Anglican Trust for Women and Children (ATWC) in Auckland. She chairs the Youth Commission of the Three Tikanga Anglican Province, of Aotearoa, New Zealand and the Pacific.[180]

*Thanks for being part of this book, O'Love.*

I'm excited be part of it, and I love that this is inter-denominational. We need more educational resources on care of creation – it is really important. I was recently talking with my Youth Commission team about how there is not much – or any at all – for young people about the environment. In the Anglican church we have liturgy for care of creation but it's not youth focused. It needs youth lingo that is easily understandable with more visual stuff and ways to engage young people.

*Where did your family come from?*

Both my parents were born in Tonga and migrated over in the late 1980s and early 1990s. I was born and raised here in Auckland, together with four other children; plus my father had three children from a previous marriage, born in Tonga. A lot of siblings – a weird mix but it worked. Onehunga has been our home, and we grew up in the Anglican church, St. Peter's Onehunga. Out of all my siblings I'm the only one still involved in the Anglican church.

My father Tipiloma is Catholic; he is from Kolofo'ou and Kolomotu'a. My mother Maile is from Ha'ano and Fotuha'a. She is Anglican, and went to an Anglican school in Tonga. I guess that informed her choice of church when she came to a new country, and the community of St. Peter's was very welcoming when she arrived.

*Was that a multicultural church or a Tongan fellowship?*

We have three strands of the Anglican Church and Onehunga falls under Tikanga Pākehā. In our early years at that church it was quite European, a Palangi church. We were the odd ones in the mix. Over the years it became more diverse with other Tongan families coming and other ethnic groups, like Asian and Indian.

My mum took a little left turn to the Anglican Church but her family are very staunch in the Tongan church, Siasi 'o Tonga Hou'eiki. When we have family gatherings they are done in the Tongan way.

*Were you brought up bilingual?*

We were raised mainly by our grandmother. She is a staunch Tongan, and growing up we were not allowed to speak English at home. So in primary school my English wasn't great. I was called a FOB[181] even thought I was born here. I could understand English and I was OK with writing, but when it came to speaking I had to stop and think before I said something. But when we had a Tongan speech competition I won the prize – I took it out! It was not until my teens that I became more confident in speaking both languages. Even now my brain is still responding in Tongan! English is a bit confused. Some people can speak off the cuff in three different languages but for me it is more of a struggle.

*And there are layers of cultural and gender expectations too; Tongan girls are not taught to speak up.*

We are taught to stay in the background. But I would look people in the eye, so people could tell that I was born in New Zealand. My grandma was very influential in my life, especially her prayer life. She would pray every morning and every evening. She would get everyone into the living room, same thing every day, and we would have to sit and listen. I was not even praying. Looking back, I appreciate it, but at the time we found it annoying. But it did help to instill a good prayer life for me. I wake up and give thanks, I go to sleep and give thanks. It built in a rhythm.

*How did you relate to the environment as a child?*

My primary school played a huge role for me because Onehunga Primary is an Enviroschool. We learned from an early age, from composting to worm bins, the '3 Rs' of reduce, reuse, recycle. Kaitiakitanga was woven into everything we did, including lunch break and after school. I was one of the Enviro Reps for my year group which meant I could leave class for a few hours per week and do composting and gardening and stuff like that. Being part of an Enviroschool built in: 'This is how we do things'. It made me aware of sustainability.

Growing up at home nothing was wasted. Living with four other siblings at the time, we were quite resourceful. We had to make do with what we had and share everything. So from a young age I was aware that the environment was important; that understanding just became my norm. At High School I was that annoying person that yelled to everyone: "Pick up your own rubbish! Don't buy plastic bottles."

*What did you go on to study?*

Leaving high school, my thinking was to study environmental science, because we look after the earth. I was very aware of all the challenges with pollution and climate change. I decided 'This is what God wants me to do'. So I did a year and a half towards a science degree. It was cool, but I lost my focus. I am a very social person. I went in with a lot of passion but got to a point where it was not connecting with me. It hit me that I should stop and take time to pray and humble myself – and there were a lot of tears. I asked God, "So what do you want me to do?" The good Lord heard my cries. That is when I was offered the Anglican youth ministry scholarship. That kick-started my studies into theology.

It made sense. If we want to care for the earth, we need to care for the humans just as much, who are part of creation – so: 'OK, I can do this. Let's do theology!' I completed a Bachelor of Theology in youth ministry through Laidlaw College and then I did a year at St John's Theological College. It has been quite the roller coaster: my weird environmental, faith and creation and youth ministry journey till now.

Before and during my study I was youth pastor at my home church, St. Peter's Onehunga. It wasn't a role that I applied for, it was just, "You're the only young person!" I had already worked with children and it felt OK to add God stuff in the mix. Last year I had a youth ministry role at the parish of Henderson, so I stayed out west for a year. Then this year I stepped into youth community work with ATWC, out east.[182] Because of Covid, and being fully vaccinated, I was deployed to the Covid Relief team. So it's been all go from then. We have been slowly figuring out a new norm with Covid, and able to explore online gatherings with our tamariki so we can still stay connected. Unfortunately, online stuff is not much fun, definitely not the same vibe as meeting together in person.

*What do you find most challenging?*

Not much … nah, kidding!! The hardest thing for me is when I can't see God in someone. Humans are such a blessing but sometimes hurt people hurt people. Dealing with conflicts has been hard, and makes me wonder 'Why am I doing this?!' I find that very confusing. It has forced me to be more resilient. God uses us to shine his light into the lives of others, but how can you continue to be a blessing to people who are behaving badly?

Especially in the Anglican Church, we have the biggest range of theology. It can be healthy to have the occasional debate and disagreements here and there – it's good to rock the boat sometimes. But sometimes people can get mean, even nasty. I have seen times where all the kindness seems to drain out of someone's body; the gentleness leaves and they focus on trying to be right and prove their point. They forget that behind someone else's theology, which is contrasting to theirs, there is a human being.

At the end of the day we are a gift from God. We can forget this, that we are to be a blessing. So please remember, you are a blessing.

*What do you see as the role of good leadership, especially when there are conflicts?*

Oh, it is really important! We can't all lead; not everyone is cut out for it. But even in following we are role-modelling good leadership. We need to be strong resilient people. We need to hold each other, regardless of what others views are; even if it's wrong, even if it's contrasting to your own beliefs and understanding – being able to hold that in God-space.

*What has your work in pandemic relief involved?*

Food and clothing has been the biggest need for families and is still a growing issue. The Covid pandemic has made it harder to navigate the use of plastic. As we give families food and supplies we just make do with what we have, even if that includes too much plastic packaging. Trying to be environmentally conscious in what you're consuming is so important, but you don't have many options if you're broke.

One of our projects is the Essential Hub. This was actually a whack idea my flatmate Hinemoa and myself literally dreamt up after having a few beersies partway through lockdown.

For this project, with the help of ATWC, we were able to connect with churches with essential resources and share them freely with people who didn't. That was one way to help, through resource rescue of essential items that people would otherwise throw away: clothing, kitchenware, bedding and toys. It was more than an Op Shop, we tried to source things that people needed and gave it to them freely.

Auckland has had a long Covid lockdown and children have grown out of their clothes. Businesses had 'click and collect' but you need to have a debit card and you need to have transport to collect what you've bought. There is quite an assumption that people have access to these basic things, but they don't. So being local has made it easier to access and redirect resources; that has been important to mitigate annoying issues that many families have faced. The Essential Hub has been a good way to support families, to help us become more aware of the things we consume. It was well received by the community.

*Have you had any experience with food rescue or initiatives to reduce food waste?*

Yup! I have helped out my mother who worked with Ananda Marga collecting food from Avondale Sunday Market that stall holders would otherwise have thrown into the trash. Some of this food is then delivered to families in Onehunga and anyone else needing kai support. They would pick out what they wanted and the remainder would be put into the community compost at Langimalie Community Garden.[183] I've also been involved in Love Food Hate Waste projects that my mother facilitated in the community of Onehunga, where a bunch of ladies got together to create dishes that could be made from left-over food. I can't remember the dishes but I know they tasted yum! So basically thanks to my mother I am food waste conscious – thanks Mum.

*What environmental issues do you see in your community work?*

The use of green spaces. How do we activate areas so that they can be well used by families in our community? How do we take care of that? At the moment with the housing crisis the use of land is very contentious: should land be developed for housing or kept as public green space?

*That is a huge issue of environmental justice: wealthier communities have nice parks and impoverished communities have impoverished local green spaces. Do kids play in the parks in the communities you work in?*

If a playground or green space looks like trash it will be treated like trash. There is litter on the ground, overflowing bins, graffiti, things are broken, so families completely avoid it. Families take their children out of their local area to go somewhere else – but in lockdown that was a 'no-go'. Having spaces to be family and interact with the environment is vital, but not easy in the neighbourhoods where many of our people live.

*And schools playgrounds are often locked in the weekends. So how do the children find ways to be outside?*

In a weirdly unsafe way, the road is the playground – obviously not the safest, and I don't think it's legal either, but you make do with what you have. If you have a ball, you just chalk up a line on the road and you have a court. Most of the housing developments do not have gardens. Pasifika families often live in areas where the houses are 'up and skinny' with not much green space they can use. But kids find happiness in the smallest things.

*Is any work being done to improve the local green spaces?*

Auckland Council has been talking about it for years – "Yes, we are going to upgrade this" – but I don't know what they are waiting for! There is lots of talk but not much walk. I know people from the community do their own hood patrol to help keep places like playgrounds safe for children. Little things like picking up trash really helps.

*How amazing would it be if a church could adopt one of those playgrounds, pick up rubbish, fix things, plant things, make it safe for kids?!*

The church in Henderson is planning to build a playground on their land. They have the idea, anyway, and awesome people to push it through. Nothing can stop the church when it wants to do something!

*What ideas do you have, or positive things you have seen, to enable people in communities to care for the environment?*

Providing workshops in schools for children to help them learn different ways to look after the environment as well as having fun. Also providing community workshops for the parents/caregivers; it gives them an excuse to get together as a community and in doing so they learn about sustainability. There are so many ideas and initiatives going on to care for the environment, but it takes strong leadership and a whole lot of commitment to create momentum within our people.

A hard thing about working in poorer communities is finding sustainable options that are easy and affordable. Our people on low incomes work so hard just to get enough to pay the rent, so don't have much spare time and energy. It can be difficult for them to care about the environment. So environmental stuff has to be enjoyable, no longer a chore but a practice you want to do. The goal for sustainability is to form good habits and stick to them. But if it ain't fun or engaging for the whole family to take part in, it won't work.

We need to mobilise families to care for the environment in their own ways. Ask them for ideas, so it comes from them, and then support their initiatives as a community.

*How do you see mission becoming more environmentally sustainable?*

Community mission needs to be God-centred. I believe God is present in creation. The environment is good, God said. If we know and understand this then the way we treat the environment will be as we treat our neighbours.

We need to go back to the roots. From my Polynesian perspective I hear stories of my grandma's family fishing and growing their own food, relying on the land for nourishment without the need for plastics. We've changed the way we do things since back then, but learning from my grandma's generation how they cooked together as a family and sourced their foods sustainably, is something I bring into my own life today.

Learning from our elders is not just about acquiring knowledge for the sake of it. There is a deeper calling for us, as learners, to reciprocate and put what we have learned into action. This helps me have a deeper connection to my Tongan ways. Indigenous environmental wisdom was present from the get-go and is still with us today. Here is where the church can acknowledge and weave God's mission into contemporary society.

*You relate to young people across cultures, and locally and nationally and internationally – how are young people affected by climate change?*

There is a range of levels of awareness and different responses to climate change. I talk about it with some young people who have no idea: "Is that the weather changing?" and I say, "It is a bit more than that!" Some young people are ignorant or don't care: "Well, if the earth is in this state, we might as well just live it up." There are a few hearty enviro fighters and climate change warriors who have made it their mission to get the word out and help organisations and churches to change.

People in the islands are very aware. For us in New Zealand we hear about climate change through the media, second-hand. But for young people in the islands it is happening to them! They are impacted directly. Their own homes are getting destroyed or flooded.

*Do you see them getting depressed about it?*

I think they more anxious than depressed. They are very worried. It is an urgent anxiousness.

We hear real life stories. People in the small islands in Tonga, and also in Tuvalu and Kiribati, are actually having to relocate their homes and move inland, or relocate from the whole island itself. The main island of Tonga is quite small and the ground is very flat. Erosion is taking away the edges of the land and villages get flooded. Most of the islands are just made of coral, there is no actual rock. Once it is eroded it's time to go.

*Climate change also means that the storms are more intense. How can they prepare for these terrible storms?*

The Anglican youth in Tonga have done CIVA training, Community Integrated Vulnerability Assessments, to prepare for disasters.[184] They figure out where on the island there is more solid ground that people can move to, looking at the geographic capacities of the island so that homes can be made more stable and less likely to be destroyed by storms. The CIVA training educates the young people to use data and tools to understand the weather and to work with their communities.[185] It has been going for about five years.[186]

*Is there a faith component? How do you think Tongan young people connect their faith with climate change?*

Their liturgy is woven in. The programme encourages their thoughts and questions. Young people are asking: "Why do we have this extreme weather? Why do we have hurricanes and sea level rise?" People start theologising at a younger age and the church can be a space to navigate those questions. I don't have the answers, I don't know why God gives us hurricanes! The important thing is to create space where young people can gather safely and openly ask these questions.

They are also having No Plastic campaigns in the islands. These things broaden the ideas of the young people from a perspective of faith and creation. How do they play a role and learn about the creation? What does it mean to not use plastic?

*What is your thinking about the theology? Is God punishing us?*

I'm definitely not a punitive person. I like to think of being restorative and reconciling. We are called to use our brains here! Even though we are challenged – and many people around the world are more challenged than us here in New Zealand – we can bring to bear all our resources and our commitment to face this huge mission challenge. We are called to work together on this. As well as finding ways to adapt to climate change we definitely also need to work to prevent it. The call is to immediate action with the intention to stop global warming.

We shouldn't just pray for a miracle when we know what we can do to prevent it. Saying it is one thing but changing our lifestyles is a whole other thing – it is hard. But in comparison to us making a few changes to reduce our carbon footprint, many other people face massive changes, like having to relocate a whole island because they are affected by extreme weather. I would love people to understand how impactful they are when it comes to doing small things. People have to start changing their mindset. Start doing some new things and stop doing other things!

*How can the church support young people to connect faith and climate action?*

More resources would be really cool, for your typical youth group to be able to weave 'care for creation' into their programmes. They might promote cycling, going op-shopping, or organise food composting – practical things that show sustainability in everyday life and educate the young people along the way.

Providing resources that actually engage is really important. We need to remember our young'uns are growing up in a digital age; the way they see and understand the world is different from our grandparents. And the lingo – so different! To connect our youth to God's Word it is important to keep God's message at the centre but share it in youth lingo so they understand.

*Where is God calling you next?*

Moving back into the Onehunga hood has reminded me of my 'Why'. I'd love to do ministry here but I need to chill for a while. I've done a few rides 'onto the next' and some good people are asking me to come work with them. But I think God is calling me into a season of rest before I go 'hundy' again.[187] It'll take some discerning to figure out where God is calling me next.

I do feel that my focus will be more in the community than in the church. The church may have a nice building but mission is 'How do we go out into the world and be who God calls us to be?' We need to take Jesus out of the church. I want to do that while still holding on to my faith. I'm young, 23, but it feels like I have had quite the journey already. I can already feel my spiritual wrinkles growing and my spiritual grey hairs!

### Action Point 66: Equip young people for a changing world

Young people aware of the issues facing our world and equipped with faith perspectives that empower positive action. A recent research project by Tearfund and Youthscape found that "9 out of 10 Christian teenagers surveyed are concerned about climate change, but just one in 10 believe their church is doing enough to respond to the climate crisis."[188]

- Talk with young people about climate change. Grapple with the theological questions together.
- Youth resources, Eco Church NZ: www.ecochurch.org.nz/youth

### Action Point 67: Look after a green space

Every child in Aotearoa needs safe places to play outside.

It is all very well to care for our local community. This is an important ecological principle. But if we stay in our middle-class neighbourhood we miss the harsh realities of social and environmental inequality. A central Bible principle is God's heart for "the least of these" (Matthew 25:40). Faith-based environmental action pushes us literally out of our comfort zone, across town.

How?

- Let God take us to places we are unfamiliar with, places of poverty, rubbish, graffiti and worse.
- Explore ways to work with local people and councils to improve public parks and playgrounds, drains and walkways. Make them safe and beautiful for kids to play in.

### Action Point 68: Rescue food

No food going to waste.

- Love Food Hate Waste campaigns against food waste, in partnership with Councils around the country. Their website includes recipes, advice and information about local events: www.lovefoodhatewaste.co.nz
- Aotearoa Food Rescue Alliance co-ordinates and supports food rescue partnerships: www.afra.org.nz
- Zero Food Waste Challenge is a new initiative aimed especially at young people: www.zerofoodwastechallenge.com
- 'Eat the change we want to see' radio interview, RNZ: www.rnz.co.nz/national/programmes/ninetonoon/audio/2018821513/food-eat-the-change-we-want-to-see

## The Moana Prayer – for the Pacific Ocean

*Archbishop Emeritus Winston Halapua*[189]

Loving and Embracing God,
You are the God of the universe and all Creation.
You create and give life, and see that your Creation is good.
We praise you for your gift of Creation.

We thank you for the Moana.
We thank you the great Oceans flowing into one another
and around the continents and islands.
We thank you for the life-giving of the Oceans,
for the oxygen, food and resources they continually provide.
We thank you that the Ocean is the home for most species,
small and great.

We are people of the Moana.
Our ancestors navigated by the stars
and crossed the waves to find new homes.
The waves breaking on the reef thunder with the message
of your constancy and your love and care for Creation.

May we hear the voices of sea creatures endangered
by the selfish greed of humanity.
May there be a deep listening to the voice of waters rising
to engulf land.
May ears be open to the groaning caused
by refusal to honour Creation.
May eyes be open to the suffering caused by power which destroys.

We beat a lali drum, alerting people around Planet Earth
to the destruction of nature and human life
threatened by climate change.
We blow a conch, calling for the worship of a God
of immense goodness.
Our forbears set our across the Moana.
We set out on a venture to protect our home – the Planet Earth
Help us to challenge short-sighted greed,
Help us to address unjust structures and practices
and to change our relationship with creation to one of care.

our ability to relate faith to rural life, for the wellbeing of all, including the land. By telling our stories of lament and of hope we made it clear that the rural church was well and truly alive.[194] We would face the realities of living with the variables of government, markets, and weather, as well as signs of a changing future.[195] Our conference in Victoria in 1996 said it all: bringing faith to bear on the practicalities of living with the land needed vision, **ecological** vision.[196]

Faith is about living in the face of uncertainty and not losing heart. 'Heart' includes both compassion and courage. My understanding is that our mission as rural churches is to bring the whole gospel to the whole community, building relationships and fostering reconciliation of land and people. We are a voice for those becoming more and more voiceless.[197]

*What makes rural churches distinctive?*

Rural church members are embedded in their community, sharing all aspects of life in that context, all of us dependent on the land for livelihood. Rural communities are held together by neighbourhood relationships. It is the nature of being rural that one cannot pick and choose who one relates to. Everybody is part of the neighbourhood, so it is a case of getting on as best one can with all others. The gospel as reconciliation therefore always has a vital part to play in rural communities. Church people often have leadership roles in the wider community and are recognised for their personal qualities. In recent decades the gospel of reconciliation has broadened with recognition of the increasing fragility of life with the land. This environmental dimension has fed more and more into our Sunday reflections. Rural life is inescapably about community relationships and ecological relationships.

Being church is about living the gospel in context. **Where** we are matters: it affects how we speak and what we talk about. Our task is to help one another discover God in the midst of our land-based context, give room for the Christ among us, and catch up with the Spirit at work in our place.

*So what of eco-theology?*

When presenting a paper on eco-theology at a conference in Christchurch in 2000,[198] I met Norman Habel, a Lutheran theologian from South Australia. He had initiated the Earth Bible series, bringing together articles that read biblical texts from the perspective of the earth.[199] This aligned perfectly with what I had been doing in Sunday sermons and in workshops with rural churches, as well as forums for local farmers on land related issues.

Scripture is rooted in the earth. In the opening chapters of Genesis the Hebrew word for human being 'adam' is linked morphologically with 'adamah' meaning ground or specifically top-soil. Abel's blood cried out from the earth (Genesis 2:7). Torah texts interweave social and environmental ethics and see right behaviour as essential to receiving livelihood from the land.[200] Prophets identify the consequences of bad behaviour as both social and environmental (e.g. Hosea 4:1-3). In the New Testament what stands out is the 'grounded' location of Jesus' ministry: parables of the land, teaching on the road, dust on their feet, learning from experience, with lakes as unpredictable as our Southern Lakes, and finding food for the crowds in the apparent wilderness. The Bible gives insights into right relationship with the world of non-human nature – if we can spot them through the layers of interpretation that have prioritised human redemption.

The real priority is set by both the beginning and the end of the Christian canon. The traditional interpretation of the opening Genesis narrative, influenced as it has been by centuries of Western culture, was that the apex of God's creation was the creation of 'man'. But that is still only day six. The real apex is on day seven, the Sabbath, which is celebration and restoration for all creation. Days one to seven place human being within an interconnected and interdependent whole. Not, "I think therefore I am,"[201] the mantra of human exceptionalism, but **I relate therefore I am**.

In the closing chapters of the book of Revelation, the holy city has been treated as the pinnacle of God's story of salvation. In fact, the focus is on what is in the midst of the city: the river of life and the tree of life, a tree first mentioned in Genesis 2 alongside the tree of good and evil. The tree of good and evil sums up all the challenges human beings face, as we see in the texts between Genesis and Revelation. The tree of life is in the centre of the city. The city epitomises both human creativity and human failings. Without the tree there would be no nourishment and no healing – no life!

*How does this relate to ministry?*

It was a no-brainer for me as a parish minister to read the Bible through the lens of rural life. There I was working in a church with crop farmers sitting next to stock farmers: how could we not read the story of Cain and Abel and think about our own struggles and grievances in getting a good harvest?[202] The book of Joel tells of drought, locust plagues and colonising armies devastating the land, putting the people's joy to shame. Likewise, rural people of our time suffer from weather challenges, biological pests and contemporary 'armies' in the form of the 'economic colonisation' of transnational companies and the demands of international markets.[203]

Often the response is to shut oneself away, with consequences for mental health, sometimes to crisis level. I came to see 'sin' as less personal fault and more what Korean Minjung call 'han' a deep-seated sense of shame and worthlessness.[204]

*Rural communities seem to feel attacked by the environmental movement. How can we engage both urban and rural people in positive conversations around sustainability and climate change?*

Urban and rural are different contexts. At times it's like we are speaking different languages. In terms of community and ecological wellbeing, much can be gained by meeting and learning more of each other's context. Sibling relationships between churches can enable mutual sharing of ideas and strategies for better earth care.

Rural churches and small churches can feel isolated and start to doubt their worth and purpose. A strong antidote to this is making contact with other rural churches, sharing stories and resources as well as pooling ideas and strategies for facing the issues that rural communities are facing.

*How did you develop your bicultural understanding?*

When a parish in Northland became a possibility for me in the early 2000s, a large part of the appeal was how different it would be. I knew I would be challenged and that my world would have to expand. Connecting with Māori was a real blessing, a gift that keeps on giving. As teina (younger sibling) to them as tuakana (older sibling), I sat at the feet of the multiple hapū (sub-tribes) of Whangaroa and their relations around the wider district. What I may have given through ministry could never match what I received.

The college students laughed when I first led karakia at school Assembly because my pronunciation was atrocious! But as I listened, and spend many days in hui (meetings), tangihanga (funerals), and Waitangi Tribunal hearings, slowly I got better. With every affirmation for my Reo I could sense that they were proud of who they were helping me become. I was simply present, but what made the real difference for me was the manaakitanga (welcome, inclusion, kindness) of the people of Te Tai Tokerau – te atawhai nui (the amazing grace) with which they received the halting attempts of a Pākehā Southlander to respect their tikanga. I was never growled at, rather I was mentored. I got feedback all right, but it was always focused on the future, in the expectation that I would be back, that I was always welcome. I learnt to stay silent during kōrero until maybe there would be a turn for me.

Patient listening was my commitment for two reasons. First it is simply tikanga Māori. That is the way to learn, starting in childhood: being present, absorbing, and when directed to, standing and contributing. I started later in life but I was determined to make the most of the opportunity. As a church minister I know the importance of listening. **Being** counts as much if not more than **doing**. Just being with people. Not racing round solving problems, not necessarily knowing the right words to say, but simply being a companion on the life journey, whatever it is that people are facing. Using words to draw out from people what is important for them; "hearing them to speech"[205] to find their way forward.

The spirituality of the North provided something that had been missing: a confident articulation of eco-theology, true to my background and to all the contexts and relationships that had educated me over the years. Northland, Māori and Pākehā, is markedly different from the south in the way that spiritual expression is a respected part of life, whatever one's personal beliefs. For Māori especially there is no question of 'Does God exist?' The question is about who we are as tāngata, relating to whenua and to Atua.[206] **I relate therefore I am.** At last I had the language to express with confidence what I knew and felt deep down. This also resonated with the guiding principles of the rural church theology we practise together in the IRCA and in our home parishes.

Hearing kōrero during this time about Christianity's legacy of collusion with colonial oppression, I realised that it is the overlay of European culture on the biblical texts that is the problem. We need to re-read the Bible from the perspective of the earth and the perspective of the people of the earth, tangata whenua – or in Hebrew the 'am ha'aretz'. Study leave spent re-reading texts opened my eyes to this perspective and motivated me to offer this as a faith resource in our Aotearoa context; working with Māori I began to live this perspective. Special moments will stay with me: together at the graveside the casket is lowered and I speak of Genesis 2 with its linking of *adam*/tangata and *adamah*/whenua, the good earth to whom we return our loved one.

It was as if, at the same time as I was in Northland with my new friends, I was back in Southland with my family. Tūmeke! (Awesome!)

For that, and much else, I give thanks ... for growing up where and with whom I did. For the perfect life-partner, unique in his own way, who let me to be myself. For our children who gave me a post-doctoral crash course in 'practical philosophy' and who offer ongoing support and friendship – and for the next generation continuing this. For people in churches and communities who let me share their lives and their place.

I have seen the struggle of farming communities to find sustainable livelihood and been a companion to the suffering of loss of land. I continue to support the ongoing battle of Māori to recover historical loss and reclaim their rangatiratanga. I have seen God in amazing people, God known always in a triangle of relationship: Tangata, Whenua, Atua.

## A Shepherd's Prayer

*Bill Bennett*[207]

God, give me an eye
to see beyond the crest of the hill;
give me wisdom to assess the task,
give me a whistle the dogs will obey,
and a loud shout to bellow at them.
Give me a caring spirit
for stock in distress,
give me courage when danger looms.
Give me strength to match the task,
give me humour when things go wrong.
Give me good mate-ship
with other shepherds.
Give me nous
to know when to call it quits.
Give me confidence in the skills I have.
Give me humility
in managing this part of your creation.
Give me that inner understanding
that no matter where I am,
and what I am doing,
you are still leading me,
for you are the Good Shepherd.

## Action Point 69: Read the Bible through ecological eyes

Hear the Holy Spirit speak true through the words of scripture as we push beneath our human-centred assumptions and listen for God's heart for the land.

- Include a creation perspective in Bible study and preaching; notice and highlight Bible references to land, animals and natural features, and honour these as central rather than purely symbolic.
- The Earth Bible Project[208]

- Book edited by Norman Habel and Peter Trudinger, *Exploring Ecological Hermeneutics* (Society of Biblical Literature, 2009)
- Book by Ellen F. Davis, *Scripture, Culture, and Agriculture: An Agrarian Reading of the Bible* (Cambridge University Press, 2009)
- *Tui Motu Interislands* has regular articles on sustainability and scripture.[209]

### Action Point 70: Strengthen rural churches through networking

Rural communities feeling encouraged and supported by the church; spaces to talk and work together on environmental action.

- Build relationships between urban and rural churches: visit, build on existing connections.
- Invite speakers from a farming perspective.
- Robyn's article 'Building Bridges in Aotearoa' on the rural-urban divide.[210]
- Rural church networks and resources, such as the International Rural Churches Association.[211] Past conference material contains a variety of treasures and the Resources page is for rural and eco-churches around the world.[212]
- Prayers and liturgies for rural churches: book by Bill Bennett, *The Shepherd's Call – Te Karanga o te Hēpara* (Philip Garside Publishing, 2018)
- Support sustainability initiatives within farming, e.g. New Zealand Farm Environment Trust[213]
- Report on sustainable farming: 'Farm planning for a sustainable future'[214]

### Action Point 71: Listen patiently

Robyn talks of the importance for learning and ministry of 'just being'. In the 'action' of ecological mission we must not forget the value of taking time to sit and listen 'hearing others to speech to find their way forward'.

- Attend to others, especially quieter people, in ways that communicate 'I want to hear what you have to say'.
- Ask open-ended questions.
- Video: 'The Secret to Talking about Climate Change'[215]
- 'Courageous conversations about climate change' facilitated process[216]
- Brené Brown – a beautiful video on the difference between empathy and sympathy[217]

# Tiddlywinks: Rosemary Biss

With a lifetime of involvement in church and community mission, together with her husband Tony, Rosemary now facilitates a group at Aotea Summerset retirement village in Porirua promoting creative recycling.

*Where does your family come from?*

My mother's ancestors came from Scotland, landing in Auckland in 1842. My English ancestors walked over the Lyttleton hill off the boat in 1854 and settled in Christchurch. Others came from Ireland and France. My great grandfather became an Anglican Priest after many years as a ship's captain.

My parents met at Ohope Beach and shared a love for the sea – we holidayed at the beach every summer. They started married life in Ōpōtiki but moved to Masterton after Dad returned from the war unwell. I learned the piano, went to an Anglican school, and decided to be a schoolteacher. I trained in Wellington and taught in an Intermediate School. Then adventure called: in 1964 I set off to England to work as a relief teacher in London, in between exciting trips around Europe marvelling at magnificent cathedrals. In 1966 it was time to come home, but I had a crazy opportunity to travel overland via Jerusalem. Gino and his new Mercedes bus took a group of us on a trip of a lifetime. An incredible 48 hours in Jerusalem left me with a better understanding and memories to dwell on for the rest of my days.

In 1969 I married Tony and we lived in Khandallah for most of our lives. Five years ago he had a stroke and we moved to Summerset Retirement Village at Aotea and we joined the Pāuatahanui Parish. I had my 80th birthday this year.

*What got you into environmental sustainability?*

It started during the Covid lockdown in 2020. We had kind offers from several younger folk to shop for us, but I turned them down. Surely I could figure out how to shop online. I was concerned about how much the younger folk had to grapple with. What contribution could I make? The thing which seemed most important was to do something about climate change. I felt: this is hard work, so let's get together and encourage each other and celebrate what we can do!

*How did the enviro group at your retirement village get started?*

In June 2020 I put a notice in the village newsletter: "Anybody interested?!" Twelve people came, all enthusiastic. The core group has stayed together ever since; it's been amazing. Over 40 residents contribute to the monthly collection. A newsletter goes to them as a reminder, which keeps up the momentum. Our meetings are good fun. I'm just a facilitator, people come up with lots of great ideas! Each one has their own task. We have reports, discussions, quizzes and videos. Last year we invited a speaker from the Sustainability Trust to talk to us about recycling.

We have an awareness box that I put items in and take along to our meetings as a discussion starter; things I pick up, like bamboo toothbrushes, dish scrubbers, cotton masks and metal clothes pegs, supermarket dockets, pill containers, polystyrene, ink cartridges, foil paper. I put in a ring from around a Marmite jar and we talked about cutting it before putting it in the bin, because a fish or bird could get stuck in there and starve to death.

Summerset management have been very supportive. Summerset nationally has committed to being carbon neutral and is part of the Climate Leaders Coalition.[218] Two villages have become 'bee friendly' with flowering plants that bees love, providing water stations and eliminating the use of harmful sprays and pesticides. The quarterly magazine has a 'Green Update' each time, showcasing their green initiatives. Our manager at Aotea is keen to encourage the recycling.

We feel very inspired by our own children. The daughter of one of our group runs an award-winning solid oral care initiative making toothpaste in a jar rather than in plastic. Tony and I have been strongly motivated by our daughter who did Plastic Free July a few years ago and has taught us so much about zero waste.

*What are the different kinds of recycling you do?*

Each month our 'Sustainability Matters! Team' sets up a recycling drop-off point in our village activities area. We have 15 labelled paper bags into which residents sort their recycling. The whole process is very sociable, talking about what items we have and who can use them. Here is what we take at the moment:

1. Newspapers. We drop these off to veterinary clinics (we go to several) and they use them to line animal cages.
2. Plastic bread bag tags. Plastic bread bag tags fund wheelchairs for children in South Africa: Bread Tags for Wheelchairs.[219]
3. Knitting wool. This is used by the Summerset craft group for projects such as beanies for the Mission to Seafarers, slippers for a local school, and little blankets for the neonatal unit.
4. Brown paper bags with handles are used by St Anne's Pantry for food parcels.
5. Soft plastics we drop into our local supermarket.[220]
6. Packaging and all kinds of items we take to a school or kindergarten for their art and craft projects: pictures, card, pretty paper, ribbon, ice cream containers, egg cartons and cardboard boxes.
7. Aluminium cans and wine bottle tops go in the metal bin at the Council recycling depot.
8. Jewellery, whether it is old, new or broken gets a new life at CanBead.[221]
9. Plastic milk bottle lids and others with recycling code 2.[222] Separately, plastic lids code 5. Both lots go to Aotearoa NZ Made: www.nzmadelimited.co.nz
10. Jam jar lids and other metal lids to McCauley's Metals.[223]
11. Toothbrushes and empty toothpaste tubes go to Terracycle.[224] Also all empty shampoo or beauty product bottles.[225] They used to take biro pens but sadly they no longer do.
12. Eco Store containers. These go to the bulk bin store and get returned to Eco Store to be made into new bottles.[226]
13. Batteries. These cannot go into the main rubbish and have to be dropped off to the Council depot or IT recyclers.
14. Anything else! The Sustainability Trust recycles a wide range of items including TVs, computers and electronics, curtains, gumboots, bottle tops, bikes, toothbrushes.[227] Mitre 10 will take plastic plant pots and seedling trays with ID 5.
15. Stamps and albums go to Anglican Mission Board.

Plus we have a regular collection for Free For All.[228] Downsizing is inevitable going into the retirement village. We all have to deal with having too much stuff. One person quoted their family as saying: "We don't want anything – when you die we will bring in the dump truck!" Which is sad, but it is practical. So at our stage of life we work hard to ensure we are living simply, and we give away what we don't need.

We value our partnership with Free for All. They take furniture, beds, tools, linen and more and they get them to people who need them. It is a wonderful, wonderful place in Porirua. They really look after people. It's like an op shop but you pay only $5 to go in and you can take whatever you like. Recently a young mother came with her two children. They were so happy; they could not believe it! There were things there that they needed very badly.

*How have folks in your retirement village responded to all this?*

People are eager for information and positive solutions. It is heartening to see the interest, and relief that there are ways to keep things out of the landfill. People love being able to pass things on to have another life. For example, the meat trays we take to a school – well cleaned of course! The kids put paint in them and use the little rollers in the tray. People ask me: "Rosemary, I've been given flowers, would the children like the paper?" "Yes, please." Or the silver paper in the tea bag box?

It has to be clear and relational, a gentle approach. People learn when you stand sorting their contributions with them – though sometimes we have to check an item with a magnifying glass to read the recycling grade! The paper bags are easy to use and everything is clean and dry and very satisfying. Folks have become confident, interested and aware.

Our group might have fizzled in Covid lockdown because we were not allowed to meet. Pandemic rules are tighter in the retirement village. Sometimes I wonder: "Are we doing enough? Is it worthwhile?" And then I think of all of the people who are depending on us to keep their stuff out of the landfill. Addressing **food waste** is an ongoing challenge. We are exploring the options, including compost systems.

*What do you enjoy about all this?*

The most beautiful thing is the sense of connection with such a wide range of people. Our group here is a regular contact with each other. It is pastoral, and it's a privilege to have a reason to keep in touch with so many interested people.

It's a myriad of little things that we can do – just tiddlywinks really, but it is good for the soul. People can hide away very easily, especially in a pandemic, and that's not good. We need to keep connections, be with people, talk, move, challenge ourselves and each other. We need to cultivate three things to keep us well: company, exercise and new stimulation. Environmental sustainability work does all three!

*What inspires you about creation?*

I have always loved the environment. I am happiest outdoors. I was only five when we left Ōpōtiki but I love to return to the beautiful beaches with overhanging pohutukawa trees. In Masterton I have happy memories of a huge veggie garden, berry bushes, fruit trees and caring for 25 chooks! We rode our bikes to school, tennis and Bible Class, swam in the rivers, and made day trips to the beaches, bush and mountains. In Wellington we enjoyed biking around the coast and along the Hutt River. At Foxton Beach we explore the wetland area through the eyes of our grandchildren. But it is the sea that I love the most! Plimmerton Beach beckons often and the Pāuatahanui Inlet is always different and just beautiful, a lovely tidal area with so many birds.

*What else are you involved with?*

It is a pleasure to join with pre-schoolers and their carers at our parish church of St Andrew's for music, craft and stories.

We are aware of the distress families are facing, especially with Covid, and the growing demand for food parcels. I love being part of an incredible team at St Anne's Pantry, the Anglican food bank in Porirua.[229] It is an absolute privilege. There is a huge community garden in Cannons Creek[230] and next to the garden an absolutely wonderful group called WELLfed that runs cooking classes.[231]

*You seem very aware of the stark differences between the wealthier suburbs and the poorer areas around you?*

Some in our group have grandchildren at a local school and they want to support it. But for me that is bittersweet, because it is a Decile 10 school in a wealthy area. When we take in all sorts of things for craft material the teachers are appreciative, but I am very aware that other schools nearby are Decile 1 and have very little. Being a schoolteacher I know how children make machines out of boxes. I was talking to a friend who teaches in Cannons Creek, and I asked her if her school would like some toothpaste boxes. She said, "Rosemary, they can't even afford toothpaste!"

*At 80 you could be taking it easy and just strolling gently on the beach! What motivates you?*

Mission is what we are called to do! It's what we are meant to do. Our Bishops Justin and Ellie have inspired our Diocese to care for the last, the lost and the least.[232]

*It really makes sense to you and you are doing something about it!*

It's nothing at all, it's just tiddlywinks – until we address food waste. There is so much more that could be done. I seem to have spent a lifetime at meetings; it was time for some hands-on action.

I married the most wonderful man in Tony. We share a love of music and choral singing, travel, cycling in Europe and supporting our children and their families. He worked as a partner in an accountancy firm, later for the Law Society and then for the Diocese of Wellington as the Trust manager. He's very patient with people and knows so much about finances. The Association of Anglican Women (AAW) has been my mainstay for 50 years.[233] I have held leadership positions in the Diocese and represented AAW on the National Council of Women.[234]

For many years we were part of St Barnabas in Khandallah, a wonderful congregation that our family grew up with. Our social justice group met in groups of five. It was fun – I love small groups. We had prayer and reading and a lunch together each month. We took on lots of projects, fundraising for medicines, promoting Fair Trade. We got the parish starting to think about the ethics of what we were eating.

When our children turned 18, they became independent and left home. It happened so quickly. One day I counted up that between us Tony and I were involved in 14 church activities, and I thought 'Oh dear!' I see women in leadership and ministry, and I would like to say to them: "Just make sure you are there for your children. You only have a few years before they fly the nest."

*How has your faith in God sustained you?*

I am blessed to be part of several faith communities: St Albans, Festival Singers, Johnsonville AAW, the Summerset ecumenical group. I felt uncomfortable with the 1970s Pentecostal movement, but I have experienced the Holy Spirit. My mother's death was a difficult time for me. My father had died young, and as the only daughter I was my mother's companion for many years; I felt that responsibility. I remember standing in our kitchen on the day before her funeral, and suddenly there was a feeling of calm, and a voice: "Rosemary." I knew I would be alright; God was with me.

When I take the time to be in a prayerful space early in the day, I am much more aware of God's hand in my life. Things happen. People phone or arrive at just the right time. I bump into somebody who needs some help, or I might need them. "Thank you God."

There was space of about 10 years after our children left home and before they had their own children. I chose to study and did the Education for Ministry (EFM) course over four years.[235] At the start I argued, "Couldn't we just jump to the New Testament?!" but we had to spend a year in the Old Testament – and now I am fascinated with the Old Testament! The EFM course opened up all the connections. I was absolutely blown away.

I sing with the Festival Singers choir performing mainly sacred music, which has been a great joy for many years.[236] I play the organ and enjoy choosing hymns that link with the Bible readings. My prayers are often in the hymns. My favourite is 'These hills where the hawk flies lonely'.

*Are there other hymns that speak about creation?*

'The majesty of mountains' 'Where the mountains rise to open skies' 'Touch the earth lightly' 'Benedicite Aotearoa' and 'O Lord My God, When I in Awesome Wonder'.[237] As an Eco Church, the Season of Creation is woven through our worship in September, including online services and children's church.

*What else is your parish Eco Church group doing?*

Helen Sharpe and Amy Ross have led the group superbly. We worked with Marie Preston putting together a cookbook *For A Healthy Planet.* We went to the launch of the diocesan Low Carbon Challenge. My challenge for three months was 'Less is More': using the dryer and the car less, using less water, less red meat and less plastic. My mentor was a member of the BluePrint Church. It was fascinating to hear about her work as an architect making plans for sustainable housing.

Children nurtured plants for the harvest festival. We have got predator control at St. Albans; they have put up six traps there, working with the Wellington Regional Council. We have a native bush restoration project; one Sunday the young ones came up and cleared the area, and planting will happen in autumn. There is a Fruit and Veggie Co-op on Tuesdays and a food swap and share box. A beach clean-up happened one Sunday. There is improved waste management signage at the parish center, and we have started a regular collection of eight categories for recycling and re-use – last month we saved 11kgs from going to landfill. We have a new noticeboard in the church foyer specially for Eco Church. It all happens quite slowly and then it gathers momentum.

*How do you see God in all this?*

God has given us responsibilities to act as stewards of his creation: to care for, manage, oversee and protect all that is his. I have looked at hundreds of Bible verses seeing the biblical connections with sustainability and learnt a lot on the way. I have watched in wonder as Eco Church became established. I believe that God had a hand in motivating and getting people together to plan a programme, in what has been a challenging year.

## These hills

*Hymn lyrics by Colin Gibson[238]*

These hills where the hawk flies lonely,
beaches where the long surf rolls,
mountains where the snows reach heaven,
*these are our care.*
Pastures where the sheep graze calmly,
orchards where the apples grow,
gardens where the roses cluster,
*these are our prayer.*

Forests where the tree ferns tower,
rivers running strong and clear,
oceans where the great whales wander,
*these are our care.*
Race meeting race as equals,
justice for age-old wrong,
worth for every man and woman,
*these are our prayer.*

Cities where the young roam restless,
lives brought to deep despair,
homeless and powerless people,
*these are our care.*
Places where the Word is spoken,
hands held in serving love,
faiths of our many cultures,
*these are our prayer.*

All that the old world gave us,
all that the new world brings,
language, ideas and customs,
*these are our care.*
Life finding joy and value,
faith seeking truth and light,
God heard and seen in all things,
*this be our prayer.*

### Action Point 72: Reuse, Reduce and Recycle everything you can

- Find out which organisations in your area take which products for recycling.
- Set up easy to access collection points, and educate people how to clean and sort items.
  Rosemary: "You want people to see that it's easy to do. I recommend a line of paper bags along a table, clearly labelled with what you collect in each one."
- Get others involved in a collaborative system to deliver items to where they can be re-used.
- Keep records and celebrate what is kept from the landfill!
- More information on your City Council website, e.g. Christchurch: www.ccc.govt.nz/services/rubbish-and-recycling/lookupitem

### Action Point 73: Involve older folks

Involve older church members, and residents in retirement villages and rest homes, in environmental action that they can manage, e.g. recycling or potting up seedlings.

Meet for coffee and chat, listen to stories, share ideas, plan, encourage and support each other. Send a newsletter to celebrate achievements and plans.

# Expanding Vision: Silvia Purdie

Ka mihi atu ahau ki a koutou: tēnā koutou katoa. Greetings!

He honore ki te Atua kaha rawa, te Tama me te Wairua tapu.
Ko koe te Kaihanga, te Timatanga, te Otinga,
te Kaikaranga, te Kaiwhakaora o te Ao katoa.

Glory to God in the highest, to the Son and the Holy Spirit.
You are Creator, Beginning and End of all things,
the one who calls, the one who sustains the world and all that is in it.

Ko Silvia Purdie taku ingoa. Nō Ingarani ōku tūpuna – my ancestors came mostly from England in the 1860s as settlers in North Canterbury. Ngāti Tūmatauenga te iwi – my husband is an Army chaplain. Kaitiakitanga te mahi – I work in environmental sustainability. Manaakitanga te kaupapa – I also work as a counsellor, supervisor, author, trainer, and am an ordained minister of the Presbyterian Church of Aotearoa New Zealand.[239]

*What experiences shaped how you feel about the natural world?*

I had an extraordinary childhood. I grew up the white girl in Pacific and Māori communities: Suva in Fiji, Kaikohe in Northland, Ruatoria on East Cape, and Nuku'alofa in Tonga. My parent's marriage wasn't great, and they split up when I was 12, but they shared a love of the outdoors. Every Saturday we'd pack a picnic and go somewhere for a walk. Every holidays we'd be off on a road trip. By the time I finished school I had travelled the length and breadth of both Aotearoa and Tonga, exploring mountains, lakes, forests, beaches and islands.[240]

My father was a Methodist missionary teacher, with a strong pacifist background. He taught geography, plus pretty much everything in those Pacific and small rural schools. He loved to inspire others to understand more about the natural world around them. As we drove across the country he would rave on about river terraces and the ages of rocks until my eyes rolled. My mother loved birds and we carried a bird book everywhere we went, as every bird call had to be identified! Together they wrote a school textbook about the environment of Tonga, laying out photos on our dining table in our little concrete block house in Nuku'alofa.

Every house we lived in they set about making a garden. Growing food to eat was just what we did. I remember their disgust when some young American Volunteer Service Abroad (VSA) volunteers next door in Tonga bought packet dry powder mashed potato. Food should be fresh!

Our favourite place in Tonga involved biking to the south coast (about 40 minutes, with my sister getting dubbed on Dad's ricketty bike, dodging pot-holes!). Pull off at a dirt track, leave the bikes under a coconut tree, clamber down a narrow gap in the cliff to a small perfect beach. Between the brilliant sand and the reef edge was a wonderland. At low tide we walked across the coral outcrops. At high tide we swam the channels. What life there, in every crevice of the pools, crazy coloured fish darting, creatures in shells. Utterly pristine, back before we invented throw-away bottles or microplastics or industrial fishing.

Through my teen and university years I lived with Mum and my sister Natalie in Lower Hutt, then flatted in inner city Wellington, enjoying the beautiful hills, river and harbour, while I worked as a University Lay Chaplain and then National Youth Co-ordinator for the Methodist Church. Two years in Taupo, newly wed, where Chris and I fell in love with the lake in its many moods. Wainuiomata was a gentle place, surrounded by regenerating bush, a place of babies – home for five years. We loved our four Dunedin years, not least for the myriad of fabulous beaches, with three lively young boys who flung themselves down sand dunes. I discovered the intense joy of seeing the natural world through the eyes of a child. I trained as a counsellor, and then I followed my husband into ministry in the Presbyterian church.

The longest time in one home was Linton, out of Palmerston North, on an army base when Chris became a military chaplain. I'll never forget arriving at that house, opening the back gate to see laid out before me wild open space with a river flowing by. In all those nine years I never lost the astonishment and gratitude to God that I felt in that moment. Gosh I loved that place. Trees grew, the river flooded and changed, and we explored it all, with kids and friends and three cats. I studied, was ordained, and began in parish ministry; at home I would be out splashing through the steam or tucked under a tree.

Recent years have been in Christchurch, and now Burnham, which has brought more places to explore and appreciate. My friend Ira bought a large rugged chunk of growing forest on Banks Peninsula. It has been amazing to see God at work in that process, and to share kaitiakitanga for that place. Regeneration and conservation is tough work. I took on the task of cutting and removing old fence wire and wild roses, and have scars to prove it.

As I reflect on my rich and diverse experience of the natural world I feel overwhelmingly grateful for the many opportunities I have had, and that I knew a time before the digital revolution and plastic pollution.

*How has God called you into caring about the natural world?*

I experienced a clear call to ordained ministry in Taizé in France at Easter 30 years ago. In a vision in worship (surrounded by candles and soft singing) I could see the Earth and it became the Communion loaf in God's hands, broken and made whole. I felt such a longing to break bread and pour the cup and share the Gospel. A decade later God renewed my call to ordination, with an even stronger sense that caring for God's creation was part of this. But you know how it is, study and work and life gets busy, and I successfully ignored this aspect of my calling for another decade. For the church, and in our ministry training, creation care was the aspect of mission which falls off the end. Yes, obviously we care about the environment, but other things are more important (?!).

It was in my time at Cashmere Presbyterian Church that I started working with A Rocha. I hosted a seminar with input from A Rocha, together with others around Christchurch who were passionate about creation care. I was so inspired by them. I figured that if I wanted to make a contribution, the most important area was sustainability. I used my study leave to write about waste and this became an A Rocha 'Rich Living' study booklet.[241] This got me into practical systems for churches to reduce their rubbish, including writing 'The Rubbish Challenge' series in 2021,[242] and co-ordinating a zero waste project for Christchurch churches.[243]

For the last few years I have convened the Christchurch group of A Rocha. We've run seminars and workshops, built up interest and connections across a real range of churches. What I love most about this is that caring for creation cuts right across denominational or theological divides. All sorts of Christians are being stirred to speak out and make a difference.

To me it is so obvious that this is a work of God in our time. The Holy Spirit is calling the church to care for God's creation. Sustainability is a trendy thing and there is a lot of media attention to environmental and climate change issues. If anything, this makes Christians suspicious of it and wary of secular agendas. My approach is to base everything I teach on the Bible. What does Bible have to say about rubbish? About climate crisis? About eco-anxiety?

A year of post graduate study last year created more space for this, including a dissertation on 'Motivations for Eco Mission'.[244] I'm interested in what actually motivates people of faith to care for creation; it's not the same for everyone. Some are practical people who want to get stuck in and do something. Others see the big picture and want to fight injustice or shift government policy. Others are relational, all about being whānau. Others seek spiritual connection, theology and prayer. It has been great to be part of establishing Eco Church in NZ as this has a breadth of ways that local churches can enhance the natural world in their life, worship and mission. There's something for everyone!

And now God is calling me well outside my comfort zone, into the wider community sector in New Zealand as I look for ways to resource social service agencies and other community groups to incorporate environmental sustainability and respond to climate change.[245]

I love the way God calls us. It is always deeply personal, connecting from the heart. And it is always global – we are part of a world-wide movement worked out in this place and time. God calls us because we matter, each and every one of us. I am privileged to have lived more than five decades and to know a growing maturing faith. These days I describe my relationship with God as a strong working partnership. I know what Jesus meant when he said that his food is to do the will of the Father (John 4:34). I know the inspiring and sustaining power of the Holy Spirit every day, as I live in full confidence of my 'mahi tahi' (working as one) with God.

I love the way God's call gathers up all of our story. I grew up a white kid in brown communities but once we moved to Lower Hutt I was part of the dominant culture. Mono-white never feels normal to me. I love to connect with people from other cultures and honour diverse perspectives. In creation care I have a heart for Pasifika communities and how they are impacted by global warming. And I'm passionate about the central place of Māori in our nation. I uphold the vital role of Māori as Kaitiaki of this land. We need to hear each others' voices.

I love the way God inspires and sustains us as he calls. One thing's for sure with creation care: the work is '2-steps-forward, 1-step-back'. It is hard, and disappointments come almost as much as the joys. But I know God constantly at work, renewing his Creation, and renewing me, and renewing the church. It is the greatest privilege to be part of this.

Another thing is for sure: we can't do this alone. God doesn't just call individuals but he raises up a people, forms teams and community and whānau. I am a networker and I love bringing people together, making connections. Stuff happens because people like each other and respect each other – and 'cut each other some slack' when we drop the ball. Calling, theology and mission are 'body' things. We are the body of Christ, warts and all.

## What are the challenges of creation care?

The main challenge, of course, is that the problems we face seem so daunting. Even with a wonderful joy-filled project like the regenerating forest on the Banks Peninsula, with increasing temperatures and risk of droughts there is every chance that the forest could go up in flames; the most common tree is kanuka, which burns really well! Fear is real and overwhelm is always a risk to be managed.

Mine is a 'big-picture' brain, so I am drawn to large-scale issues and solutions. And God meets me there and pushes me further out! The Spirit of Christ drops these 'what-ifs' into my mind and I can see it, I can picture it. 'What if churches of every stream started caring for creation in their local area?' 'What would that take?' 'What if every community agency had an environmental sustainability strategy, and was resourcing their staff to integrate care for people with care for the environment?!'

These 'what-ifs' are energising and scary at the same time, because having seen it I cannot turn it off. I can no longer not engage with that vision. It is God's call for me personally, and God's vision for me expands me. It's no good saying to God, "I'm too little for that vision." He just doesn't buy that!

When you step out in that vision, God has already cleared the way. Not every time, by any means, but a lot of times there are amazing 'coincidences'. In my Place Consultancy work I have found someone's name and phone number and just called them. They have no idea who I am, and I start raving on about environmental sustainability in social services. And heaps of times the person has said, "Gosh, funny you should ring, I was just thinking about that!" One person was sitting at his computer struggling with an assignment on the topic. Other people recently had someone ask them about it and they didn't know how to respond. God prepares the way. Then what happens next is often frustration and disappointment. Occasionally one conversation leads to another one and it grows and leads on into partnership. Mostly, though, people are too busy, other demands are too pressing. Especially with Covid, people in the community sector and in the church simply don't have the spare mental capacity or sheer energy to tackle something new. Environmental sustainability feels big and hard and all too much right now.

God's mission to renew the face of the earth through renewed people[246] is as wonderful as it is fraught. Moving with the Holy Spirit in partnership with the Creator requires that we significantly enlarge our capacity for frustration and failure. God does not seem to mind setbacks.

In church ministry I expected that everything we did would succeed and everyone would be happy. It sounds completely bizarre to me now, but I really did! The church is allergic to failure. I remember the chairman of a church funding trust telling me there was a "black mark" against me because the youth ministry project they had helped fund had not gone as well as we had hoped. When I applied for a creation care project the following year our application was dismissed. God does not work like that. God does not measure success or failure the way we do. He gives us a D for Determination, an E for Effort, and a F for Fearless Faith!

Perseverance to me looks like being kind to myself and others. Especially in the Covid pandemic, in and out of lockdowns, we have all had to learn to sit more lightly with our plans. Adjust, let it go, find something else to do, another way around. And it's OK to do less. My relationship with God is a rock solid foundation soaked through with grace. There is always more love, more mercy, more possibilities. I am learning to trust completely in God's timing.

*What do you encourage churches to do?*

Three specific things I would like to highlight here. The first is around mental health and wellbeing. I have been applying my counselling, pastoral and theological training to the question of how the climate crisis is affecting people. I encourage everyone in pastoral care roles, especially those working with young people, to learn more about climate change and to face the building storm of emotions. How do you feel about global warming? How do those emotions impact how you live and work and sleep and relate to others? We have to notice and honour our own responses.

Then we have to create space for other people to be open about how they feel. Many children and young people feel overwhelming waves of hopelessness and pointlessness. Why bother going to school when the world is being destroyed? Eco anxiety is defined by Glenn Albrecht as "the generalized sense that the ecological foundations of existence are in the process of collapse."[247] If this is becoming a defining feature of our time, what does this mean for how we create community, do children's programmes and provide pastoral care? Panu Pikhala calls the church in our pastoral care to "the encounter of different emotions and anxieties related to the environmental situation, with the purpose of finding meaning and even joy in the midst of a tragedy."[248] I believe that taking environmental action together as faith communities is the only way we can offer substantive hope.[249]

The second specific action I would encourage churches to do is to host seminars. People in our communities are hungry for good information and space to discuss what we can do about environmental crises. Churches can speak into this: advertise a sermon series, invite a panel for a public forum, hear from scientists, and politicians, and climate activists, and theologians, and psychologists.

Third, we definitely need to shift our 'norm' around the end of life. My grandparents' generation chose to break with tradition and not be buried in cemeteries. They were motivated by a concern for the environment: they did not want to see more and more land being covered in concrete in memorials to the dead. Unfortunately we now know that cremation is just as bad for the environment. The intense heat required for cremation uses a huge amount of power. When a body is cremated all the carbon is released into the atmosphere as carbon dioxide, adding to global warming. The ash left behind is toxic, mostly salt and residual chemicals.

All credit to the Natural Burials team who have worked with councils around the country to create eco cemeteries, where bodies are enabled to gently return to the earth without adding toxins. Trees are planted instead of tombstones, so that the burial site becomes forest.[250]

My family is in the process of making this shift in thinking and practice around death. We recently visited Makara Cemetery out of Wellington, where several of our whānau now lie, and it was amazingly beautiful and peaceful. The grandkids explored the bush and lay around on the grass, feeling connected with those they remember. It is a real God place.

*So what is God's heart for creation?*

My theology comes out in liturgy. I hear God's heart in Proverbs 8. The early church recognised Jesus in the voice of Wisdom, and this shaped their conviction that Christ was with God from before time and in all of Creation. This is how I hear God's cry for us today:

## Here I am, crying out

*Litany by Silvia Purdie*

Here I am, crying out – can you hear me?
I am Wisdom, I am Christ, I am Creator and Saviour and Sustainer
I stand at this crossroad, I stand at your door – do you welcome me?
I cry out and my voice is True and my word is Life.
My determination is Justice and my gift is Love.
For all time **I was**, for all Creation **I am**, for all that's to come
**I will be.**
I saw the foundations of Earth. I saw the birth of Life.
I am God's rejoicing!
Every fragment, every atom, every corner of the universe
I see, I hold, I adore.
In every creature, every wave, every moment
I breathe.
And here I am, crying out – can you hear me?

I call to you, arms wide open – step toward me,
fling yourself headlong!
I catch you as you trip and fall, for you are entangled,
wrapped around and around by
power cables and strips of plastic and cords of debt,
labels and fears and data,
dragged down by effort on effort on effort.

Love, you try so hard
but only I can release you.
Stand still, let it all fall away
here in the favour of God, who sees you
with equal measure of Judgement and Affection.
Stand still, and look! Here is another way.
Share my delight, for you and for all things, all things, all things,
till you too are the voice of Wisdom.

**Action Point 74: Pastoral care that addresses climate anxiety**

All those offering pastoral care, especially with young people, reflecting on their own emotional responses to climate change, and able to engage in constructive conversation about this with others.

- 'Climate Change and Mental Health' webinar by Silvia: www.conversations.net.nz/mental-health
- Eco-Anxiety and Wellbeing resources, Eco Church NZ: www.ecochurch.org.nz/eco-anxiety-wellbeing
- Book by psychiatrist Dr Hinemoa Elder: *Aroha: Māori wisdom for a contented life lived in harmony with our planet – whakataukī (proverbs) for emotional and environmental healing* (Penguin Books, 2020)

**Action Point 75: Host seminars on environmental topics**

Invite the wider community to events where they hear a range of perspectives and are able to discuss, network and inspire action.

- Find a speaker on the A Rocha website, or ask for help from the Eco Church NZ team.
- Invite New Zealand Christians in Science: www.nzcis.org

**Action Point 76: Encourage eco funerals**

Natural burial as a normal way of honouring a life and returning a body to the earth.

- Visit your nearest Natural Burial cemetery: www.naturalburials.co.nz
- Discuss natural burial in your church.
- Find out which funeral directors in your area do natural burials.

It is helpful for a family to have already made this decision prior to a death, as it is a very different approach, e.g. no embalming, which may have implications for such things as the timing and process of a funeral.

**Action Point 77: Compost**

All food and garden waste, as well as compostable paper, rots down and is transformed into food for the earth.

- Composting resources at Eco Church NZ, including tips for setting up composting or a worm farm at church: www.ecochurch.org.nz/compost
- Video of Silvia's husband Chris (The Compost Master!) on how to make compost, The Rubbish Challenge (Step 5): www.conversations.net.nz/rubbish-challenge

# In God's Will: Skye Finlay

Skye is an 18-year-old small business entrepreneur, striving toward a sustainable fashion label, SALT, that she felt God put on her heart. She lives in Paraparaumu with her parents and two sisters. She is a part of ARISE Church in Kāpiti.[251]

*Let's start at the beginning, where did your parents come from?*

They come from a background of faith and creativity. Mum is Kiwi with Scottish ancestry and Dad is from Scotland. They met at Iona. I have lived here in Paraparaumu my whole life. My two sisters and I love living here, near the beach and the Waikanae River. We spent every summer of our childhoods at our caravan on the East Coast at Pōrangahau Beach, always in the water.

*What was your faith experience as a child?*

Our family went to the Union church in Kāpiti. I remember the family services, all about the community. It was a place of familiarity, knowing the people. I remember praying and I always knew that God was listening to me. We stopped going to that church over time as we grew older. My sisters and I went on our separate journeys of faith; you start to form your own perspective on things.

A close friend went to Arise church. She always asked me to come to Youth on Friday and I always say no but she kept asking. She was persistent and it paid off. I went, and my third time I gave my life to Jesus. I was quite emotional but it wasn't 'wake up the next day a different person'. It was a progression. I came to Youth, then to church, then serving on Kids Team. I felt at home. Serving connected me in.

At Arise, church is a vision that we are in together. If you want to be a part of the vision, join a team, get connected with the people around you, and work together to build the kingdom – which is awesome! I came to church to serve and each time I came I grew my relationship with God.

*How would you describe your relationship with God?*

I'm a very emotional worshipper. When someone prays for me I just cry! I start singing a cool song and I cry. It's like when you're standing in a forest, or if you're in the ocean, I feel connected to this whole presence. When I worship I feel full and sure. All the worries go away. I stand in thanks. Words speak to me in worship – like in the song today the words were: "Jireh, you are enough. You're always enough. And I'm loved. I'm chosen." That speaks to me a lot. I look up at the sun and I feel that God is with me – and I'm stoked about that! Sometimes I'm sad, and I can spend time with God to get comfort. No matter what the occasion is, God is there in that moment. I can always feel it. It is a heart and spirit response.

The first time I really truly knew God's Spirit within me was at our church's summer camp last year. I received the gift of Tongues. The preacher was praying for the room to receive new gifts. He was saying "Start speaking – if it's in God's will for you to have that gift, you will speak it right now." So I opened my mouth and words came out. I fell to my knees, crying. I got really shaky. I couldn't stop, I couldn't control it. "What is this?" – but I knew it was God. Some leaders took me aside and prayed for me, but I still couldn't stop. I somehow knew: there is a person who has a prayer for me. I said his name and he was called over. He prayed for me in Māori, and instantly my body relaxed.

*Did that total flooding of the Spirit change you?*

Yes, definitely! It changed the way I know God. No one can take that away from me. No one can tell me that didn't happen. I know that he is always within me and always will be within me. I didn't specifically ask for that gift but he gave it anyway, because it was in his will. Even at our lowest, God is always caring and always has the right answer. Even if we don't feel in the space to ask, he knows what we need before we ask.

*So how has God called you, as you left school and started a business?*

I did not have a solid idea of what I wanted to do: maybe environmental science like my sister, or design. In Year 12 I went to our church's July conference. I was still quite new to the church; I wasn't fully engaged in the worship, I was just standing there watching. And a vision was put in my head, like a whole new memory that felt suddenly familiar. It was words and pictures and feeling, all in one. God told me, "Skye, you are not going to go to university. You are going to start a fashion brand." He also told me that it will lead into growing sustainable practice.

It all sounded pretty crazy. I went home and told Mum: I'm not going to go to university. I have been sure ever since. This is what I was made for. God has a plan for everyone – but for most people it is not such a literal thing. You are designed for a purpose. To know my purpose at 16 years old was astonishing.

*What does that look like in practice?*

I saw a vision and tried to make it happen. Last year I did the Young Enterprise Scheme. It's a business course for high schools, with mentors and workshops. It was a great opportunity and I loved it. I got the award for the top sole trader in Wellington. It gave me a good start on my fashion business, up-cycling second-hand jeans. Denim is an easily recognisable thing, and sustainable – it just felt right. The creative side is using denim in new ways to create new shapes and designs. I started a little side-hustle making clothes, sold on Instagram and slowly built up a following.

The name 'Salt' was there from the beginning. I felt God wanted me to use the name Salt, but initially it was just a cool name – the ocean is salty. Then we had a sermon on salt and light and it clicked for me 'That's why!!' It is Matthew 5:13-17: "You are the salt of the earth. If the salt is not salty anymore, how can it become salty again? You are the light of the world." We are to enhance the flavour of this world! We can bring light to others by allowing God to use us and be a vessel for him.

It also intertwines with sustainability. Enhancing the flavour of old things to give them new life is what God does. People can assume 'There's nothing for me'. They look down on themselves and assume the worst. But God has something big for everyone. He takes the old and gives new life. With clothing, and with the world's natural resources, God wants me to enforce the new life of things by re-creating old materials into something new.

*What have you learned about starting a business?*

Initially I thought I would be more into the creative side than the business side, but I have really enjoyed both. It has not been as hard as I expected to start a business, though Covid has made it harder. It is a 'one step at a time' thing. Lots of people are very willing to help young business owners, and business owners in general right now. I have help from Creative HQ in Wellington.[252]

Starting a business involves setting up a website, and it helps that I can do the design myself. Instagram has been my main format and target market.[253]

*How can churches encourage new business?*

Just supporting and having each other's back. When I launched my products people said: "That's amazing! It's really cool to see this vision come to life." It is encouraging to know that people are behind you. Some other people at our church are also starting businesses, which is awesome.

It is about living our calling. A platform is a platform; you build it and that builds connections and opens doors. It is specific for everyone. If God intends for you to own a business, he already knows who will be involved, what will come of it, and how you can grow as a person of influence. You can make such an impact by being an outwardly Christian employee or business owner even if it is not an explicitly Christian business.

*What do you understand about sustainable business practice?*

When you're starting up, you know your morals, where you stand. It's easy when you're starting small: I do everything myself so it's easy to say it is ethically made, because I made it. I'm not handcuffed to my sewing machine! It's my choice.

I will learn more about sustainability as I get older and as the business grows, like: "Do I supply a product from here where it's much cheaper but I can't trust it, or do I go to this person where it's more expensive but I know exactly where it came from and I can trust it?" Those sorts of decisions definitely come up. Being in relationship with God means being able to make the right decision because I am not just operating in my own strength.

*Why does the sourcing of materials matter for sustainability?*

You want to know where your materials come from, to feel OK about selling it on and wearing it and promoting it. It is being authentic and genuine with people, being transparent. It's hard though. I would love to have a fully locally made or sustainably made wardrobe. That would be my goal. But most of the stuff I buy is second hand, because it's the cheapest option and is sustainable.

My goal is to create a massive brand that stays true to my roots in God. I would love in the future to be able to provide healthy well-paid great jobs to get people out of awful working conditions.

*What are the harmful environmental impacts of the fast fashion industry?*

The environmental impact of fast fashion comes from always needing the new thing – creating consumer demand which drives the whole mass production of bad quality clothes. With consumerism and the media there always has to be something new and more, more! Which means things are always getting thrown away. That is not sustainable.

To see the environmental impacts you look at how something is made and where the waste goes. Shipping the products around the world has a massive carbon footprint. The clothing industry has fabrics made from plastic, massive industry associated with poor working conditions, the carbon emissions from transport, and waste is a big thing.

Clothing waste gets shipped to poorer countries. Or waste fabric or clothes are dumped in landfill and it goes in a hole in the ground. It just sits there. Plastic fabrics – acrylic and polyester – do not rot down. But even if it is made of organic materials, if it ends up in the landfill, that's not a win. You can buy organic cotton, but if the garment is not made well it could still end up in landfill after a few months.

There are great sustainable options out there. The best thing is clothes that last or that you can recycle. I love denim because it is durable. If a pair of jeans rip, you can cut them up and reuse them. The best alternative, and the best way to live, is that everything can be recycled, so that we can be self sufficient and don't have to use a landfill.

Sustainable clothes like denim don't need to be washed as much. Micro plastics in fabric is a major problem. When you wash plastic-based clothes the micro plastics get flushed into the waste water. It soaks into the ground and goes into the ocean. It gets into the fish and the seafood and the whales.

*How does that affect you, thinking about what is happening to our oceans?*

It used to affect me a lot. That was the reason I went vegan, because I felt very in touch with the environment. I didn't understand God as much, so all I had was empathy for people and empathy for the environment, which can be very overwhelming. I still have empathy but I also have God, to reassure me that everything will be OK in the end. He is the one in control.

*What would you say to young people who are stressed about what is happening with the environment?*

It is really hard. When I was 12 I watched *Cowspiracy* and lots of videos of animals inside the meat industry. Immediately I decided, "I am never eating meat again." The grief can be consuming. But it is not sustainable to live in sorrow for what is happening in the world. It is great to be conscious of it and to dedicate your life to make the world better. But we don't live in a perfect world with no waste or suffering.

*So you don't think God wants people to live in anxiety and grief for the environment?*

No! God definitely gives people empathy and the ability to tune in with other people's emotions and also with the environment's metaphorical emotions. It is definitely a gift to be able to look at the environment, to see what's happening and feel the desire to make a change – because it's his environment, and we are called to be stewards of our things and stewards of the environment. But I don't think God ever wants people to be living in complete sadness and grief and despair all the time – because if you are so sad you don't want to live!

My priority is always to invite people into relationship with God. If something is in God's will then it will be sustainable. It will have good effects and it won't detrimental to the environment.

I have recently stopped being strictly vegan. Our family still very ethically conscious of our food but we now eat some good quality local meat and fish, and I know I am more healthy for that.

Focus on what is good and what you can control. And take care of yourself. Don't break yourself over the environment – because how can you help fix the world if you are broken?

*So has experiencing God balanced this out for you?*

It has helped me understand why I cared. I knew from the beginning that I wasn't just a silly little girl who watched too many animal videos. I felt it so strongly but I didn't understand why. As I grew to understand God and understand my identity in him, I knew that the reason I feel this is because it is part of my calling. He wouldn't give me that empathy towards something that I didn't have the ability to change. He gave me that for a reason. Through him we have the power to create change, when we make the most of the gifts we are given.

*Can you share what your family has been through over the past year?*

A year ago we were having renovations done in our home, and dust was left behind. The next day we discovered that it was asbestos. Because we were there overnight without realising the dust was asbestos, we moved it all around the house and into all of our things. Once we found out, it was too late, it was everywhere. We had to get out of house straightaway and we have not lived there since. Almost all of our stuff was destroyed because of the toxic dust, all our appliances and clothes, all the linings of the house, every book and piece of paper, everything. Only a few things were saved, things that could be sealed so they are safe to touch, a few pieces of art and photos.

*How has changed your relationship with stuff?*
It has changed a lot. I could give away any of my things now. But before this happened I was very attached to things; I found sentiment and value in objects. It was so weird – on the day the asbestos happened I was on the train coming home with my friend. We were talking about what we wear and I said to her: "I don't know what I would do if all my clothes got chucked away. I love my clothes so much!" And it happened, that same week! I lost all my clothes. It was traumatic. We were so confused. "What is happening? What is the next however-long going to look like?"

The main learning for me is that my identity is not found in what I own or what I can buy. Jesus said that in Matthew 6:21. The closer I get to God the more I understand it. We are not called to buy and buy and get what's next all the time. Mostly we don't see it as wrong: everyone owns stuff, everyone has to wear clothes, everyone has to buy food and furniture. The call is to not let stuff own you. Losing everything made us face that.

*You have been homeless. You had a taste of what it is to be a refugee.*
The worse day was the day when we knew that everything had to get thrown away, and we couldn't go back home. We were in the hotel together, with our dog. We just sat there. But we had a roof overhead and a hot meal. God had his hand over us, even when it was really hard. We always had enough. Even when we had nothing, we still had enough.

*Not many people in New Zealand have experienced anything like that. You had to grieve for what you lost, and you also had to be grateful for the simple things.*
Exactly. It's so much more healthy to be grateful than to think about what we used to have and don't have anymore.

It is still not finished. We still have long legal battles going on. And it could turn out so badly. It could just be a completely unjust situation that we never get redemption from.

*It's not just the tragedy of everything you lost, but it is also a massive injustice.*

It is a very, very hard and heart-pulling thing to let go of the anger that human error caused so much complication in our life that we were not in control of.

Something that was said at church recently was: God is actually not 'Just' in our terms. His will is not always going to feel fair in our eyes, but he does what he knows is best for us. It is so much better to let it go than to always be thinking about "Oh, this happened to me and I didn't get my repayment."

*I honour that journey. God is in it and transforming the situation, but not necessarily fixing it.*

We were never promised a beautiful house and heaps of fancy glossy objects. God never told us that we were going to have that. But he is making a way for us. We have always had what we need.

A message comes to mind about Hosea. The Lord told him that he was destined to marry a prostitute and he was: "Why?! Why do you want me to marry a prostitute? That's not right!" And God said, "You are going to be a living metaphor for the people around you to inspire hope and new life." Hosea had to suffer the hardship, because she wasn't a faithful wife. In those days, it was an awful thing; a prostitute would never get married. But God said to him, "I want you to do something that no one else would want to do, and you are going to teach so many people that listen through it." That could be what is happening for us. God knew that we were strong enough to handle it.

*That is a big calling. You are amazing. You're so articulate, and you are only 18. And God has given you a wonderful young man to do life with.*

He is also called to Christian fashion, so that's pretty crazy. It is going to be an awesome journey ahead.

"The Lord will guide you always; he will satisfy your needs."

*Isaiah 58:11, NIV*

## Jireh

*Excerpts from the song by Elevation Music*[254]

Jireh, You are enough, so I am enough
I will be content in every circumstance
I'm already loved, I'm already chosen
I know who I am

If He dresses the lilies with beauty and splendor
How much more will He clothe you
If He watches over every sparrow
How much more does He love you

"Now to him who by the power at work within us is able to accomplish abundantly far more than all we can ask or imagine, to him be glory in the church and in Christ Jesus to all generations, forever and ever. Amen."

*Ephesians 3:20-21, NRSV*

## Action Point 78: Wear your ethics

Stop supporting the 'fast fashion' industry, with its massive pollution, waste and unethical employment practices.

• Provide a repair service so that clothes last longer.
• Celebrate second hand clothing, with fashion parades, clothes swaps etc.
• Find and promote local and ethical clothing sources.
• Learn more about environmental issues in the clothing industry.
• 'Ethical Fashion Guide' Tearfund NZ: www.tearfund.org.nz/ethicalfashionguide
• 'Choose Slow Fashion' GenLess: www.genless.govt.nz/for-everyone/everyday-life/choose-slow-fashion
• With a bit of research you can find out if clothes are being made by people who are underpaid, businesses that don't have good work ethics, e.g. Good On You: www.goodonyou.eco

***Action Point 79: Support Christians in business and sustainability in business***

Christians leading in environmentally friendly business practices across the full range of businesses.

* 'Join the Low-Carbon Economy' GenLess: www.genless.govt.nz/for-business
* 'Embedding sustainability into your business model' New Zealand Trade and Enterprise: https://my.nzte.govt.nz/article2/why-sustainability-matters-to-business

***Action Point 80: Integrate evangelism and concern for the environment***

People invited into faith in Christ that directly connects with their worries for the world.

***Action Point 81: Teach 'you are enough' and 'you have enough'***

Strong Biblical faith teaching that confronts consumerism's drive for 'more' and 'new'.

* 'Lead us not into temptation: Christian responses to consumerism' PhD thesis by Christchurch Anglican priest Carolyn Robertson: https://ourarchive.otago.ac.nz/bitstream/handle/10523/8361/RobertsonCarolynJ2018PhD.pdf
* 'Responding To Consumerism In The World And The Church' by Glen Marshall, Freshstreams: https://freshstreams.net/wp-content/uploads/Consumerism-Glen-Marshall.pdf
* There is a host of books, blogs and sermons online about the spiritual practice of Simplicity, such as 'The Discipline of Simplicity' Prayer and Possibilities: www.prayerandpossibilities.com/spiritual-discipline-of-simplicity

as an equal, rather than something that I had authority or dominion over. Learning about how indigenous peoples relate to the environment helped convince me that we are part of creation. It is only through balanced relationships, with our environment and with each other and with our communities, that all of creation can flourish. That anchored the way I understand God: God is part of creation, God is in creation, God is creation. I now have a much more relational way of seeing and doing mission – not 'over above' but 'together alongside'.

*How would you respond to those who say that humans can exploit the earth because God gave us dominion over the earth in Genesis?*

Lala: I hear that a lot: "We can do whatever we want because God gave it to us, and we are superior." I don't believe that! My answer is: "We have to go back to who God is." What does it mean to be made in God's image? Our father God looks after us and loves us unconditionally. Our God-given 'dominion' is our responsibility to continue to do what God started from the beginning. As children of God, the image of God, having this relationship with God, then it is our job to do what God does – and that is to care, to love. Not that everyone agrees but that's what I say to people.

Amy: We are part of creation, we are totally integrated into it. We are dependent on it. And creation is dependent on us and our behaviour. You can't just exploit it in an unbridled manner to gain resources for yourself. That is going to end in disaster for you and everyone else – which unfortunately is where the Industrial Revolution and the Enlightenment has led us.

*Are humans the problem?*

Amy: I hear people asking, "Would the earth be better off without the people?" My response is that as humanity we do have an important role, just not a 'top-down' role. Creation thrives when human beings carry out our caretaker role properly. Scientists like Robin Wall Kimmerer describe how the natural world thrives when humans facilitate its growth.[256] Indigenous cultures have a beautiful emphasis on reciprocity. The Bible describes mutual relationships between God, land and people. Like Deuteronomy 28, where Moses lays out the lists of blessings and curses that are promised for the Israelites depending on whether they follow or don't follow God's instructions for Shalom holy living. These are not just consequences for people but also include blessing and curses for the land. So if the people's relationship with

God is in good shape, if their hearts are turned towards him and they keep the Law, then the crops, animals and land they depend upon will flourish.

Diana: Creation needs people to be an active part. Especially in Aotearoa, with all our introduced predators, and mammals like deer and pigs. If humans were suddenly wiped out, I suspect that the birds would come off second best. There is definitely responsibility for us to act, and to act now.

*What obstacles to environmental mission do you encounter?*

Eliala: In the Pacific Islands we are a collective society, but increasingly there is tension with individualism. When we grew up everyone knew how to care for each other. Now there is more talk about individual rights, and there is a break-up of the bond between communities. People want to use resources as they like, and to dispose waste as they like, because it is their 'right'. It disrupts our idea of community, and is destructive to the environment. Collective care is a God principle.

Faaolataga: The biggest challenge I see is the impact of technology, especially on our young people. They now see another world, a virtual world, through technology, rather than look at the here and now. I say: "Look outside. Look who is here in your whare. Look to the back and at the front – that is creation." We are trying to shift the focus away from I.T. and Facebook to care for creation.

Jill: Some people in my church still believe that climate change is not real: "It's just the earth doing its natural process" and "God is in it all anyway" and "It doesn't matter because Christ is going to come back and save us." I find that really frustrating and hard and challenging.

I also see Christians who sincerely believe that the environment is important, but continue travel the world, without realising the impact that is having on the planet. For a long time the church taught that is belief that matters the most: do you believe in God and heaven? And the cult of the individual is so embedded in Western Christianity. So what 'I' believe matters, and what we 'do' does not matter as much.

Diana: One obstacle is that change feels just too hard. Unspoken within people's reactions can be: "I don't want to accept environmental responsibility because it means I will have to change the way I live." That can be daunting. I approach it as a journey, just one step at a time. Bike a bit more. Buy one less plastic bottle. Another obstacle is that enviro friendly options still tend to cost more.

Silvia: Two challenges I would highlight. The first is the pervasive sense of overload, both in the church and just generally in our society at the moment. We are still in the midst of a global pandemic, which brings so much fear and hassles and fatigue. Climate change and environmental degradation hover over us with threats of doom, and that can diminish people's capacity to engage in positive solutions. I am so inspired when people turn fatigue and stress into creative action. God is absolutely in that!

The second issue we have to address in the church is our fear of offending people. There's a hard-core minority who are opposed to science in general and evolution in particular. Fair enough, but what frustrates me is that other Christians tiptoe around questions of science and creation, out of politeness. We need more teaching about science and God's involvement in the natural world, and space for tough discussion, or Christians will be stuck as helpless passengers on the ride to global disaster.

*How do you see creation care in the life of the church?*

Amy: People say to me: "Isn't it cool that the churches are now catching up, through Eco Church, with the environmental movement?" But I think: "How sad that it feels that way to them. Actually this was part of church mission all along." To me it is central to what it means to be in relationship with God in this world. It is a fundamental part of living as part of creation. That is what we are, and who God is. It is all so connected. Through Aristotelian Western dualism the material and the spiritual were separated. We split the body from the soul, mind and spirit. There has been such a disassociation between us and creation, and God and creation, in an other-worldly expression of faith. So now when it seems like creation care within churches is 'catching up', I would say: "No. It has been part of faith from the very beginning."

Faaolataga: I treasure the Samoan value on the central role of women in nurturing the creation. In my culture there is a sacred connection between the mother and the earth. Mothers nurture families and children, and the environment. This is vital in the church also.

Jacynthia: I think of the Pink Floyd album cover to 'Dark Side of the Moon'. A line of bright light enters a prism and the light that comes out of the prism is multicoloured, filling out in every direction. That is a wonderful analogy for God's presence in our lives. There is no one way to serve. There is no one lens to understand God. There is a plethora of colour, which all adds to the God that I love, the God that I serve, and how I shepherd God's people.

Silvia: I love the way this book has shown that diversity. Each of you has shared your own stories of how you've experienced God's speaking – how the living Word has been bringing to birth new things and forming you as people. We ourselves and our own words become part of the living Word of Christ, in a unique way in our time. To me that means that we are part of an emerging mission movement.

*Christa, what are the theological issues here, as you see them?*

Christa McKirland:[257] To understand the relation between God, humanity, and creation, the imago Dei question is very significant. I have focused in my own study on how the original Hebrew readers would have understood being made in "the image of God." Further, how did 'images of god' function in nations around Israel? The uniqueness of the Hebrew understanding is so interesting. In Israel's story, the Image is both distinct from God but it is also intimately bound to God, and this relates to our conversation about our theology of creation care. While God is God, and we are not, humans have a unique identity bound to a unique function as creatures made in God's image.

Compare this to Israel's surrounding neighbours in Egypt and Mesopotamia, where only the king could be the image of the deity. What is beautiful in Israel's story is it is not just limited to the royal class; all humankind is made in God's image. Genesis 1:27 is a democratisation of the imago Dei.

Another important difference is that for Israel's neighbours the image was the deity: the king was the tangible presence of the god. The image was actually that god in human form – an instantiation of the deity. For

Israel, God continues to be God, as the creator/creature distinction is maintained. The Image is not all of God, but works as a mediator. It is as mediators that we were meant to have dominion. Such a dominion was never meant to be a control over the created order, but a stewarding of the created order so that all might flourish.

On this account, being in the 'image of God' is a vocation, and this also comes through in the New Testament. To be made in the image of God is a royal priestly vocation. In my understanding, the best way to translate Genesis 1:27-28 from the Hebrew is: "In the image of God he created them, male and female he created them, so that they would have dominion." It is a 'cohortative' one leads to the next; people are made in the image of God so that we function as royal priests within creation. It is a beautiful pairing; their identity and their function are inextricably linked.

To be made in the image of God is to expand the presence of God in the world. We are meant to be the manifestation of God's care for the world. So if we take the Genesis mandate seriously then Christians would have to be on the forefront of caring for the world, because it is literally why we were created!

And this has already come out so beautifully in our discussion.

I had this epiphany about four years ago, working on my doctorate in the University of St Andrews: 'Oh! So it really matters how things came onto my plate'. If I take the creation care mandate seriously: 'How have I cared for creation with what is on my plate to eat? And what goes on my body to wear?'

I hear in the church a tendency to let the perfect become the enemy of the good, which is paralysis: 'Living sustainably might be too hard so I won't try'. However, as beings made in the image of God, intended mediators of God's presence, and wise stewards of creation itself, how do we encourage each other to interrogate our choices ethically?

There is no theological justification for not caring for creation. I have come to see that care for the created order is part of what it means to be human. It is part of my neighbourly care. And it is an extension of God's presence on this planet. As well as our Hebrew origin story, we also have a crucified Messiah: it costs him everything to be the ultimate mediator of God's presence on earth. As the true image of God, Jesus is both a mediator of the divine presence and the divine presence itself. Yet that status did not keep him from becoming human and dying on our behalf. So all of my excuses are completely undermined from Genesis all the way through to Revelation – we have no legs to stand on, with a faith earthed in an embodied Jewish Messiah! I am passionate to help the church realise that we don't have an option in our care for all that is other to us. Creation care is part of the ontological core of what it means to be human, and the Christian story reveals this important truth.

*So what is your hope for the new heavens and new earth? What does that mean to you?*

My daughter Raya is now five years old. She often asks me, "Mommy, when is heaven coming to earth?" I reply, "Sweetie, I don't know. That is up to the Triune God, but we get to be a part of that right now!" I have actually been talking with her about her priesthood. Being royal priests is part of being made in the Image of God. So her priesthood impacts on how she cares for our neighbours next door and the rollypollies (slaters) and the worms in our backyard.

Amy came and did a workshop at our church, and taught us about how to be an Eco Church. That prompted a discussion with my partner Matt about composting our waste and starting a worm farm. So over lockdown my family began composting and worm farming – which as an American is all very new to me. I'm trying to be a steward of that royal priestly mandate that I understand scripturally. How do I communicate that to my five year old? "Raya, this is how you get to see God's presence manifest in this world." And she is like, "Can we save our banana peels so I can feed the worms?!" We connect that to what it means to be human and walk in our priestly calling. That calling is epitomised in Jesus as the perfect Prophet, Priest and King. He is our prototype – the true Image of God. So we think it through – what does that look like? How can we extend the presence of God in the world?

As for the new heavens and new earth, I don't know what that is going to look like. But I do know that it is 'already but not yet'. We are meant to participate in the trajectory of what God is going to bring about in fullness. What I hope is that the church can be a window revealing a people who are actively living into the reality that is our future.

## Hiccups

*Poem by Ana Lisa de Jong, Living Tree Poetry*

There is death and unrest,
grief and turmoil.
But the world has hiccuped before,
held her breath, settled.

We are children in a sandpit.
If we could retreat back
into space we might see how,
of this world large swathes
on sea and land
are calm harbours,
farms and forests, prairies, grasses,
mountains.

Where any stirring is more often the wind,
or the sea, the rustling of a deer or a cow grazing at the fence line –
looking at us with brown,
lash fringed pools of eyes.
Indeed much of what goes on in nature,
the small skirmishes for territory,
the cracking of an iceberg, goes unheeded,
remains unknown.

Not for lack of importance,
but more for want of a witness.
Fear will always echo,
and catch like dry tinder in a forest fire.

Might we be ones then that speak of
peace as a lake in the mountains,
quiet and still,
mirroring the peaks and the sky.

That anyone who hears us can
breathe a little clearer,
and see the world for what it is
when mankind is left of centre.

And, even still,
if enough of us practice,
hope might catch the edge of the rising sun
to light the sky with a burning flame.

Maybe – or maybe just settle
gently into hearts soothed and mending,
as a child burrowing under blankets
listens to its mother's song.

## Blessing

*Silvia Purdie*

May you know God's call through all your story.

May you hear God's Word through all your soul:
    "This world matters to me. You matter to me!"
    "Jesus is well pleased with you!"
    "You will be alright. I am with you."

May you feel the embrace of God,
    and so reach out to awhi others.

May God bring you friends, young and old, of different cultures,
    to partner with you in caring for creation.

May God stir you with holy fire for our beautiful fragile world
    and sustain you with courage for the challenge.

May God give you peace with every breath,
    a still centre in the building storm.

Kei a koe te mārie o te Atua, te pono o te Atua, te ora o te Atua.
The grace, the truth and the life of God be yours.
Mā te Atua koe e manaaki.
God bless you and keep you,
so you will be a blessing
to the people and the places you connect with.
Amen.

# Book List

*A New Zealand Prayer Book, He Karakia Mihinare o Aotearoa*, The Anglican Church in Aotearoa, New Zealand and Polynesia (1988). Available online at: www.anglicanprayerbook.nz

Colin Bell & Robert S. White (editors), *Creation care and the gospel: Reconsidering the mission of the church* (Lausanne, Tyndale House, 2016)

Bill Bennett, *The Shepherd's Call – Te Karanga o te Hēpara: Prayers and liturgies for rural Aotearoa New Zealand* (Philip Garside Publishing, 2018)

Wendell Berry's novels: *Hannah Coulter* (Counterpoint, 2005) and *Jayber Crow* (Counterpoint, 2001)

Dave Bookless, *Planetwise: Dare To Care For God's World* (Intervarsity Press, 2017)

Barbara Brown Taylor, *An Altar in the World: A Geography of Faith* (Deckle Edge, 2010)

Barbara Brown Taylor, *Learning to Walk in the Dark* (Deckle Edge, 2015)

Helen Clark, *Climate Aotearoa: What's happening and what we can do about it* (Allen & Unwin, 2021)

Joy Cowley's wonderful books include *Aotearoa Psalms* (Pleroma, 1989), *Tarore and Her Book* (Bible Society NZ, 2009) and most recently, *Veil Over the Light* (Fitzbeck Publishing, 2018)

Ellen F. Davis, *Scripture, Culture, and Agriculture: An Agrarian Reading of the Bible* (Cambridge University Press, 2009)

Neil Darragh (editor), *Living in Planet Earth: Faith Communities and Ecology* (Accent Publications, 2016)

Ana Lisa de Jong's poetry collections: *Release from Darkness – Words for Spring, From Beauty for Ashes – Words for Autumn, and A Garment of Praise – Words for Summer* (Humanities Academic, 2021)

Celia Deane-Drummond, *A Primer in Ecotheology: Theology for a Fragile Earth* (Cascade, 2017)

Tom Doig (editor), *Living with the Climate Crisis: Voices from Aotearoa* (BWB Texts, 2020)

Jonathan Edwards, *Images or Shadows of Divine Things* (Praeger, 1977)

Charles Eisenstein, *Climate: A New Story* (North Atlantic Books, 2018)

Hinemoa Elder, *Aroha: Māori wisdom for a contented life lived in harmony with our planet* (Penguin Books, 2020)

Francis, *Laudato Si'* (Vatican Press, 2015)

Kathy Galloway & Katharine M. Preston, *Living Faithfully in the Time of Creation* (Wild Goose, Iona Community, 2021)

Norman Habel & Peter Trudinger (editors), *Exploring Ecological Hermeneutics* (Society of Biblical Literature, 2009)

Nicola Hoggard Creegan, *Animal Suffering and the Problem of Evil* (Oxford, 2013)

Nicola Hoggard Creegan & Andrew Shepherd (editors), *Creation and Hope: Reflections on Ecological Anticipation and Action from Aotearoa New Zealand* (Wipf and Stock, 2018)

John Ikerd, *A Return to Common Sense* (R.T. Edwards, 2007)

Elizabeth Johnson, *Creation and Cross* (Orbis, 2022)

Naomi Klein, *On Fire: The Burning Case for a Green New Deal* (Penguin, 2020)

Naomi Klein, *This Changes Everything: Capitalism vs. the Climate* (Simon & Schuster, 2014)

Catherine Knight, *Nature and Wellbeing in Aotearoa New Zealand: Exploring the connection* (Totara Press, 2020)

Johannes Luetz & Patrick Nunn, *Beyond Belief: Opportunities for Faith-Engaged Approaches to Climate-Change Adaptation in the Pacific Islands* (Climate Change Management series, Springer, 2021)

Bill McKibben, *Oil and Honey* (Griffin, 2014)

Douglas Moo and Jonathan Moo, *Creation Care: A Biblical Theology of the Natural World* (Zondervan, 2018) and DVD series: 'Creation Care Video Lectures: A Biblical Theology of the Natural World'

Nelle Morton, *The Journey is Home* (Boston: Beacon Press, 1985)

Roy Rappaport, *Ritual and Religion in the Making of Humanity* (Cambridge University Press, 1999)

Rich Living study booklet series, including: *Waste* (by Silvia Purdie) and *Transport* (by Nicola Hoggard Creegan), A Rocha NZ: www.arocha.org.nz/rich-living-booklets

Charles Ringma & Irene Alexander (editors), *Of Martyrs, Monks, and Mystics: A Yearly Meditational Reader of Ancient Spiritual Wisdom* (Cascade Books, 2015)

Jay Ruka, *Huia Come Home* (Ruka, 2018)

Suzanne Simard, *Finding the Mother Tree: Uncovering the Wisdom and Intelligence of the Forest* (Allen Lane, 2021)

Dick Tripp, *The Biblical Mandate for Caring for Creation* (Avery Bartlett Books, 2011)

Ruth Valerio, *L is for Lifestyle: Christian living that doesn't cost the Earth* (IVP, 2019)

Ruth Valerio, *Saying Yes to Life: The Archbishop of Canterbury's Lent Book 2020* (SPCK)

Christine Valters Paintner, *Earth, Our Original Monastery: Cultivating Wonder and Gratitude through Intimacy with Nature* (Sorin Books, 2020)

Sally Welch, *Outdoor Church: 20 sessions to take church outside the building for children and families* (Bible Reading Fellowship, 2016)

Nicholas Wolterstorff, *Educating for Shalom: Essays on Christian Higher Education* (Grand Rapids, MI: Baker Academic, 2004)

Selwyn Yeoman, *Is Anyone in Charge Here? A Christological Evaluation of the Idea of Human Dominion over Creation* (Pickwick, 2020)

David Young, *Wai Pasifika: Indigenous ways in a changing climate* (Otago University Press, 2021)

# Endnotes

1  For more on this: Ruth Valerio, *Saying Yes to Life* (SPCK, 2020), 157-158.

2  A mihi, or greeting, based on John 1:1-5, bilingual with the Māori Bible.

3  All contributors have been encouraged to speak with their own voice and perspective, but this does not imply endorsement of all the views expressed either by A Rocha Aotearoa New Zealand or by the global A Rocha family.

4  I wish to pay tribute to the work of Neil Darragh in telling creation care stories of Kiwi Christians, especially Catholics, and Kiwis of other faiths, in his wonderful book, *Living in the Planet Earth: Faith Communities and Ecology,* 2016; available from Accent Publications: www.accentpublications.co.nz/product/living-in-the-planet-earth

5  Community organisations are fluid so people and websites change; if a web link does not work, some online research will find more awesome people doing awesome things. Please let the Eco Church NZ team know about other initiatives. I have only linked to not-for-profit organisations; sustainable businesses are growing rapidly and I would also encourage readers to explore these online.

6  The first verse of 'E tū kahikatea' a song written by Hirini Melbourne. Used with permission from the Melbourne Whānau.

7  Translation supplied by the Melbourne Whānau.

8  Hirini Melbourne was a Māori composer, musician, poet, university lecturer and activist. His waiata (songs) and his ability to connect with people across a wide spectrum played an important role in the revival of Māori culture, and introducing the world to the beautiful rich sounds of traditional Māori instruments. I met him once at Pipitea Marae in Wellington, and vividly remember his dynamic energy and infectious love of the power of music in community.

9  Hirini Melbourne. Used with permission from the Melbourne Whānau.

10  As evidenced by the contributor's stories, many New Zealanders have a mix of Māori and Pākehā ancestry and can identify as either or both. Also, Aotearoa is home to people with ancestral links to every nation on earth – we are a diverse bunch!

11  Anglican Women's Studies Centre: https://anglicanwomen.nz

12  Copyright: the poems in this book by Ana Lisa de Jong are used with permission. 'Stories' and 'Dumb' are published in *Release from Darkness – Words for Spring*. 'A Change of Heart: A Poem for the Planet' and 'Plenty' are published in *From Beauty for Ashes – Words for Autumn*. 'Soft Beast' and

'Turning Point' are published in *A Garment of Praise – Words for Summer*. Each publication is printed by Humanities Academic Publishers, 2021. 'Absence' 'Hiccups' 'Mustard Seeds' and 'No Explanation' are previously unpublished. To read more of Ana Lisa's poetry, or to make contact about her books or use of her work: www.livingtreepoetry.com.

13  Eco Church NZ: www.ecochurch.org.nz

14  'About Us' A Rocha Aotearoa New Zealand: www.arocha.org.nz/about-us

15  Te Ao Māori refers to Māori culture and world-view. Te Reo refers to Māori language.

16  Orama Christian Community: www.orama.org.nz

17  Pohutukawa are a native tree, known as the Kiwi Christmas tree for their brilliant red summer blossom. Their branches can grow out over rocks and beaches.

18  Cambridge Carbon Footprint: https://cambridgecarbonfootprint.org Cambridge Centre for Christianity Worldwide: https://www.cccw.cam.ac.uk

19  The Lausanne/WEA Creation Care Network: http://lwccn.com

20  Eco Church in England and Wales: https://ecochurch.arocha.org.uk

21  Living Tree Poetry: https://livingtreepoetry.com

22  Godspace Light: https://godspacelight.com

23  Northumbria Community: www.northumbriacommunity.org

24  'Refresh' is published by Spiritual Growth Ministries NZ, and Ana Lisa is a regular contributor: www.sgm.org.nz/refresh-journal

25  'Lectio 365' app provided by 24-7 Prayer: https://24-7prayer.com/resource/lectio-365

26  Traditional Māori whakataukī or proverb.

27  Forest Church UK: www.mysticchrist.co.uk/forest_church. Wild Church Network: www.wildchurchnetwork.com

28  Pope Francis, Laudato Si' paragraph 84.

29  Brother David Steindl-Rast, OSB 'On Gratefulness and the Body' from 'Encounter with God through the Senses': https://gratefulness.org/resource/on-gratefulness-and-the-body-from-encounter-with-god-through-the-senses. Also 'Art and the Sacred': https://gratefulness.org/resource/art-and-the-sacred

30  Then Inter-Church Trade and Industry Mission, now Workplace Support.

31  'The Climate Crisis: Defence Readiness and Responsibilities' New Zealand Ministry of Defence: https://defence.govt.nz/publications/publication/the-climate-crisis-defence-readiness-and-response

32  Philippians 4:8. "Finally, beloved, whatever is true, whatever is honorable, whatever is just, whatever is pure, whatever is pleasing, whatever is commendable, if there is any excellence and if there is anything worthy of praise, think about these things." (NRSV)

33 'Precarious Nature' exhibition by Toi Moroki: https://coca.org.nz/exhibitions/
precarious_nature
'Poetry and the Environment' Poetry Foundation:
www.poetryfoundation.org/collections/146462/poetry-and-the-environment.
'Wild Creations' a joint project between Creative NZ and DOC:
www.creativenz.govt.nz/news/wild-creations-combines-art-and-environment-
to-tell-conservation-story

34 Grace Vineyard: https://grace.org.nz

35 Sam and Jen Harvey have now planted a church in Napier - Bay Vineyard:
www.bayvineyardchurch.org/the-leaders

36 Ruth Valero: https://ruthvalerio.net

37 A Rocha Aotearoa New Zealand: www.arocha.org.nz/resources

38 'How To Save The World Podcast' by Waveney Warth and Tim Batt

39 The Hope Seminar 2019:
www.arocha.org.nz/resources/the-hope-seminar-christchurch

40 Superhome Movement is working to make NZ houses healthier and more
sustainable: www.superhome.co.nz

41 Yunus Social Business Centre: https://research.lincoln.ac.nz/our-research/
faculties-research-centres/the-yunus-social-business-centre
Ani Kartikasari's academic profile, Lincoln University:
https://researchers.lincoln.ac.nz/ani.kartikasari

42 *The Ecology of Indonesia* series (Periplus Editions, 1996)

43 The Tribe Church: www.thetribe.org.nz

44 A Rocha Canada: https://arocha.ca

45 A Rocha Kenya: www.arocha.or.ke

46 Para Kore, Working towards Zero Waste: www.parakore.maori.nz

47 Self-Assessment Worksheet, Eco Church NZ:
www.ecochurch.org.nz/self-assessment-worksheet

48 The Story of Stuff: www.storyofstuff.org

49 'Connecting communities one repair at a time' Inspiring Communities:
https://inspiringcommunities.org.nz/ic_story/connecting-communities-one-
repair-at-a-time

50 Community bicycle maintenance groups include Bike Hubs in Auckland:
www.ecomatters.org.nz/on-bikes/bike-hubs, and the Aranui Bike Fixup in
Christchurch (on Faceboook)

51 Rolleston Christian School: www.rollestonchristian.school.nz

52 Te Ara Kākāriki, Greenway Canterbury Trust: www.kakariki.org.nz

53 Banks Peninsula Conservation Trust, Tui Project:
www.bpct.org.nz/our-projects?id=26

54  Five Ways to Wellbeing resources from the Mental Health Foundation of NZ: https://mentalhealth.org.nz/five-ways-to-wellbeing

55  'Tools for Environmental Action' DOC: www.doc.govt.nz/globalassets/documents/getting-involved/students-and-teachers/in-the-environment-series/tools-for-environmental-action.pdf

56  'Creating Catalysts for Change' Waikato Enviroschools: https://waikatoenviroschools.files.wordpress.com/2017/03/catalyst-for-change-resource-2017.pdf

57  'Inquiry and action learning process' Science Learning Hub: www.sciencelearn.org.nz/image_maps/92-inquiry-and-action-learning-process

58  'What is Action Learning?' Family and Community Services, New South Wales: www.ngolearning.com.au/files/Others/learningseries/WhatisActionLearning.pdf

59  Urban Vision is a missional order of the Anglican church; teams live in community with rhythms of prayer, mission and hospitality.

60  Caritas Advocacy work: https://caritas.org.nz/advocacy

61  Read more about ADJust, Diocese of Auckland: www.ecochurch.org.nz/stories/adjust-green-up-and-give-challenge

62  Creation Care Study Programme (CCSP): www.creationcsp.org

63  Japan Exchange and Teaching Programme (JET): http://jetprogramme.org/en/

64  Suzanne Simard, *Finding the Mother Tree: Uncovering the Wisdom and Intelligence of the Forest* (Allen Lane, 2021).

65  Barbara Brown Taylor, *An Altar in the World: A Geography of Faith* (Deckle Edge, 2010) and *Learning to Walk in the Dark* (Deckle Edge, 2015).

66  Two of my favourites by Wendell Berry are *Hannah Coulter* (Counterpoint, 2005) and *Jayber Crow* (Counterpoint, 2001).

67  The Great Kaikōura Whale Count is on Facebook.

68  Christine Valters Paintner, *Earth, Our Original Monastery: Cultivating Wonder and Gratitude through Intimacy with Nature* (Sorin Books, 2020).

69  'Tips for a Blessing of the Animals Service': Five Leaf Eco-awards, Australia: https://fiveleafecoawards.org/resources/tips-for-holding-a-blessing-of-the-animals-service

70  South West Baptist Church: www.swbc.org.nz

71  Adventure Specialties Trust: www.adventurespecialties.co.nz

72  A significant book that formed my thinking is *Huia Come Home* by Jay Ruka (2018).

73  G. Barrow 'Being well in the world: An alternative discourse to mental health and wellbeing' *Pastoral care in education*, 37(1) 2019, 26-32.

74 Julia Torquati 'Environmental education: A natural way to nurture young children's development and learning' YC Young Children 65(6) 2010, 98-104.

75 Tearfund NZ: www.tearfund.org.nz

76 L.K. Corlew 'The Cultural Impacts of Climate Change: Sense of Place and Sense of Community in Tuvalu, A Country Threatened by Sea Level Rise' PhD Thesis. University of Hawaii Manoa, 2021.

77 'About Tuvalu' UNDP: www.pacific.undp.org/content/pacific/en/home/countryinfo/tuvalu.html

78 United Nations Framework Convention on Climate Change: https://unfccc.int

79 Thanks to New Zealand Government MFAT Aid.

80 Breadfruit, bananas and swampy taro are important sources of food in Tuvalu. Aid projects tend to focus on short term tangible results by planting tomatoes, cabbage and some foreign vegetables not common to Tuvalu daily diet. This is not long term food security.

81 National Disaster Management Agency (Civil Defence): www.civildefence.govt.nz
Council for International Development (CID): www.cid.org.nz/about-us/humanitarian-network

82 Profiling project through the Negotiated Partnership Program SAFE.

83 Initially the project focused on modern slavery and sustaining livelihoods, but we are collecting all other data to better prepare our partners for any disruptions and disasters that may come.

84 Roy Rappaport, *Ritual and Religion in the Making of Humanity* (Cambridge University Press, 1999).

85 This is also a quote from the *Thor Ragnarok* movie directed by a Taika Waititi in 2017, when King Odin reminded his son that their nation "Asgar is not a place, it's a people."

86 Urban Kai aims to grow nutritious, locally grown, climate resilient kai (food) and to educate, enable and equip the wider community along the way. It is the urban farming collective of Common Unity: www.commonunityproject.org.nz/urban-kai-farms

87 More about Elise at Common Unity: www.commonunityproject.org.nz/urban-kai-blog/2021/11/10/internduction-spring-2021

88 Wendell Berry, *The Selected Poems of Wendell Berry* (Counterpoint, 1999).

89 Presbyterian Women Aotearoa New Zealand: www.presbyterian.org.nz/national-ministries/presbyterian-women-aotearoa-new-zealand

90 Malua Theological College in Samoa: www.malua.edu.ws

91 The lyrics of the famous song 'The green, green grass of home' by Tom Jones, 1967.

92  Samoan term for family – aiga, and whanau i Maori term.

93  Samoan term for family elders – tua'a/lauao sinasina and Māori term – kaumātua/whaea.

94  Tusi Pese EFKS-Hymn Book # 356. 'Swell the Anthem' Songs and Gospel. p.352.

95  Te Paipera Tapu, Putanga Reorua. The Holy Bible, NRSV, bilingual edition, Bible Society New Zealand; 2012, p.830.

96  Prayer based on: Isaiah 44, 2 Chronicles 7:14, Jeremiah 29, Ezekiel 13, Lamentations 3-5, Matthew 6, 2 Corinthians 5, Philippians 4 and Timothy 1.

97  Hughes Place Community Garden is on Facebook: www.facebook.com/hughesplacegarden

98  Have a Heart Trust: https://haveaheart.org.nz/hughes-place

99  'Community pantries filling the gap for the 'have nots' in Taranaki communities' Taranaki Daily News, 14 October 2019.

100  Advivia: www.advivia.org/Englisch

101  The German Catholic priest Ignaz Franz wrote the German lyrics ("Großer Gott wir loben Dich") in 1771 as a paraphrase of 'Te Deum' a Christian hymn in Latin from the 4th century. It became an inherent part of Christian ceremonial occasions, mainly as a conclusion song. Due to its memorable melody and theme it is one of the most popular hymns and prevalent in German-speaking communities. We sang it at my wedding. (Ira)

102  Nicholas Wolterstorff, *Educating for Shalom: Essays on Christian Higher Education*, ed. Clarence W. Joldersma & Gloria Goris Stronks (Grand Rapids, MI: Baker Academic, 2004).

103  Au Sable Institute: www.ausable.org

104  E3, Scripture Union: www.sunz.org.nz/youth/e3

105  I recently came across Circlewood's *Ecological Disciple* blog by James Amadon which elaborates on this worldview shift. Amadon argues for seven shifts that are necessary to reconnect theology with the environment. It would make a great sermon series!
Eco Disciple: www.ecodisciple.com/blog/seven-shifts-we-need-to-make
Also: www.ecodisciple.com/blog/how-have-you-shifted

106  A prayer from *The tree of life and the life of trees: A Rocha 2012 Environment Resource Pack*, written by Dave Bookless, A Rocha UK: https://atyourservice.arocha.org/en/tree-of-life-and-life-of-trees-2012-resource. Used with permission.

107  'Indigenous Voices on the Planetary Crisis' video: https://youtu.be/5FSUXBGx1_I

108  Incantation of the Hokianga, composer unknown, still sung on northern marae.

109 Whānau is family, hapū is sub-tribe. Oranga tonutanga means 'wellbeing or sustenance' (*Te Aka Online Māori Dictionary*, https://maoridictionary.co.nz)

110 Aroha is love. Manaaki and tiaki are aspects of care-taking.

111 Marae are Māori cultural centres. Hui are any kind of meeting or gathering.

112 Whanaungatanga is relationality.

113 Whakapapa is genealogy.

114 Jacynthia Murphy, *submission to Aotearoa Multi-Faiths Climate Change UN COP26*, October 2021.

115 A whakataukī or saying in Māori referring to the retention of cultural language and practices.

116 *A New Zealand Prayer Book, He Karakia Mihinare o Aotearoa*, The Anglican Church in Aotearoa, New Zealand and Polynesia, 1988, p.407.

117 For more on Papatūānuku: https://teara.govt.nz/en/papatuanuku-the-land.

118 Karakia are prayers or incantations. Tinana is the physical body.

119 *A New Zealand Prayer Book, He Karakia Mihinare o Aotearoa*, p.385.

120 Ibid., p.837.

121 Mana is prestige, authority, status.

122 *A New Zealand Prayer Book, He Karakia Mihinare o Aotearoa*, p.409.

123 'Prophetic Indigenous Voices on the Planetary Crisis – Aotearoa and Polynesia' video, Anglican Indigenous Network: https://youtu.be/pkijdqwnsjg. Search Youtube for other videos in the series.

124 United Nations: www.unep.org/resources/publication/1st-draft-post-2020-global-biodiversity-framework

125 COP26: Opening Ceremony – World Leaders Summit: www.youtube.com/watch?v=oofxDQQKE7M

126 Caira Supervision: https://caira.org.nz

127 A detailed story of the battle for Manapōuri and its significance in NZ history, NZ Geo: www.nzgeo.com/stories/manapouri-damning-the-dam

128 Forest and Bird: www.forestandbird.org.nz/about-us/our-history

129 Coal Action Network Aotearoa: https://coalaction.org.nz

130 Just Transition, NZCTU: https://union.org.nz/just-transition

131 NZ Parliament submissions website: www.parliament.nz/en/pb/sc/make-a-submission

132 Anglican Women's Studies Centre: https://anglicanwomen.nz

133 Called South, Anglican Diocese of Dunedin: www.calledsouth.org.nz/on-line-worship

134 Te Wānanga o Aotearoa, Ngā Mahi ā te Whare Pora – Weaving, Certificate in Māori and Indigenous Art: www.twoa.ac.nz/nga-akoranga-our-programmes/

maori-and-indigenous-arts/kawai-raupapa/certificate-in-maori-visual-arts-nga-mahi-a-te-whare-pora-level-4

135 Several organisations around the country offer Treaty training, such as Network Waitangi Ōtautahi: https://nwo.org.nz

136 Harakeke weaving: Te Wānanga o Aotearoa offers courses. Find a workshop near you. Watch online tutorials and join NZ Flax Weaving: www.youtube.com/playlist?list=PL3viv_wougoI9e2MqSVGk1h1DFh-pcSrx

137 'Indigenous Māori Knowledge and Perspectives of Ecosystems' Harmsworth & Awatere, Manaaki Whenua – Landcare Research: www.landcareresearch.co.nz/uploads/public/Discover-Our-Research/ Environment/Sustainable-society-policy/VMO/Indigenous_Maori_ knowledge_perspectives_ecosystems.pdf

138 *Bay Buzz*, January 2022: https://baybuzz.co.nz

139 Iona's 'Wild Goose' publications are a rich source of eco-friendly worship material: https://iona.org.uk

140 Presbyterian Support Otago: https://psotago.org.nz/services/families/buddy-programme

141 Newspaper article: 'Mega solar panel farm could be solution to energy poverty in Hawke's Bay' Stuff: www.stuff.co.nz/business/108627982/mega-solar-panel-farm-could-be-solution-to-energy-poverty-in-hawkes-bay

142 Interview: 'Hastings Church hatches solar plan to reduce energy poverty' 23 November 2018, Radio NZ: www.rnz.co.nz/national/programmes/ninetonoon/audio/2018672495/ hastings-church-hatches-solar-plan-to-reduce-energy-poverty

143 Karakia, kōrero, waiata and kai: prayer, talk, song and food.

144 Manaakitanga: hospitality.

145 Mokopuna: grandchildren

146 NIWA is the National Institute for Water and Atmospheric research: https://niwa.co.nz

147 Mauri is the life force. Maunga is the mountain. Mahi is the work.

148 1080 is the common name for a biodegradable poison called sodium fluoroacetate, used often in aerial drops to control predators: www.doc.govt.nz/nature/pests-and-threats/methods-of-control/1080

149 A large tract of land (500 ha) is owned by Mana Whenua (local tribal people) on the Northern slopes of Karioi.

150 Karioi Project education: www.karioiproject.co.nz/education

151 Litter Intelligence, Sustainable Coastlines: https://sustainablecoastlines.org/about/our-programmes/litter-intelligence

152 It is well worth reading up on the Raglan story at Xtreme Zero Waste: https://xtremezerowaste.org.nz/our-story. Watch video: https://youtu.be/-DOOkKqR29I

153 Para Kore: www.parakore.maori.nz

154 The Anglican Communion internationally agreed on Five Marks of Mission in 1984: www.anglicancommunion.org/mission/marks-of-mission. Other churches, such as the Presbyterian Church of Aotearoa New Zealand, have a similar mission framework: www.presbyterian.org.nz/about-us.

155 Meister Eckhart 'When I was the stream' translated by Daniel Ladinsky, in Love Poems from God: *Twelve Sacred Voices from the East and West* (Penguin Random House, 2002).

156 Lala Simpson: https://www.lalasimpson.co.nz/ Highly recommended: search Lala Simpson NZ on video – so much fabulous music!

157 'This Pretty Planet' by John Forster & Tom Chapin, © Limousine Music Co. & The Last Music Co. (ASCAP): used with permission.

158 Christiania Bikes: www.christianiabikes.com/uk

159 Cashmere New Life: www.cnl.org.nz

160 A lovely newspaper article on James Hamlin and family is 'Trailblazer James Hamlin on a mission' NZ Herald, 12 January 2019: https://www.nzherald.co.nz/northern-advocate/news/trailblazer-james-hamlin-on-a-mission/2D3EZYSBLBRFYNAWGGJLEIJTFI/

161 Spiritual Growth Ministries Aotearoa NZ: www.sgm.org.nz

162 Charles Ringma and Irene Alexander (eds), *Of Martyrs, Monks, and Mystics: A Yearly Meditational Reader of Ancient Spiritual Wisdom* (Cascade Books, 2015).

163 Pope Francis, Laudato Si' (Vatican Press, 2015).

164 Bellyful has grown into a nation-wide charity: https://bellyful.org.nz

165 WELLfed, Nourishing communities through food and connections: https://www.wellfed.kiwi

166 Low Carbon Challenge: https://anglicanmovement.nz/lowcarbon

167 'Get One, Give One': https://anglicanmovement.nz/getonegiveone

168 Love Food Hate Waste: https://lovefoodhatewaste.co.nz/food-waste/what-we-waste

169 Lecture entitled "Science and The Cosmic Christ: the meditative axis in the environmental movement" 2021 Eco-Theology Seminar, Wellington Theological Consortium: http://wellingtontheology.org.nz

170 Jonathan Edwards, *Images or Shadows of Divine Things* (Praeger, 1977)

171 From *The Assisi Compilation* written in the 13th Century.

172 Charles Eisenstein, *Climate: a New Story* (North Atlantic Books, 2018).

# Action Points Index

Lightning Source UK Ltd.
Milton Keynes UK
UKHW020657050722
405403UK00010B/747